THE UNBROKEN GENERATION

Youth Voices of Belarus 2020

Skaryna Press, 2024
London, UK

Editors
Elena Korosteleva, Victor Shadurski

Illustrator
les

Translation from Belarusian and Russian *M. R.*
Style editors *Thomas Clifton* and *Paul Hansbury*
Glossary and design *Ihar Ivanoŭ*

ISBN 978-1-915601-54-4 (Belarusian and Russian)
ISBN 978-1-915601-53-7 (English)

© Authors, 2024, texts
© les, 2024, illustrations

The students' accounts of their treatment at the hands of the Belarus state are heart-rending, compelling and occasionally humorous. This collection of essays gives us authentic and personal insights into the dashed hopes of a generation, yet the authors are never hopeless and their determination to see change in the country that they call home remains steadfast throughout — in that sense they are 'unbroken'. Such insights into the events of 2020 cannot be found elsewhere. An important book.

Dr Paul Hansbury, Warwick University

Unbroken Generation is a powerful testament to our era, which is marked by horror, challenge, terror, deprivation, and fear. Yet, it is also an era defined by courage, creativity, and the emergence of bold individuals who have sacrificed everything for freedom. This book bears witness to the heroism of many young Belarusians who dared to challenge oppression and refused to break. A must-read for reflection and inspiration.

Franak Viačorka, Senior Advisor to Sviatlana Tsikhanouskaya, Chief of Staff

Powerful personal narratives that draw close parallels to the 'Weiße Rose' student resistance movement against the Nazi regime in Germany during the Second World War. This history, and the strength of student reflections, give the country hope to continue their struggle for a free and democratic Belarus.

Berend de Groot, former Head of Cooperation EU Delegation to Belarus

Students represent the future of any society. With these testimonies from Belarusian students, who have had to pay a high price in their fight for freedom and democracy, we can be confident that Belarus has a bright future as the heart of Europe.

Tatiana Termacic, Council of Europe

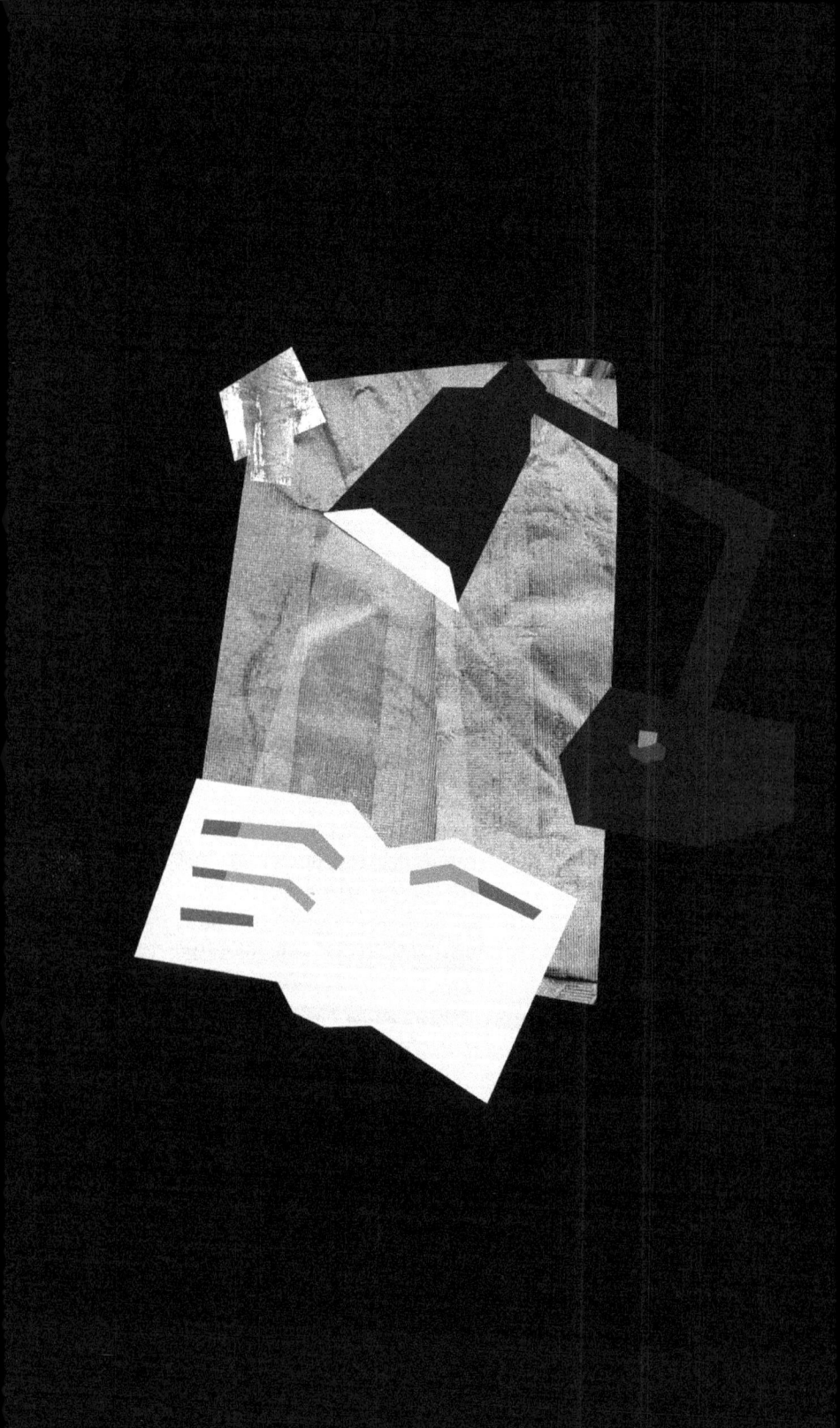

CONTENTS

Introduction	7
Acknowledgements	14
Belarusian Students Against the Authoritarian Regime	17
Remaking Historical Events: Reality With Dystopian Elements	45
I Believe Belarus Will Become a Country of Happy People	53
No Regrets	63
How to Vote in Elections and Go to Jail When You Are Nineteen Years Old?	71
A Country Under Two Flags	83
The Only Thing We Had Was Hope	91
A Revolution of Unfulfilled Hopes	101
A Belarusian is Belarusian To Another Belarusian	115
Feeling Love, or The Events Of 2020 in My Life	123
How To Look Happy	133
Muffled Voices: A Student's Personal Story About the Events of 2020	139
(No) Dreams of Belarusian Students	151
I am Determined Not to Give Up	163
Burn to Shine The Light!	169
An Imprint of a Worldview	181
I Have Been Fighting Fires for Three Years	189

From The District Honour to The Police "Wanted" Board	197
The Lost One	205
We Do Not Choose The Times, We Live in Them	223
(Non)Cultural Essay	231
History Is Full of Surprises	241
Observing Elections in Belarus Is Dangerous	251
How I Became a Protest Coordinator	261
I Do Not Consider This Time Wasted	273
The Way	281
Afterword	288
Glossary	292
Note on Transliteration	296

INTRODUCTION

Elena Korosteleva
Professor of Politics & Global Sustainable Development
University of Warwick, UK

This book represents a collection of essays written by student participants of Belarus' 2020 protests. Many of them ended up in jail, having experienced first-hand the maltreatment by Lukashenka's regime. All of them had to flee their homeland as a result. Yet, their young voices today — which in this book, we refer to as the UNBROKEN GENERATION — resonate stronger than ever before, giving us HOPE for the future, and BELIEF in ourselves, in the process of becoming THE PEOPLE.

I feel very privileged to write this introduction while co-editing the book with my colleague and mentor Professor Victor Shadurski, Belarusian State University, now in exile too. Being an educator all my life and having to undertake a difficult journey myself, leaving Belarus in the mid-1990s, I am humbled by courage and determination, and more so, by love and faith recounted by every author of this book, including the organiser of this project whose name we must keep anonymous for the purpose of their safety. After all the tribulations the authors had experienced, including taking on the arduous journey of an émigré, in my view, they will always remain victorious in standing up to the regime, and feeling positive about their future.

In what follows, I will provide a summary of the events in 2020 especially for those who may be coming for the first time to this page in the history of young Belarus. This stoical journey of resistance as depicted by the young people in this monograph, captures their passage and transformation from being effectively an 'absent' or 'missing people' (Sadiki and Saleh 2024) with no rights or voice, to becoming the most vociferous generation of their time. They bravely stood up to the autocracy, taking their resistance to a new level — PEOPLEHOOD, a powerful political force that will haunt Lukashenka until his regime is swept into oblivion ushering in a new era of Happy and Fear-free Belarus, a single vision recounted by all the authors of this volume. I will then briefly explain the structure of the book and conclude by remembering the trauma of this unbroken and yet very fragile generation of the Belarusian youth: while brave and determined, they all had a deeply distressing and disturbing experiences from the hands of the regime, and they need to find their way back into a happy and positive future. Their storytelling is one way of doing so…

Belarus 2020: the rise of Peoplehood

Each book is a journey unlike any other, and for me this journey is so different to what I normally write as an academic: in a way, this is my personal reflection on the events of 2020, and their aftermath.

For the Belarusians this journey began in the early 1990s, when a new political entity, called Belarus, emerged, perhaps unwillingly and frightfully, after the break-up of the Soviet Union. Not many people, including the leaders themselves, may have anticipated this newly attained independence, and yet, they all embraced this opportunity, for better or worse. In practical terms it was an almost impossible undertaking: economically, the country did not have its own substantive resources, having served as an assembly shop for the USSR, or indeed any currency to prop up its failing infrastructure devoured by hyperinflation and the dire consequences of Chernobyl (Marples 1999; White et al. 2005). Operationally, having no prior culture of political debate, newly formed representations fended more for their own interests, failing to agree on a unified vision for a democratic future (Wilson 2012; Korosteleva et al. 2024). This would have been a normal process of maturing, for a fledgling democracy, to learn its way, by trial and error, into a world of sovereign states, if this were not cut short by the arrival of Alexander Lukashenka. An opportunist and a demagogue, he initially encapsulated the hitherto marginalised and unheard voices of the 'absent people', to betray them after, and use them for his own ambitions and wealth ensuing in the longest-holding presidency to date across the post-Soviet space, with a robust police state to support him — or what Victor Shadurski aptly termed as 'the Leviathan' in his latest book (Shadurski 2024).

Needless to say, there have been multiple attempts to dislodge Lukashenka from power, through electoral challenge, mass protests and growing civil society, but he always succeeded in thwarting the opposition, by force and fraud, deploying the oppressive state machinery to quell dissent. The year 2020 and his presidential (re)election were set to be like any other: with major presidential candidates — *Viktar Babaryka*, *Siarhei Tsikhanouski*, and *Valery Tsapkala*, amongst others — allowed to canvass, only to be arrested (or flee the country) soon after; and with Lidiya Yarmoshyna, the infamous head of the Central Election Committee, readying to confer Lukashenka's victory once more as she had countless times before. And yet, the year of 2020 turned out to be different, in many ways, becoming a watershed year for Belarus now and then, where 'the now Belarus' was no longer afraid to stand up to the dictator. The year 2020 birthed a mesmerising groundswell of people, united in their indignation, in response to yet another fraudulent election, and more so, to the unprecedented levels of brutality and violence, with which Lukashenka's regime was trying to 'convince' the people of his victory. People stood up against the dictator, in their hundreds of thousands, across the whole country, from the capital to provinces, representing all walks of life and rallying around a single candidate — *Sviatlana Tsikhanouskaya*, who replaced her arrested husband, Siarhei, to become an accidental embodiment of people's power in Belarus 2020.

These people, being hitherto 'absent', unseen and unheard, protested for nearly six months, almost daily, peacefully wanting change, demanding dignity and respect — or in the words of a Belarusian poet *Janka Kupała* (1905-7), simply 'To be called People' (*Ludźmi zvacca*):

> And, say, who goes there? And, say, who goes there?
> In such a mighty throng assembled, O declare?
> Belarusians!
> [...]
> And what is it, then, for which so long they pined,
> Scorned throughout the years, they, the deaf, the blind?
> To be called people!

А хто там ідзе, а хто там ідзе
У агромністай такой грамадзе?
— Беларусы.
[...]
А чаго ж, чаго захацелась ім,
Пагарджаным век, ім, сляпым, глухім?
— Людзьмі звацца.
(1905-1907)

The price of being called 'people', peacefully, turned out to be very high. Following the election on 9 August 2020, nearly fifty thousand were arrested, including up to two thousand political prisoners, and a few murdered or 'disappeared' by the regime. Nearly ten percent of the population had to flee the country. Months of confrontation have been followed by years of incarceration and sickening torture of detainees in custody where many, including minors, were forced to kneel for hours, beaten, deprived of water and food, verbally abused, and raped. Among them were the authors of this book.

Arrests, cruelty, physical and moral torture continue to date — that is, four years on, at the time of writing.

And yet, as one of the authors reflected, in this hell of darkness and brutality, something beautiful was born — protestors and sympathisers gradually morphed into something bigger than a crowd of people being thrown together for different reasons. Through solidarity, self-help, care and love for each other, they suddenly found themselves on the path of becoming a PEOPLE, dignified and thirsty for change, who no longer wanted to be treated as narodets (a Russian derogatory notion for 'people'), bydlo (animals), ovtsy (sheep), narkomany i prostitutki (drug-addicts and whores), which Lukashenka's regime repeatedly called them (Korosteleva & Petrova 2021). The acute sense of injustice suddenly galvanised an emergence of unity and a strong desire for the dignity to be human. This single moment signified the birth of a new transformative force — the peoplehood — which was ten thousand times superior to an organised crowd, and which, with time, will pave the way to a proud and united nationhood — the Belarusians. This is exactly what this collection of powerful young voices tells us about — the rise of the oppressed, the emergence of a new transformative force, creative and morally pure, which under no circumstances, at home or in exile, can be straitjacketed back into the oppressed past, or silenced any longer. Just listen to their voices in this enchanting and powerful read.

The structure of the book

The book opens with a chapter that explains how this initiative came about as a project supported by the European funding Science at Risk. It explicates the complicated conditions which young people had to endure to survive in Belarus, unhelped and stifled by and education system rigid and intolerant of dissent at all levels. These young people were also undermined by the decades of servitude their 'educators' had to endure, many of whom as a result succumbed to the regime, embarking on the road of betrayal by (and) volunteering as informers for the regime. At the same time, the author clearly highlights the importance of international collaboration and continued support for civil society, without which it would have been impossible to raise this new UNBROKEN generation of young people, or to arrive at the level of mobilisation experienced in 2020 and beyond. This is further attested to by a relative ease with which many of them adapted to their life abroad with most being able to find a job, or continue to study, and volunteer to help, especially to the Ukrainian refugees, following Russia's aggression of 2022. This support, the author concludes, is needed even more today, to give this unbroken generation the strength and motivation to return home, to rebuild the country and live on, happy and affirmatively, post-Lukashenka.

The book continues with individual storytelling, representing twenty-five different voices, of young people, from many universities in Minsk, who rose up in indignation demanding change, and who were incarcerated for their right to speak. They all came differently to the protests: some through student movement, others as bystanders unwilling to accept cruelty and injustice of the regime; but all — mobilised by compassion and the desire for freedom, and all grown to identify themselves as Belarusians, even in exile.

Their stories are so poignant and moving in the volumes of suffering, struggle, belief and maturing, they had to endure. They all recount their individual journeys, and yet all of them are driven by a common vision to see Belarus free, and by the moments of epiphany some of which I summarise below:

> A peaceful, long and difficult path to a victorious end is our self-identity, the visiting card of the Belarusian protest.

> The majority of Belarusians want to have a new way of life, but are not yet ready to accept the norms of a civilised world. People are simply used to waiting for orders from above on how to

behave, but fundamental change in their worldview must begin with them, at a micro level.

Not resisting Lukashenka would have been akin to not opposing Hitler on the eve of World War II. I believe that Belarusians proved that they are worthy of their dream!

The continued existence of Lukashenka's regime gives me an incentive to live. After all the pain that so many people have been through, you realise you ought to see him overthrown.

There were many disappointments, yet they were vastly overshadowed by the admiration and love I felt for my people. I have never seen so much support, solidarity, rejection of evil and violence that I saw in these days of August-December 2020 in Belarus. I saw these thousands of worthy people, patriots of their country. And I was proud to be among them.

I was surrounded by the very essence of beauty — the women in white. I didn't know whether this beauty could exist anywhere else. It was like the white nymphs emerged from the canvas. Did the ancient Greeks know whom they were painting?

I have become more compassionate and kind towards people, but what is most significant is that I feel even more Belarusian than ever before.

These stories are left unfinished, without a summary or a defining conclusion in this volume, similarly to that in life. This is done deliberately, to highlight the ongoing and unstoppable journey to freedom for all our authors. For now, this journey continues in exile, but there is a sense of affirmation among them that there will be a moment of rebirth and return to their homeland, victorious. They all reiterated their belief, when asked to revisit their essays two years on: their conviction and commitment to a new Belarus remains unwavering and seems stronger today than ever before.

Trauma and the ways to heal

I wish to conclude this introduction by recalling the pain and grief, physical and mental, witnessed by these young people during the brutal events of 2020. They all seem to be haunted by the images of their stuffy and foul cells; harsh voices and shadows of their tormentors in balaclavas; and a sense of being defenceless in the face of the complete lawlessness of the regime. This is, of course, countered by warm feelings of solidarity and love they all had experienced, while in prison, but the dark side still occasionally prevails.

This is the TRAUMA of this generation: it is raw and naked; it violated their body and mind, and it is not easy to forget, or forgive...

As Slavoj Zizek, a Slovenian philosopher, commented once: "The essence of the trauma is precisely that it is too horrible to be remembered, to be integrated into our symbolic universe. All we have to do is to mark repeatedly the trauma as such" (1991: 272).

Marking the trauma could be done in many ways, especially when seeking to forget it and heal. However, while still being on an unfinished journey of claiming freedom and justice, with Lukashenka still in power, back at home, the experienced trauma is calling for remembrance rather than forgetting.

This book is precisely that: it is retelling us the story of horror, and torture, of crime and violence, as these young people's way of healing and also fighting, and for us all — to remember the price of freedom, and the need to continue fighting as long as needed. I will conclude this piece with reference to Anatoly Liabedzka's diary, 108 Days and Nights Behind the KGB Bars, published in 2013: "It is good the book is published today. It is good that the author has not parked it on a shelf while waiting for change and democracy in Belarus. We need this truth now. The way it is, raped, beaten, and naked". We need this truth, the storytelling, bare and harrowing, and yet UNBROKEN and affirmative of a new future, as our young voices powerfully testify to.

Long live Belarus!

Live forever!

References

Korosteleva, E & I. Petrova (2021) 'Societal Fragilities and Resilience: The emergence of peoplehood in Belarus', *Journal of Eurasian Studies*, https://journals.sagepub.com/doi/full/10.1177/18793665211037835.

Korosteleva, E. et al. (2024, in Belarusian) *Belarus in the XXI Century: Between Dictatorship and Democracy*. London: Skaryna Press; for English version see Routledge 2022.

Liabedzka, A. (2013) *108 days and nights behind the KGB bars*. Belgorod Press.

Marples, D. (1999) *Belarus: a Denationalised Nation*. Taylor & Francis.

Sadiki, L. and L. Saleh (2024) *Revolution and Democracy in Tunisia: a Century of Protestscapes*. OUP.

Shadurski, V. (2024, in Belarusian) *The Rise of the Belarus Leviathan*. Białystok.

Wilson, A. (2012) *Belarus: The Last European Dictatorship*. Yale University Press.

White, S. et al. (2005) *Postcommunist Belarus*. N.Y. & Oxford: Rowman and Littlefield.

Zizek, S. (1991) *For They Know Not What They Do: Enjoyment as a Political Factor*. London: Verso.

ACKNOWLEDGEMENTS

This publication was financially supported by the Warwick Ukraine-Belarus Hub (WUB-hub) from the Research England Policy Support Fund at the University of Warwick funding.

The essays published in this volume were created for the 'Belarusian students against the authoritarian regime' projected supported by the Science at Risk fund (Director Dr Philipp Schmedeke). All authors consented to their publications in Belarusian, Russian and English, as part of the monograph. Most names are anonymised for safety reasons.

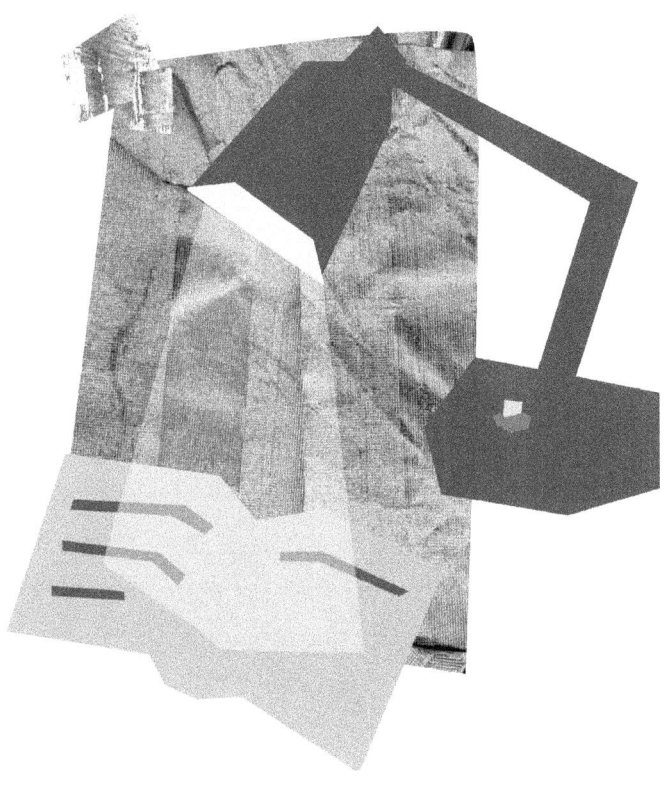

BELARUSIAN STUDENTS AGAINST THE AUTHORITARIAN REGIME

A teacher

who is proud of their students and believes
in their wonderful future in democratic Belarus

The Republic of Belarus, which is a medium-sized European state in terms of area and population, is considered by many politicians and experts to be one of the least recognisable countries having unobtrusive national characteristics. The authoritarian power established there as a result of the coup d'etat (November 1996) gave reason to former US Secretary of State Condoleezza Rice in April 2005 to call Belarus "the last dictatorship in Central Europe."

It should be admitted that the situation in the post-Soviet state, that is, close political and economic dependence on neighbouring Russia, was of little interest even to its closest democratic neighbours. However, in the summer of 2020, Belarus unexpectedly found itself in the spotlight of the world's topical debate. The reason for the heightened interest in Belarus was the mass peaceful protests against the authoritarian ruler, who had once again grossly falsified the presidential elections. Belarusians were now being seen as a nation that had challenged the pro-Moscow dictatorship and sought to establish a democratic state.

The illegitimate ruler, relying on a large repressive apparatus and moral and financial support from Moscow, managed to suppress mass resistance. As the protests subsided, the Belarusian issue began quickly to disappear from the European political agenda. With the beginning of large-scale Russian aggression in Ukraine (February 2022), which was supported by official Minsk, the attitude towards Belarus was increasingly negative.

In our opinion, one must clearly distinguish between a dictatorship and the Belarusian people, who are hostage to an aggressive regime. As the leader of the country's democratic forces, *Sviatlana Tsikhanouskaya*, figuratively stated, while Ukraine is fighting in the real war, Belarus is waging its own quiet war. However, the Kremlin's goal in this case is absolutely identical — to turn a sovereign country, with the help of the Minsk dictator, into another colony subordinated to Russia. In her speech in the European Parliament on 13 September 2023, *Tsikhanouskaya* called for support for the European aspirations of Belarusians, "bringing relations between democratic Belarus and the European Parliament to a new level and institutionalising cooperation."

We believe that democratic countries should keep Belarus in their focus, because counteracting the existing authoritarian regime is not alone the task of those who support change, who continue to be subjected to brutal repression within the country, and who are also forced to flee abroad en masse. The creation of a democratic Belarus in the geographical centre of Europe is an important prerequisite for peace and security in the entire region.

One of the most pressing problems of modern Belarus, calling for special support from the international community, is political prisoners of the dictatorial regime. According to the representative of the United Transitional Cabinet, former political prisoner Volha Harbunova, the number of people behind bars in Belarus for political reasons could reach five thousand. International human rights organisations recognise 2,290 people convicted over these three years (2020–2023) as political prisoners.

Tens of thousands of Belarusian students openly challenged the aggressive regime in the summer and autumn of 2020. Like other opposition-minded Belarusians, they were persecuted by the dictatorship. Thus, according to an analysis conducted by the

Association of Belarusian Students, as of 12 November 2021, there were 492 politically motivated detentions of students, 246 politically motivated expulsions, and 52 criminal charges against students in Belarus. At least 529 people testified to pressure from the leadership of universities for their civic position.

Students languishing in prisons and forced to flee their country are in dire need of international solidarity and support. The story of their struggle and suffering, courage and resilience should serve as an antidote to the virus of authoritarianism and tyranny, in whatever forms and in whatever states they may appear.

The project methodology

The implementation of the Science at Risk Foundation's project, Belarusian Students Against the Authoritarian Regime, began in April 2023.

Over the next months, twenty-five authors composed their essays, highlighting the most striking events of their personal development that shaped their civic position. The texts are for the most part emotional, filled with personal experiences. The young men and girls speak about the reasons for their rejection of the authoritarian regime and assess various forms and methods of resistance to the illegitimate power. Many essays expose the repression that students suffered because of their civic activism. Young Belarusians pose questions and try to find answers themselves. What happened in Belarus in 2020? Why did the protests become so widespread? How did the authoritarian government manage to suppress large-scale popular protests? What does the future hold for Belarus?

Young men and women representing various social groups, big cities, and rural areas, arrived at their civic choices in different ways. Some authors, during their school years, under the influence exerted by their parents or conversations within informal social groups, came to recognise the ineffectiveness of the ruling regime's policies and the pressing need for fundamental reforms. For other authors, the events of 2020 in Belarus proved to be an eye-opener: the irresponsible policies of the authorities during the Covid-19 pandemic and the machinations and violence of the dictatorship during the presidential election campaign. All the authors demonstrate strong empathy. Like many Belarusians, they could not remain indifferent to the unprovoked violence of the authorities in

2020, as a result of which many protest participants were killed and maimed by the "security forces".

All project participants took an active part in public life while at university. This gave them positive experience and helped develop leadership qualities. More than half of the authors were actively involved in an alternative youth movement that faced not only a lack of support, but also persecution by the government well before the events of 2020 unfolded.

Most of the authors were unable to complete their studies in Belarus and were forced to look for opportunities to continue their education outside the country. Six female students were sentenced to long prison terms on false charges. Most of the participants were subjected to administrative arrest on one or more occasions under Article 23.34 of the Administrative Code, well-known in Belarus, "Violation of the procedure for organising or holding mass events."

All project participants studied at the bachelor's and master's levels in Minsk, but at different universities: Belarusian State University, Belarusian State Pedagogical University, Belarusian National Technical University, Belarusian State University of Culture and Arts, Belarusian State Academy of Arts. Most of the essay authors studied in the humanities and social sciences.

As noted above, currently all essay authors are forced to reside outside of Belarus. In many cases, the authors avoid specifics due to fears of persecution of their loved ones who remain in their homeland. Young people write very briefly about their studies and work abroad and are reluctant to talk about the difficulties of adapting to new conditions. Being extroverts and optimists by nature, they do not want to concentrate on current temporary difficulties, prefer to look into the future with optimism, and try to share their plans. It is noteworthy that all our authors continue to actively participate in the Belarusian democratic movement. There is extensive information about some of them in the independent Belarusian press.

Obviously, using the example of the twenty-five essays presented, it is not possible to show a comprehensive picture of the processes that have taken place and that are still ongoing within the vast Belarusian student community. Nevertheless, the texts that we have received provide a clear account of the young people's participation in protests against the authoritarian regime and indicate the sentiments expressed by them. Drawing upon their own experiences, the authors demonstrate the romantic and highly idealistic character traits that are innate to the leaders of student protest movements. The essays allow us to conclude that universities retain great protest potential, which will certainly manifest itself in the future.

The main contradictions of Belarusian education under an authoritarian regime. Driving forces and forms of democratic protests

The examination of texts produced by students, combined with analytical publications from Belarusian and international researchers, enables a deeper comprehension of the adverse developments within the Belarusian educational model, including in the sphere of higher education and helps to identify the primary contradictions inherent in the current system. Its degradation is becoming increasingly noticeable as the dictatorial power intensifies its intervention in the content and forms of education. The mass participation of university students and faculty in the 2020 protests against the illegitimate government was a logical outcome, stemming from the disagreement of the majority of Belarusian society with the regime's antiquated domestic and foreign policies.

Belarusian higher education under dictatorship is an example of a degrading dead-end model

Belarusian higher education, despite the significant intellectual, material and technical potential accumulated in previous decades, in the current authoritarian conditions, clearly represents a dead-end model. Internationally, it can only be used as a negative example for countries intending to reform their educational systems. The degradation of the Belarusian higher education system began almost immediately after the establishment of a personalist dictatorship in the country in November 1996.

Over the course of nearly three decades, the authoritarian government has persistently escalated its efforts to curtail academic freedoms, tightly centralise the educational system, and infuse teaching and research with ideological agendas. The ruling administration associated the prospects for the development of education in Belarus mainly with a return to outdated Soviet practices of the 1960s–1970s. The year 1996 witnessed the termination of rector elections at Belarusian universities, turning them into executors of the will of the so-called presidential vertical power structure and requiring their appointments to be personally endorsed by the authoritarian leader. Rectors were then compelled to fill managerial positions at lower levels with individuals who were loyal to the authorities. The impact of academic communities on the governance of educational, research, and developmental activities has been noticeably diminished year after year. Intensified ideological pressure from above has been exerted on the content of educational courses, particularly in the humanities and social sciences, with a heightened focus on the history and culture of Belarus.

After 2020, the process of degradation of the Belarusian higher education system has noticeably accelerated. The interference of the administrative-command and propaganda apparatus in university activities has assumed alarming proportions.

Belarusian secondary education is one of the regime's main tools for suppressing dissent among youth

Many essay writers have mentioned their school studies. Their assessments of secondary education are contradictory. It was during their school years that the project participants developed an interest in studying specific subjects, which highlights the role of individual teachers. However, almost none of the students noted the positive function of secondary schooling in the shaping of their political views and values. They emphasise that the process of civic education took place mainly in the family and in informal youth groups. School, on the contrary, shaped conformism and social passivity. With rare exceptions, it did not set the task of developing critical thinking. According to one of the authors, the most difficult thing was to comprehend the "culture of silence" that was persistently instilled in schoolchildren from the first days of school: the notion that they should simply listen and do as their superiors, both adults and educators, commanded, not raise unnecessary questions, etc.

One project participant recounted an instance where, when asked about the dispersal of peaceful protesters demonstrating against election fraud in December 2010, the history teacher responded that "only idle onlookers gathered in the square, who got what they deserved, as there was no need for them to be there". The Minsk schoolboy was not only surprised by the teacher's reaction, which caused him to lose respect for her, but also by the silence of his classmates, who in private conversations admitted that their parents had voted against Lukashenka, yet did not stand up for their friend in class. The example given is not a single one; both students and teachers have spoken and continue to speak out on this topic. The authorities imposed penalties on the students' slightest expressions of open criticism not just on the students themselves, but extended those sanctions to their teachers and school principals too.

Scathing criticism has been directed by project participants at the teaching methods used for social and humanitarian subjects in secondary schools, especially history, social studies, and Belarusian literature. According to ex-pupils, the majority of teachers confine themselves to the textbook content without expanding beyond it. The emphasis in ideological education is often placed on the events of the Great Patriotic War (the Soviet part of the Second World War). The authoritarian regime's persistent invocation of the war theme as a propaganda tool appears neither new nor original.

Indoctrination within the school system persisted through the compulsory publication of propaganda-filled wall-posted newspapers and the mandatory holding of information sessions that extolled the activities of the dictator.

It is widely known that the administrations and teachers of Belarusian schools made up a significant part of the precinct election commissions — the basic link in the system of election fraud. This serves as an additional argument reinforcing the notion that the Belarusian school is not conducive to the development of a civic mindset, owing to its subordinate position within the administrative-command structure. The notion of schools serving as the principal institution for fostering an attitude of unwavering compliance with the authoritarian regime prompted extensive discourse among Belarusians in the aftermath of the 2020 events.

The BSU Lyceum, from which several of the essay authors graduated, stood out as an exception within the broader context of secondary education in Belarus. They write that the teachers and students at the lyceum loved their country and were concerned about its future. The lyceum students openly and frankly discussed current political news in class: the Maidan in Kyiv, the annexation of the Crimea and Donbas, the shortcomings of the presidential election campaign, and other hot topics. The lyceum students and their mentors organised days of the Belarusian language and culture and tried to use the national language more often in communication.

The lyceum was an atypical educational institution for Belarus, so it is no coincidence that after 2020 the management and teaching staff of the lyceum were subjected to persecution.

The positive impact of international cooperation on the development of Belarusian universities

However, even under dictatorship, Belarusian educators and learners retained the capacity freely to develop their knowledge and creatively apply their skills. These opportunities were preserved thanks to the achievements of the democratisation and internationalisation of the Belarusian academy in the final stages of the USSR and during the years of the parliamentary republic. Despite the policies of the authoritarian authorities, some progress in the higher education system after the coup d'etat in 1996, as in some other areas, was achieved. This was facilitated by the introduction of modern technologies, primarily in the domains of information and communication, which opened up virtually boundless opportunities for freely acquiring knowledge and engaging in international dialogue.

The education of Belarusian youth was bolstered by an extensive network of partnerships with foreign universities and active involvement in international student exchange programmes. The European Union programmes TEMPUS, INTAS, Copernicus, Sixth Framework Programme, Seventh Framework Programme, Erasmus Mundus, Erasmus +, Horizon, and so on made a positive contribution to the internationalisation of universities and to increasing the efficiency of their activities. German programmes and foundations (DAAD, Goethe Institute, state, party and private foundations) provided invaluable assistance to the academic community of Belarus. A promising solution was the accession of Belarus (May 2015) to the European Higher Education Area (Bologna process). It is known that the participation of Belarusian and Russian universities in the Bologna process is currently suspended.

The existence of critical sentiments across university communities triggered mounting discontent among the ruling authorities. In an effort to tighten their grip on the academic community, the authorities resorted to a strategy of negative personnel selection (appointing unpopular but loyalist individuals to leadership roles) and created obstacles to international exchanges and the implementation of joint projects with specialists from democratic countries (long and complex registration of projects, ideological control over their content, lack of Belarusian funding, and others).

The situation changed dramatically by the summer of 2020, when a significant part of society, including the university community, expressed its dissatisfaction with the existing authoritarian system. According to a wide range of evidence, Lukashenka lost the presidential election held on 9 August 2020. However, the dictatorship responded to the legitimate demand for change with violence and brutal repression that continues to this day.

The role of alternative education in the formation of civic activism

Many students were actively engaged in diverse non-formal educational initiatives organised by non-governmental public associations and funded primarily through foreign grants. These projects largely focused on human rights advocacy, the advancement of student self-governance, the promotion of Belarusian national culture, and charitable endeavours. In her essay, one of the participants noted how drastically the Belarusian summer school on human rights, which she completed after her second year at university, changed her life. The knowledge and skills gained there stimulated her active life position. Another of the essay authors completed a special volunteer student leadership programme, after which she arranged a waste separation project in her academic building. We can continue quoting such examples.

Democratic-minded students sought to convey their views to their peers, sometimes using Aesopian language. When one of the essay writers was assigned to give a paper in class, she prepared a text about her hatred of tomatoes. She named "Signor Tomato" as the reason for her dislike, because this character passed stupid laws. According to the girl, her classmates and the teacher highly appreciated the performance because they understood well who the student had in mind.

Growing criticism of the dictatorship amid its irresponsible behaviour during the Covid-19 pandemic

According to many experts, it was the ruler's irresponsible behaviour and his offensive rhetoric during the pandemic that convinced the population of the low quality of the Belarusian government. The awkward actions of the authorities during the Covid-19 crisis (denying the severity of the infectious disease, refusing to implement necessary preventive measures, and concealing accurate statistics) provoked justified outrage among many Belarusians. According to the majority of the essay writers, the authorities' mishandling of the pandemic served as a precursor to the widespread protests that occurred before and after the 2020 elections.

The arrival of the pandemic in Belarus, the overcrowded hospitals, and the spike in mortality rates amidst the government's contradictory actions spurred the rapid development of civil society initiatives. For many students, participation in volunteer projects to support doctors during the Covid-19 pandemic was their first experience of social activism and at the same time stimulated their interest in the political situation in the country. The authors of the essays are convinced from their own experience that Belarus is pursuing a disastrous policy of "pacification" towards the prevailing public mood. The essence of this approach is the authorities' concealment of substantial, sensitive information and the imposition of restrictions on its publication in the media. During incidents like the Chernobyl nuclear power plant accident, pandemics, and other disasters, citizens were left with incomplete knowledge, relying mainly on unofficial channels for information.

Regarding the coronavirus, the authorities systematically manipulated the statistics. Consequently, the people did not have access to the exact figures for the sick and deceased in the country, despite the fact that the scale of the disaster could not be fully hidden. Classes continued uninterrupted in schools and universities, even as many of the students and teachers fell ill. During this time, in an effort to satisfy his own vanity, Lukashenka ordered the staging of mass sports and propaganda events. Even school teachers and university professors actively involved in ideological work condemned the president's attitude towards the situation.

Participation of students in the presidential election campaign (May–August 2020)

For the vast majority of essay authors, participation in the 2020 presidential election was the first event of this kind in their lives. Through their parents, older peers, and even the media, they had gained knowledge about the fraudulent nature of past elections in the country (2001, 2006, 2010, 2015) and the suppression of local opposition protests in the first days after they were held. Most

Belarusians, including the project participants, anticipated that the situation in 2020 would likely unfold as it had in the past, without sparking widespread public indignation. However, the subsequent events shattered the previous notions held by many Belarusian citizens. Belarusian society, weary of the authorities' irresponsible policies, unexpectedly and openly expressed its outrage en masse against the actions of the dictatorship, which fully impacted students who became active participants in all stages of the election campaign and the ensuing mass protests.

Working in initiative groups of opposition politicians

The official start of the election campaign in May 2020 was marked by the registration of presidential candidate initiative groups. One of the first surprising developments of the political campaign was the swift formation of a large initiative group, numbering over ten thousand people, in support of the opposition candidate *Viktar Babaryka*. Many students joined this initiative group. One of the project participants describes their work within one initiative group, collecting signatures in backing a candidate. Even at the stage of gathering signatures, members of the initiative groups for candidates like *Viktar Babaryka*, *Sviatlana Tsikhanouskaya*, and *Valery Tsepkalo* faced persecution by the authorities, despite the legality of their actions. The repression later extended to Belarusians who had signed in support of the nomination of these opposition candidates, particularly impacting representatives from government agencies.

Independent observation of voting

Democratically-minded students assumed a direct role in monitoring the elections. Perceiving their low electoral rating, the authorities undertook unprecedented actions to impede independent observation at polling stations, with the intent of concealing the genuine voting results.

It required personal courage to register as an independent election observer. Owing to the real threat of persecution, there was an insufficient number of independent observers to ensure their presence at all polling stations. This issue was especially pronounced in the regions. Thus, in August 2020, less than half of the polling stations in the Viliejka district had independent observers. Participation in election observation independent of the authorities had become a common cause for repression, including criminal prosecution.

On election day, one of the essay authors, who had been legally registered as an observer at a polling station in a rural school in the Viliejka district, was prohibited from directly entering the voting room. The observer was then asked to leave the school building under the pretext of a complaint about his alleged polling of voters. After persistent threats from the police, the observer felt compelled to obey the unlawful order. Eyewitness accounts indicate that police threats, including the display of weapons, were directed at independent observers at numerous polling stations.

A project participant who was forcibly appointed as an official "observer" at the elections from the school where he worked shares his impressions of the atmosphere at the polling station. It turned out that even before the end of voting on election day, as calculated by independent observers, the overall turnout was more than 100%. This convincingly proved that the voting results were falsified.

Independent observers recorded widespread fraud at polling stations, especially during early voting, which began six days before the main voting day. Thus, according to one of the essay contributors who registered as an independent observer at her former school, on the first day of early voting, she counted 28 people who came to cast their ballots, yet the official ballot result reports indicated 97 voters. The following day, the polling station commission reported a figure of 400 voters, which was implausible. The observer did not receive a response when she inquired about the commission's significant distortion of the information. On 8 August, the eve of the main election day, she was compelled to hastily depart the polling station due to the threat of detention.

Public rallies on election day and the next two days

The atmosphere at the polling stations on election day, with a large contingent of Belarusians visually manifesting their rejection of the dictatorial leader (wearing white bracelets on their wrists, folding their ballots into an accordion shape, and adorning themselves in a combination of white and red clothing) implied that the authoritarian government had lost. Immediately after the close of voting on the evening of 9 August 2020, thousands of Belarusians, including participants in the project, went to their polling stations to view the result certificates detailing the distribution of votes between the candidates. By law, these result certificates were required to be posted in a publicly accessible location. However, on orders from above, the overwhelming majority of election commissions did not display the result certificates, which were drawn up with major violations. The result certificates of only 1,310 polling stations (22.7%) out of 5,767 nationwide were made public.

In response to the legitimate demands of people to see the voting results, reinforced police arrived at the polling stations and began making arrests.

Late in the evening and throughout the night, clashes erupted on the streets of Belarusian cities between citizens who rejected the falsification of election results and the so-called security forces. Stun grenades, rubber bullets, batons, and water cannons were used against unarmed demonstrators. Access to the internet was blocked in Belarus. The clashes went on for several days and nights, with thousands of Belarusians being arrested and subjected to violence. According to one of the essay authors, he and a friend were detained on the first night of protests, from 9 to 10 August, while returning home. After their arrest, the young people were beaten and then taken to the police station, where they were forced to kneel, keep their hands behind their backs, and lower their heads to the ground. The detainees, including women, were made to remain in this position for approximately two hours.

Another project contributor was detained on the night of 10–11 August. He was shocked by the huge number of people who had been arrested and brutally beaten, compelled to kneel throughout the night with their faces to the ground in the police stations. They were not permitted to lift their heads, access the toilet, or even ask for water. That night, those who were apprehended were gripped by a serious fear for their lives. Later, independent media would write that the frightened dictator gave the "security forces" complete carte blanche for violence against the protesting Belarusians.

Women's chains after the news of brutal violence against demonstrators

Once the internet became available, Belarusians were bombarded with an immense number of messages, images, and videos that exposed the beaten and injured protesters in the post-election protests. The disturbing online content provoked feelings of shock and anger even among those far removed from political engagement.

The authoritarian ruler was forced to release most of those detained on 9–10 August. Experts, whose assessment is also reflected by the essay writers, suggest the dictator was swayed by the threat of strikes. The authorities were aware of the protest sentiments taking hold at major factories, which could have resulted in significant problems for the economy.

The initial response to the inhumane violence in the immediate aftermath of the fraudulent elections was the formation of women's chains of solidarity. Women of diverse ages, dressed in white and carrying flowers, gathered in the centres of Minsk, *Hrodna* and other cities across the country. These courageous actions helped give rise to the narrative about the female face of the Belarusian protests. Many essay authors also shared their recollections of these events.

The largest demonstration in the history of Belarus (16 August 2020)

A festive atmosphere was palpable at the massive march in Minsk on 16 August, which stands as the largest demonstration in Belarus' history, attracting several hundred thousand participants. The overall mood is conveyed by one of the project participants: "That day showed how many of us there were, all striving for the same goal — common good, wellbeing and a happy future. On that day I became confident that we, Belarusians, would succeed".

The festive atmosphere persisted until the end of August 2020, up until the point when the dictatorship, having secured moral and material backing from the Kremlin, resumed the mass arrests of protest participants. The events of those August weeks, the hopes for change, and the belief in the strength of the Belarusian nation are emotionally captured in the texts of all the project contributors, without exception. In the students' view, the large-scale protests facilitated the unification of hundreds of thousands of concerned Belarusians, enabling them to recognise their collective power and declare their identity as a free and democratic nation. Unquestionably, the events of the summer and autumn of 2020 constitute the most important stage in the formation of the Belarusian nation, a fact highly appreciated both domestically and internationally.

The solidarity and unity exhibited by participants in peaceful demonstrations, neighbourhood activities and gatherings, and other acts of mutual support enabled the birth of a patriotic slogan: "A Belarusian is Belarusian to another Belarusian." It signified that Belarusians who opposed the authoritarian regime were characterised by more than just common political beliefs — they were also united by respect for each other and a spirit of mutual support. As such, the opponents of the dictatorship managed to showcase their most admirable human and national qualities throughout the mass demonstrations. The protesters demanded peaceful solutions to pressing conflicts and championed the observance of freedoms and human rights. At the mass marches that brought together hundreds of thousands of Minsk residents and visitors, volunteers placed packages of drinking water along the route of the demonstration columns and hung bags for collecting garbage. The high level of civic culture among the participants was evidenced by the protesters removing their shoes when standing on the benches.

Student protests after the start of the academic year

The start of the academic year saw representatives of the Belarusian academy sustaining their involvement in the Sunday protest marches as part of common columns, while simultaneously launching their own protest initiatives including strikes, pickets, rallies and meetings, demonstrations, and issuing open protest letters, declarations, video messages, etc. The numerous protest addresses and petitions put forth three primary demands: to stop the violence, release all political prisoners, and hold new democratic presidential election. These events are discussed in detail across the essays contributed by all the project participants.

Creation of university protest communities in social networks and instant messengers

Towards the end of August and into September 2020, collective chats began appearing across all higher education institutions. Almost immediately, these chats coalesced into regional and national networks. The leaders of these groups on social media and instant messengers assumed the primary coordinating and organisational role in challenging the dictatorial regime, which alarmed the authorities. This led to the arrest of the creators of independent online communities, as well as active authors and commentators.

Revival of the activities of student democratic associations

As the protest movement gained momentum, long-standing democratic student associations, such as the Belarusian Students' Association, a coalition of university associations led by the National Student Council (established in May 1988), were reinvigorated. The Belarusian National Youth Council RADA (BNYC RADA) and the Public Bologna Committee were also involved in the coordination of student democratic initiatives. BNYC RADA was created in 1992 to consolidate the activities of youth organisations in the fields of representation, promotion, and protection of their interests. The organisation is an associate member of the European Youth Forum. As a result of the repressive policy of the authorities towards civil society, BNYC RADA was deprived of official registration in Belarus in 2006. This happened again in 2021 during the campaign of mass liquidation of civil society organisations. The BNYC RADA's authority was acknowledged through the appointment of its leader, Marharyta Vorykhava, as an adviser to *Sviatlana Tsikhanouskaya* on matters pertaining to youth policy and students.

Mass student demonstration on 1 September 2020

Several thousand young people participated in the student protest in Minsk on the first day of the new academic year, marching to present petitions with numerous student signatures to the Ministry of Education. Due to interference from the police, the demonstration was prevented from reaching its intended destination and had to alter its route several times. According to various reports, around seventy participants in the peaceful protest were detained on 1 September.

Other student actions took place on that day. So, students of the Academy of Arts held a flash mob: wearing black, they stood in a line near their educational institution with their mouths taped shut.

Fearing student protests in the lead-up to the academic year (27 August 2020), the dictator ordered that students engaged in democratic actions be drafted into military service. University rectors immediately complied with this unlawful order, using it as another mechanism to punish democratically minded young men.

Student solidarity action on 5 September 2020

Another manifestation of collective student solidarity was associated with the brutal detention by riot police (special police unit) of students at Minsk State Linguistic University, who performed an excerpt from the musical Les Misérables in English in the hall of their educational institution. The following day, 5 September, several hundred students assembled near the main building of the Linguistic University, waving white-red-white flags and chanting "Shame! We won't forget, we won't forgive!" The protest was joined by the teaching staff and parents, who were outraged by the actions of both the police and the university administration for allowing violence against their students.

Student columns from other Minsk universities tried to get through the cordons of "law enforcement" to the Linguistic University. Dozens of students were detained that day.

Student participation in the national strike on 26 October 2020

The Belarusian opposition leader, *Sviatlana Tsikhanouskaya*, called for a nationwide strike on 26 October 2020. On this day, student activists, despite resistance from university administrations, managed to organise several protests, including marches by students from two Minsk institutions along the city's central avenue. The MSLU protesters, backed by some faculty members, were also able to reach Independence Avenue that day. Students from various institutions tried to unite near the main BSU building, but their efforts were thwarted by the police. Protests also took place at other universities in Belarus, such as in Brest and *Hrodna*, where young people held sit-ins and pickets at the entrances to their universities.

On this day, for propaganda purposes, the Ministry of Education of Belarus released a statement claiming the student actions were sporadic in nature and did not disrupt the educational process in the country. Although this statement did not correspond to the real situation, it should be recognised that large-scale, public student protests noticeably decreased after 26 October 2020.

It should be noted that open protests only involved a small portion of students and teaching staff. This can be attributed to various factors, primarily the learned fear of Belarusians regarding potential reprisals from the authorities. One could also point to the stance of some young Belarusians who adopted the example set by their elders in the willingness to adapt to the dictatorship and pursue career advancement under any conditions.

The dictatorship had consistently demonstrated its decisiveness and cruelty in suppressing dissent throughout all the years of its rule, especially during election campaigns. Participating in protests required personal courage. Many demonstrators, aware of the risks of arrest, tried to prepare for the worst-case scenario by bringing a change of clothes, necessary medicines, hygiene products, and memorising important contact numbers.

Repressive actions of the dictatorial regime agains students as a means of retaining power

"Black Thursday" in the history of Belarusian students.
The fabricated students' case

On Thursday, 12 November 2020, the KGB detained ten activists of student strike committees and initiative groups, as well as one lecturer, who became hostages of the so-called students' case. Another BSU student was arrested two weeks later. The list of the accused included students from Belarusian State University: Ksieniya Syramalot, Yahor Kaniecki, Tatsiana Jakielchyk, Illia Trakhtenbierh; the Belarusian State Pedagogical University: Yana Arbieyka and Kasia Budzko; students expelled from Belarusian National Technical University: Victoryya Hrankouskaya and Anastasiya Bulybienka; expelled from the Academy of Arts: Maryya Kalienik; expelled from the Minsk State Linguistic University: Hleb Fitznier; the lecturer from the Belarusian State University of Informatics and Radioelectronics, Volha Filatchankava; and a graduate of Belarusian State Medical University, representative for youth and student affairs of the Office of the Democratic Forces of Belarus, Alana Gebremariam.

Although many of the students had not personally known each other prior to their arrests, they were all implicated in a single group criminal case. According to the case materials, those arrested were "local coordinators who administered themed Telegram channels, personally called for participation in protests, produced and distributed leaflets with calls to action, organised participants, provided material support, and reported on the movements of police officers." The nature of the accusations, the conduct of court hearings associated with the so-called students' case are reminiscent of the political trials of the Stalin era.

On 14 May 2021, after six months of "investigation", the "trial" began (Judge Maryna Fiodarava), during which the young men and women were charged under Article 342 of the Criminal Code of the Republic of Belarus "Organisation or active participation in group actions that grossly violate public order." It was evident to all the accused from the outset that this trial was fundamentally an unlawful proceeding. The speeches of the prosecutors, the questioning of witnesses, the remarks of the judge had nothing to do with real justice. As the participants in the students' case recalled, on the day the verdict was announced, they agreed to carry out their last student protest action — to come to the court hearing with the element of fire in their clothes. The imprisoned students alluded to the sacrifice of Charles University student Jan Palach, who in January 1969 protested the aggression of the USSR and its satellite countries by setting himself on fire in the centre of Prague.

On 16 July 2021, at the request of the prosecutor's office (Anastasiya Maliko and Raman Chabatarou), eleven defendants were sentenced to 2.5 years in prison, one defendant — to 2 years. The student activists in the "cage" heard the verdict in handcuffs, which were not removed even during the court hearing. Except for one student, none of the defendants in the case admitted their guilt. The young people delivered a final speech in which they conveyed not only faith in their lack of guilt, but also stressed their unwavering commitment to continue fighting for human rights, freedoms, and a democratic Belarus. Thus, one of the illegally convicted students tried to convey her dominant emotions at that time: "I could not and will not put up with unjustified violence against civilians, turn a blind eye to it, or pretend that everything is fine. I still believe in the honour, dignity, and justice inherent in people. I'm not going to confess to something I didn't do."

Human rights activists recognised the arrest and trial of the students as politically motivated. At the same time, it became a real disgrace for representatives of Minsk universities and the entire Belarusian higher education system. Vice-rectors, deans, deputy deans, and faculty members testified for the prosecution against their own students. They were compelled to declare openly that students who had gathered during breaks between classes in campus buildings, having tea and singing popular songs, were allegedly disrupting the educational process. However, the so-called witnesses were unable to provide any adequate arguments to respond to the lawyers' poignant questions. In our opinion, the authorities deliberately made this so-called trial public and based the charges on the perjured testimony of academic personnel in order to humiliate the universities and demonstrate their unenviable position within the authoritarian system.

Administrative arrests and criminal prosecution

In addition to the women involved in the so-called students' case, ten of the essay authors were subjected to administrative detention under Article 23.34, with several even facing detention twice. In total, more than forty thousand people have been administratively detained in Belarus since 2020, with the reasons for arrest varying widely. One of the project participants was detained after a student rally on 5 September, while another was arrested for carrying both the national historical flag and official state flag at a football match in Minsk, in an apparent effort to appeal to the nation's divided populace for reconciliation.

Arrests remained ongoing in Belarus even after the open protests had subsided, as the authorities deliberately worked to sustain a climate of fear and despair. In the autumn of 2022, a project participant who was a lawyer by profession was arrested and spent fifteen days in a temporary detention centre. She was outraged by the conduct of court proceedings. The woman, known for her calm nature, was falsely accused of causing a scandal at the police station while already undergoing interrogation. The judge's conduct, ignoring the lawyer's arguments and simply reading a pre-written verdict, was indicative of the degradation not only of specific "servants of Themis", but of the entire legal system in dictatorial Belarus.

Torture in places of detention

A sophisticated array of torture methods existed in the temporary detention centres, including denying detainees access to hygiene products, keeping windows closed in overcrowded cells or failing to operate the ventilation, withholding opportunities for walks or showers, and waking inmates multiple times throughout the night. The cell lights were never turned off, forcing the people to cover their faces with clothing at night.

Prisoners on political charges were forced to wear yellow signs on their prison uniforms, indicating that they belonged to "extremists". The regime imposed on these prisoners was more severe, characterised by persistent badgering, threats, and unjustified, relentless punishments from the prison administration. As recounted by the women who were incarcerated in the colonies, the administration's directives to establish unbearable conditions for the political prisoners originated from the very top. The authors attest that it was the prisoners' solidarity, mutual aid, letters from family members (while other mail did not get through), occasional news about support for the repressed, and confidence in the justness of their choice that enabled them to endure.

We believe that the resilience and dignity displayed by young political prisoners, as well as the targeted torture inflicted upon innocent prisoners of conscience by the Belarusian authoritarian regime in its detention facilities, merit in-depth examination and reflection in both scholarly and creative formats.

Intensifying repression after Russian troops began invading Ukraine

Political repression in Belarus did not cease even after the conclusion of the large-scale public protests. Another wave of protest activity and related arrests took place following the Russian invasion of Ukraine on 24 February 2022, which was carried out in part from Belarusian territory with the backing of the Lukashenka regime. The first Belarusian political prisoner arrested and convicted for her anti-war position was Danuta Pieradnia, a twenty-year-old student of the Faculty of Romance-Germanic Philology at Mahilioŭ University. Her sole offence was that on 27 February 2022, she posted a message in one of Mahilioŭ's independent online forums denouncing the criminal conduct of Vladimir Putin and Alexander Lukashenka and urging participation in an anti-war demonstration. The next day, she was arrested and charged under two articles of the Criminal Code of Belarus — Article 361 (calls for actions intended to undermine national security) and Article 368 (defaming the President of the Republic of Belarus). Immediately after her arrest, Danuta was expelled from the university, with the administration falsely informing her fellow students that she had withdrawn for family reasons. The student was ultimately sentenced to six and a half years in prison. The KGB included her on the list of terrorists. This status entailed more sophisticated forms of repression and mistreatment of political prisoners, such as restrictions on visits, phone calls, letters, parcels, etc.

Continued degradation of the illegitimate regime's policy in the field of higher education

In its operations, the authoritarian regime has started more extensively to employ totalitarian methods. The practice of pressing criminal charges against Belarusians merely for owning and reading scientific books deemed extremist by the authorities has expanded. Arbitrary, random searches of the information stored on mobile devices have become commonplace. The active "purge of personnel" at universities has persisted, as propaganda efforts and control over the content of teaching and research intensified. Western countries in general and their universities in particular were broadly declared hostile to Belarus. Teachers and students were actually prohibited from contacting their foreign counterparts, as well as the Belarusians compelled to flee the country.

The "mindset" of representatives within the dictatorial vertical power structure is evident from a report published in state media about a meeting of high-ranking officials from the Presidential Administration (on 24 May 2023). The topic of discussion was "The organisation of ideological and educational work in higher education institutions of Belarus." The central theme of the speeches was the assertion that "underestimating the significance of ideological and educational work is fraught with consequences." According to the Lukashenka administration, bolstering ideological efforts is essential to ensure "there is no misgiving in entrusting the country to those who will exit the premises of a school, vocational institute, or university tomorrow." The antiquated and ineffective approach of the officials is apparent. They believe that internet technologies, social media platforms, and Telegram channels adversely affect the worldviews of students. In the opinion of these "statesmen," the information young people receive is inherently disruptive and destructive in nature, instilling alien values, generating a negative disposition towards society and the state, and provoking confrontational, and sometimes even criminal behaviour. The most pressing problem in universities is the formalistic approach to organising ideological activities. Belarusian officials have acknowledged that the so-called Youth Union, which operates under tight control, is not viewed as a leading public organisation by either university leadership or students themselves. This information provides insight into where the efforts of propagandists and ideologists will likely be focused in the near future.

At the meeting, the findings of sociological surveys of student youth carried out in October–November 2022 by the Institute of Sociology of the National Academy of Sciences were presented. The authorities expressed displeasure that such values as conscience, honour and dignity were named as priorities by a mere 18% of respondents, love for the Motherland by 15.6%, and humanity and helping people by 14.3%. In contrast, 57.8% of respondents selected "prosperity and money" as their values. According to the survey, one-fifth of the students surveyed do not identify as "patriots" and the same proportion are uncertain about this "honourable status".

The authorities were especially alarmed by the reduction in the share of young people eager to join the armed forces, as well as the increasing appeal of Western celebrations like Halloween and Valentine's Day among Belarusians. Officials from the ruling administration were also incensed by "the desire of young people to go abroad to get an education and in search of work." The "deficiencies in the work of the university teaching staff" were once more identified as a major contributing factor. It was suggested to correct the situation by forcibly showing propaganda films aimed at discrediting the peaceful Belarusian protests.

Even the most superficial glance at the actions of the authorities shows that they have nothing to offer young people except threats and outdated Soviet dogmas, which demonstrated their meaninglessness decades ago. The authoritarian government does not and will not enjoy the support of young people, except for a small group of pro-government careerists and "security officials". Continuous repressions have no long-term prospects in this direction either.

The degradation of government policy and its consequences are manifested in the so-called "new" forms of ideological work. Thus, on the eve of the above-mentioned meeting (23 May 2023), an incident occurred at BSU that received wide publicity in independent media. The core of the issue was that a video emerged on social networks in which a law student was coerced into publicly apologising for his criticism of the faculty administration and the pro-government Youth Union. This video, which was recorded with department and university logos in the background, was not only a violation of human rights, but also a gross violation of academic freedom. Previously, this practice of coercing public apologies was employed primarily by representatives of the repressive security apparatus. This time this criminal technique was used by representatives of the university. Another moral failure of local universities was condemned by human rights organisations, many public structures and initiatives, including the Association of Belarusian Students, BNYC RADA and the Public Bologna Committee.

Persecutions in Belarus, including at universities, have not stopped. The authorities, with the backing of university rectors, maintain their efforts to stir up an atmosphere of fear and social apathy. "Purges" of employees and teachers objectionable to the regime are still being carried out, and students are being arrested. However, even in such difficult circumstances, signals are emerging from Belarus that protest sentiments persist among teachers and students, which will manifest themselves with full force at the opportune time.

Servile behaviour of university administrations and some teaching staff

There is ample evidence, including that coming from the authors of the essays, that the primary tool in the hands of the authoritarian government for repressing students has become the leadership and staff of universities. The low moral standards of this category are highlighted by their behaviour being contingent on the prevailing circumstances in the country. When the situation was uncertain, university representatives attempted to adopt a neutral stance, even exhibiting sympathy towards the protesters. However, as the dictatorship solidified its grip, they opted blindly to follow directives from above. Many dean's office staff transformed into assistants to the police, prosecutor's office, and military commissariats, monitoring the actions of "suspicious" students and endeavouring to prevent informal youth activities.

The current situation in Belarusian universities, especially in the field of administration and teaching of social sciences and humanities, shows that a future democratic Belarus will face a serious personnel problem. It is obvious that employees who have tainted themselves by participating in repressions against their colleagues and students will not have the right to work at universities, so personnel for the future Belarus must be trained now.

Belarusian students after leaving Belarus

All the essay authors were compelled to leave Belarus out of fear of persecution by the regime. This process occurred in diverse ways, at varying times, and through different methods, each case entailing a distinct level of peril. Until February 2022, Ukraine provided the most viable exit route from the country, as Belarusian citizens did not require a visa to enter. The students had ample reason to believe that the Belarusian security services could include them in the lists of persons prohibited from leaving the authoritarian state.

Following the outbreak of the large-scale war in Ukraine, the essay authors more frequently selected Georgia as a destination country, as Belarusians do not need a visa to travel there. Many authors, including those involved in the so-called students' case, have refrained from disclosing the details of exit from their homeland, which had become perilous for them to remain in. The majority of the project participants are currently studying or working in Poland, Lithuania, the Czech Republic, Georgia, Germany, and Latvia.

The process of finding their footing in a new country proved challenging for nearly all the young men and women. They have provided scant information detailing the difficulties of their adaptation to the unfamiliar living conditions abroad, including those stemming from a lack of proficiency in the language of their forced place of residence or a low level of fluency in it.

Without exception, all the authors remain actively engaged in diverse solidarity initiatives and cultural events organised by the Belarusian community abroad. Each one has voiced their aspiration to return to Belarus as soon as circumstances permit.

Conclusions and recommendations

The preceding analysis enables us to formulate several key conclusions and recommendations.

The narratives of Belarusian students protesting against Lukashenka's illegitimate dictatorship, and the personal bravery of young people in the face of brutal repression, hold significance not only for Belarus. They constitute an integral component of the contemporary and prospective pan-European student movement, and should garner the interest of national and international student organisations. By their individual example, Belarusian students highlighted the hazards of authoritarianism, which attempts to obscure its factional interests with professed concern for the common good and demagogic claims about safeguarding ethics and morality. Belarusians have been immunised against the ideology of dictatorship, an inherent aspect of which is xenophobia, homophobia, and other inhumane manifestations. Belarusian students, like all other compatriots compelled to leave their homeland for safety reasons, can share their experiences with residents of their current host countries. This experience holds particular significance for European youth at a time when certain EU member states are witnessing a surge in the popularity of radical political movements that draw upon the purportedly successful track record of authoritarian regimes, including in Belarus.

In our view, the fate of Belarusian students who have endured repression amidst the "quiet war" in Belarus merits greater attention from the media in democratic countries. While the imperative of objectively directing state and public focus to supporting Ukraine's courageous fight against large-scale Russian aggression is understandable, this should not diminish the significance of the topic of democratic Belarus, which is waging its own struggle against the Kremlin's imperial policies and its Belarusian accomplices.

Thus, the dramatic events of the Belarusian political anomaly (a brutal dictatorship in a European state in the twenty-first century) are of paramount importance for educating and shaping the values of current and future generations of young Belarusians and their international peers alike. The primary objective of the project undertaken by the Science at Risk Foundation is to alert citizens of democratic nations about the perils of authoritarianism, while illuminating the path to freedom for those living under oppressive regimes.

Given the context outlined, we are of the opinion that the capacity of Belarusian student and youth organisations functioning beyond the borders of Belarus may be more actively engaged. Extending material and moral backing to these organisations would help them amass the requisite experience and expand their connections with national, pan-European and global student bodies.

Increasing the number of educational and research scholarships allocated to Belarusians could be a tangible expression of solidarity with those who have challenged the authoritarian regime. Such support would also represent a promising investment in the creation of a stable and democratic Belarus that Europe needs, as well as the training of potential specialists for the future Belarusian academy.

In our opinion, it is necessary to strengthen individual support for current students of Belarusian universities (undergraduates, MA and PhD students). For various reasons, they do not have the possibility to study abroad; they are forced to exist under dictatorship and the repression of academic freedom. At the same time, many of them not only maintain, but also intensify their critical attitude towards the authoritarian system. It would be fair to increase their opportunities to participate in international educational and research programmes. Naturally, when conducting such events, confidentiality is required.

City N, January 2024

REMAKING HISTORICAL EVENTS: REALITY WITH DYSTOPIAN ELEMENTS

Hrybočak

A bit of context to our lyrical heroine's childhood

I was born in a little village in Belarus. On the one hand, this was a positive: I was surrounded by nature, had more liberty of sorts, and a chance to build a foundation for my personality in isolated conditions. On the other hand, it was a rather closed system where a fast internet connection appeared quite late, and the main sources of information were those one could not consider independent.

From childhood, my mother instilled a love of nature in me, as I often went to pick berries or mushrooms with her. When I started school, I immediately decided that I would study chemistry seriously. I'm sure you would understand me if you had seen my chemistry teacher. She was a very charismatic woman! And she immensely impressed the child that I was with her hairstyle, because it looked very much like Einstein's iconic hairdo. I was faithful to my word and studied chemistry with enthusiasm. However, step by little step, biology started creeping into my life. The more I learned about various phenomena, the more I liked this science.

I studied in a Belarusian-language school until the 10th grade, and then the school was closed. I'd like to add that we local residents tried to defend our school and make it function at least for one more academic year. A meeting was organised for a public debate between the authorities and local residents. The village hall was full of people. Everyone was tense. Everyone realised that this was a mere formality, since the decision to close the school had already been made. The moderator said we could speak and ask questions. And here I was, sixteen years of age, feeling extreme injustice, and even some contempt for the officials present. Therefore, I decided to express my position. I don't remember exactly, but, in general, I spoke about how important that year had been for me and for other students and teachers. By the end of my 'performance' I had tears in my eyes. Some time passed before I learned that, because of my speech, the bonus was revoked from the headmaster's salary, and he was given a warning. I felt hurt, it was painful to realise that because of my sincerity another person was punished. That's how I got to know the way the government uses "pressure levers" and punishes anyone it wants.

My relatives suggested that I move to the city for one academic year and offered for me to live with them to continue my studies. I think that relocation had an impact on my further behaviour, because after a couple of years I started living 'out of suitcases'.

I can honestly admit that I was little interested in politics at that time, which lay somewhere far away from me. I remember asking adults in my teen years: why was Lukashenka the only president, why did they elect him alone? The reply I received was: "And who else can we elect?" With that, no one was able to give a coherent answer as to why they continued to vote for him. Even as a teenager I found this strange, but there was no way to talk to someone with opposing views about it. And here I take my hat off in respect to the system of education.

When I look back, I feel very scared, ashamed and sad. I did not think too much about my national self-identity, because my primary aim was to enrol at university. Belarusian history in the textbooks and during classes was presented in a very formal and distorted manner. And the teachers almost never went beyond the material that was given in the textbook. It is ironic that the emphasis in ideological education was on the events of the Great Patriotic

War. And now the ideology of the illegitimate government broadcasts a pro-aggressor position.

And what was it like there?

My choice of subject specialism was very well-considered; I wanted to continue to study for my master's and postgraduate degrees. I wanted to do what I liked, to engage in research. Commenting on the teaching process itself, I can say that with minimal state investment, an enormous effort of the university lecturers made it a quality education. For the rest of my life I shall remember a conversation with one of the university staff about the most important word in the world — that is "attitude": to oneself, to other people and to being. Actually, it would be interesting to know his opinion about the events of 2020. At the beginning, the administration had a relatively democratic stance towards the protests at the faculty, they did not even call in the riot police. Unfortunately, due to security reasons, I cannot tell you more about my studies.

Until 2020, I was almost completely focused on my education. And my activities had little to do with the political agenda. A clear feeling that something was wrong appeared during the anti-integration rallies. It made me wonder what was going on outside my own world. From that moment, I restarted my acquaintance with Belarusian history and culture. Afterwards, repressions rolled out in front of my eyes, as though it were a natural state of things. It was impossible to stay in the country any longer, to prefer one's own peace and well-being when violence became a norm in the country. I think that the main motive of my own protest is opposition to violence. It is difficult to talk about any changes in society or the regime, if people's basic right to security is not guaranteed.

I was very lucky during the peaceful protests. At one of the actions, during picketing near the infamous metro station, I received the best gift ever. It was already getting dark, but people were not going to leave. I was standing by the roadside with a *white-red-white* flag on my phone screen, a popular picture for picketing at that time. And suddenly a man approached me and simply gave me a *white-red-white* flag. It made me so happy. I had this flag with me on all other marches. Thank you, good man!

I want to thank the people who saved me during a police 'snatch' at one of the rallies, offered me tea and then took me to a safe place. In fact, I was often helped by strangers to get to the site of the marches or to leave a dangerous place. In general, during the protest period, the support and unity of the people was very motivating. There was a sense of a common cause. People came out into the streets for the sake of everyone else's freedom.

Different feelings arose during these actions, and I experienced emotional swings. You get ready for each rally as if it were for the last time: a change of clothes, a first-aid kit, hygiene products, a raincoat, you memorise all the important phone numbers. I should possibly mention that I was very scared during the marches. However, one expression (unfortunately, I cannot recall the original source) helped a lot, the meaning of which is that you need to pretend to be brave, at least for a few minutes, when you have to do something you're afraid of. That was a unique and positive experience of the rallies and marches. I keep a persistent association in my mind now: Belarusians are incredible. For me, everything happened for the first time: clashes with the riot police, the detention of my friends, and the fear for my life.

My decision to join an independent student organisation was an important personal move, because I felt that I was not doing enough just by going out into the streets. Communicating with numerous strangers at once was somewhat embarrassing for me. It sounds funny now. I am glad I made this decision. It was a very foundational one, and it pushed me to end up at this very point. I met so many wonderful, interesting, and intelligent people. These people have influenced my life in one way or another.

These three years have hardened many; and I like to think that I am among them. My only regret is that I could have acted more decisively, if I may say so.

At first, all my efforts and activities were synchronised to fight against the regime, and then an additional task appeared: to help others cope with the outcomes of the violent government actions. I'd like to point out that it is not difficult, and in addition, it is very important to support political prisoners with postcards. This is something that can be done both anonymously and remotely. And the main thing is — almost everyone can do it. I wrote my first postcard to a friend who was detained for several days. The first time I experienced a slight moment of dissonance, because I did not think that in 2020 I would write a postcard to someone for a reason other than just *postcrossing*, especially someone in a prison.

The tense period came after the active protest wave subsided. In addition to the general standby mode, "vigilance" mode was activated. Incarcerations for a period of several days were replaced by years of imprisonment. You become more careful. More mindful. The bitterest thing is that many photos had to be deleted so that there would be no additional grounds for detention. You had to recheck constantly whether something remained or appeared on one's phone that could be a reason for detention. Now I might not even write back to my friends when I see that there is a police van under my windows.

One of the most difficult moments for me was the detention of my colleague, with whom I shared the same flat at the time. I can't forget it when I had to gather the most necessary things with a torch, looking for a place to move to temporarily in a matter of minutes. The fact that we did not know what he was detained for and what to prepare for did not save the situation. It's hard to describe my feelings that night. There are many things I would like to share... I hope that one day I will be able to do it openly and fully. But that is it, so far...

Emigrant's life

I really want to look at my relocation to another country as a journey, albeit an indefinite one. It hurts when I hear the stories of people who were also forced to emigrate earlier, in 2010, and in 2015. But I don't want to develop this wind-up thinking and convince myself that I will never return to my Motherland.

After several years of living under constant stress and fear of losing freedom for my opinions, relocation has had a positive effect on my physical and mental well-being. It is as though a gun has been removed from my head. It has become easier to breathe. And other people are still forced to stay in this hell. Every day.

My first six months in emigration have been spent on adaptation, as I was moving into the unknown. During the entire period abroad, when I faced various problems, there was not a single case of not receiving help from Belarusians when requested. It is so impressive. It is impressive, too, how strong the diaspora, the community of Belarusians, is. It makes me sad to think that all those wonderful initiatives, projects, and organisations are in exile now. How many interesting and worthy things could be done within the country! Personally, I have more opportunities for education, because there is at least a chance safely to organise various programmes and events abroad. At the moment, I continue to engage in social activism. I keep adapting to new conditions.

I feel like an unwanted stranger in emigration. I realise that people are different everywhere, but when you face discrimination and persecution, it throws you off your stride. And you begin to harbour a prejudiced attitude, and expect to face intolerance. I think that I will never be able to say that I belong here. I will always be a stranger. I often see my homeland in dreams which also picture my illegal return there for a few days, but soon, in my dream, I have to leave again. I even began to like those nightmares, because in them, I can see people who are dear to me.

If you put it in one sentence, it is abroad that I feel safe for my physical freedom, but psychologically it is still difficult, very much like at home now.

I am glad that I have managed to make friends, there is even a sense of a family that you have created yourself. There is support and care for each other. And things do not seem so bad.

The beginning is chronological, the end is messy

Over the past five years, the aspiration to try and get an education and to become a specialist has not diminished. Apparently, I was not mistaken about my choice. By the time of the final revision of the essay, I had already become a little closer to the implementation of my plans. Even the bureaucratic system in another country failed to break me.

All in all, if you delve into self-reflection, thoughts like "I won't be able to do it", "maybe I should just let the situation go..." begin to appear. It scares me, because this was never typical of me. I think that this is one of the most sensitive moments when I am ready to give up. But so far I have survived it, which means I continue to fight!

I would like to learn about the emotions and the feelings of those who followed criminal orders of their commanders. How does it feel to realise that you have become that very villain from fairy tales, whom it is impossible to treat with sympathy?

I want to return to my homeland. While I am young, everything seems to be easier to cope with. But that will soon change. I don't want to put up with the fact that the "Belarusian question" has remained a burning issue for so long — whether it is a period of three years or three hundred years ago. No matter how I read it, the continued existence of Lukashenka's regime gives me an incentive to live. After all the pain that so many people have been through, you realise you ought to see him overthrown. I hope this will happen not because of a physiological condition, but thanks to the activities of Belarusians who oppose the violent regime. I hope that fewer and fewer people will say that they are outside of politics and that it does not concern them. I hope there will be more personal and public awareness, and violence will become impossible to ignore.

If I were to write about a hypothetical future, I want to see Belarus free and independent of both internal oppression and external pressure; to see the path to the process of self-determination and development; to make personal efforts to liberate our Motherland and take part in its growth. A lot of high-sounding and pathetic words here. Will I be as good as my words? Will they come true?

The answer is to come in time.

City N, December 2023
favoritefungus@proton.me

I BELIEVE BELARUS WILL BECOME A COUNTRY OF HAPPY PEOPLE

Aliaksandra P.

I was born in Minsk and I lived there until November 2022. Since childhood, I have wanted to help those who needed support. This inspired me to choose my education in law and work in this field. My professional specialisation was human rights law and refugee law, although I did not discover this area immediately.

After finishing school, like most applicants, I did not have a clear idea of my future profession. However, after hearing about the Faculty of International Relations at Belarusian State University, I felt that this institution would help me gain various beneficial skills and knowledge that I could put to use.

In my first year of university life, I desperately tried to understand the branches of law, imagining how, as an adult, I would work with them, but each time the future seemed blurry. Everything changed in my second year when I met people who told me about refugees on the border of Belarus and Poland. That moment became a turning point in my life. I was extremely distraught that people fleeing persecution could not find a safe home. These emotions motivated me to action, and I began to study it thoroughly, as well as human rights law.

I was lucky to be born into a family that always encouraged my ambitions, supported, and protected me. I remember telling my parents about my desire to study human rights, and the mixed emotions that followed. My dad said that this was a noble cause; however, remembering 2010, he warned me that in Belarus this was too dangerous a career. I understood this well, but at that time I no longer saw my future work in a different field.

It gave me great pleasure to study at the faculty, although exams always created a lot of stress. In seminars, we were often free to think and discuss. You could see students' sparkling eyes when the tutorial was interesting; and the manner in which the information was presented made it obvious that for most teachers it was important not only to convey knowledge, but also to involve students in the process of learning.

During the entire course, I studied human rights and refugee law in depth, both at Belarusian State University and elsewhere, completed internships and participated in volunteer programmes. With the help of various organisations, I looked for humanitarian aid possibilities and organised educational events, translated articles and interviews, conducted legal research and lodged complaints and appeals to national and international bodies. It seemed obvious to me that support and assistance to vulnerable groups was vital for creating a democratic society based on solidarity and respect for human rights. At the same time, I often had to explain why some people were forced to leave their home countries and should not be judged. It was essential to help others overcome prejudices and present an objective picture to them in order to avoid disapproval and stigmatisation of migrants and start to present everyone as bearers of inalienable rights.

My goal after graduating from university was always clear: to work as a human rights activist in a non-governmental organisation. I felt no anxiety about this decision because I believed that I was doing everything right within the bounds of the law and morality. It was on the verge of my graduation when the protests began, although they had not yet reached the mass scale that we saw in the following months.

My activities after graduation

Soon after graduating from university, I found a job I embraced. My quick employment was greatly facilitated not only by the knowledge acquired at the university, but also by my active participation in volunteer programmes. I began working remotely with refugees in European countries, helping them to understand the procedure of applying for refugee status, as well as how to appeal a refusal of protection. On behalf of my clients, protecting and asserting their rights, I also prepared complaints to the European Court of Human Rights, UN committees, and other international organisations.

Besides my main job, I continued to help other organisations on a volunteer basis. A particular need for this occurred in August 2020 when the entirety of Belarus was shocked by the news about torture and ill-treatment. I won't forget the moment when I was at home and I heard my mother crying in the next room. When I asked what was happening, she showed me interviews of several people who came out of *Akrescina* and who described the violence they faced. By that time I knew something about torture in places of detention in Belarus, but my mother's tears and the shock that someone could be so cruel impressed me more than anything I had read about in books and articles before. It has left a deep impression in my memory. As long as it was possible, I assisted human rights activists in collecting and systematising information about torture. When they began to detain those volunteers, I moved away from this activity, guided by the advice of colleagues and my emotional state.

Peaceful actions

Like many others, I took part in peaceful protests. I don't think I could have done otherwise, given my commitment to justice. I believed that through our joint efforts we would manage to change things peacefully and ensure a future free from dictatorship. I believed that my future children, studying history at school, would see "2020" in their textbook table of contents and would proudly tell others that their parents contributed to the struggle for freedom in Belarus.

I will never forget the Freedom March on 16 August 2020. That day showed how many of us there were, and we were all striving for the same goal: common good, wellbeing, and a happy future. On that day I became confident that we, Belarusians, would succeed, because we were supported by the majority, fighting for truth and justice. The information about torture and detention was frightening of course, but it did not seem as if it would last forever, because the lesson from our childhood taught us that good triumphs over evil which means we need to move on and fight.

Looking back, I understand that Belarusians did everything they could. I don't think we were defeated just because the government didn't change. I consider it a victory that we took off our masks and found out who truly values freedom and who is ready to betray their neighbour for the sake of money and power. We showed both ourselves and the world what real Belarusians are like and what we have to go through.

Detention

In 2022, when the world community began to switch attention to the war in Ukraine, many thought that mass arrests in Belarus had stopped. However, this was far from the truth. The machine of repressions did not stop. It continued to increase its power. In the autumn of that year, I was detained. Like many others, there were neither grounds for the arrest, nor was there a detention report.

Law enforcement officers came to my flat and carried out a search, threatening me with a long prison sentence, without explaining any reasons. Later they took me for interrogation which lasted for more than four hours. There I learned that I was taken as a witness in a criminal case about protests, but I was only indirectly associated with those who were charged. I had studied advice about behaviour during interrogations, but it did not actually help me. When I referred to specific legal norms and tried to refuse to testify against myself, they threatened to make things worse for me and my loved ones. Despite the fact that I ultimately gave all my testimony, they did not release me, but placed me in a solitary cell without light or windows. They did not allow contacting my family and did not even give me any water. At night, they brought me to *Akrescina*.

I learned about the essence of the charges against me only the next day during the court trial. It was conducted in a remote mode: I was in someone's office at *Akrescina*, under the supervision of security guards, and in front of a laptop with a poor internet connection. My family managed to hire a lawyer, who explained that I was accused of resisting a police officer. According to the detention report, during the day I was walking near the district department of internal affairs when a police officer approached me and said that I was suspected of possessing extremist materials. The report said that instead of obeying, I began to scream, resist the officer, and wave my arms. Despite my being already in custody and under interrogation at the time specified in the report, the court, without even a recess for a decision, considered that they had no reason not to trust the law enforcement officer, the only witness, and sentenced me to fourteen days of detention. The only advantage of this court hearing was the opportunity to tell my family through a lawyer that I was healthy and that I was not physically assaulted. Later on, the lawyer told my family that, despite her long experience with similar cases, this trial was one of the most morally difficult for her, and I think it was due to my endless stream of tears and shock from completely fictitious accusations.

During my two weeks of imprisonment at *Akrescina*, I met scientists and business people, nurses, lawyers and expelled students. All of them were detained because of their political opinions. Some were assaulted, and the police tried to convince them that they did not know or understand anything, that girls should get their nails manicured and not meddle in politics, that prison is inevitable for all of us.

We were kept in poor conditions, even unbearable sometimes. They didn't give us personal hygiene products, or open the window, or turn on the ventilation; they didn't allow outdoor walks, or let us take a shower; they woke us up several times every night. The light in the cell was never turned off, so at night we had to cover our faces with clothes. One day, the light was accidentally switched off in our cell which shocked us so much that we could not utter a word. To appear in almost complete darkness just for a minute seemed like a miracle to us, something we did not appreciate in ordinary life.

There were often so many people in the cell that some had to stand at night because there was no way to lie down. It was forbidden to sleep during the day, but in a few corners on the floor, where the video camera did not cover the area, it was possible to rest for a short time. In general, the day was divided into several parts: getting up, cell search, breakfast, lunch, dinner and lights out. Sometimes between breakfast and lunch, several people were summoned for so-called preventive talks. Usually these talks were limited to explaining why the individual was detained, but sometimes they helped us to approximately determine the time and the weather outside. Our usual pastime was word games; however, towards the end of my sentence they arrested a girl who knew several folk tales by heart. We closed our eyes and felt calm when the fairy tales were told; it helped us forget our experiences for a brief moment.

Although the conditions were terrible, they were not the worst thing. The fading hope for the future was worse. Hope waned every time someone returned to the cell after serving their sentence, and reported new charges of violating criminal articles. It was completely impossible to be certain that you would be released, since every second person was detained again, sometimes immediately after leaving the gates of *Akrescina*.

There seemed to exist an unspoken rule in the cell: don't cry, even if you want to badly. Considering that there were usually about seventeen people kept in a seven-square-metre room, each girl realised that it was vital to maintain moral stability without aggravating the atmosphere. Despite the difficulties, we understood and supported each other. We offered help every time we could. I remember when I got into the Isolation Centre for Offenders (ICO) cell for the first time, I told the girls that I had not been given food for two days. Without further asking, they gave me bread and water and offered me some Valerian — all they had. We always shared our stories, advice and experiences, even with the girls we hardly knew. Everyone in the cell was kind, intelligent and interesting. This fact, I believe, demonstrates the uniqueness of the current institutions of detention in Belarus.

In addition to the girls in the cell, another source of support was communication with relatives, which was limited to the transfer of information through those who managed to leave *Akrescina*. If information got through, the fact became clear after a few days, because new medicines were provided by relatives. If there were medicines, it meant our loved ones were not detained. Later I learned that only a small part of what our family members sent was actually passed to us.

Everyone in custody became immersed in their choices. Remembering the past, I tried to analyse what should have been done to avoid arrest. I must admit that, because of moral pressure, the question inevitably comes to mind: was it worth going to protest marches in the first place and expressing your discontent? Wouldn't it have been easier to live in line with their orders, but at least outside the prison walls? Only over time did the realisation come again that submission and silence are the goal of the

Belarusian authorities, and that one cannot give in to this pressure. In such situations, we must not forget that it is not the protester who is wrong, but the one who suppresses any opinion that is unacceptable to the dictatorship. Keeping this in mind is especially hard when you are haunted by thoughts that your long-cherished plans for the future may never come true.

After being released, the first thing I did was breathe in the fresh air. The second thing was to hug my family and cry. I left Belarus a week later, fearing that I would have to go through imprisonment for a second time. Despite the fact that memories of *Akrescina* are hard, I still keep in touch with the girls from the cell. Each of us follows the events that take place in the lives of each other, we communicate as much as we possibly can, and we are ready to help each other. The traumatic experience we went through, contrary to the expectations of the authorities, has only brought us closer, and it is producing positive results.

Life after Akrescina

Two shocking events — my arrest and emigration — have overlapped, causing serious moral difficulties. Despite the support of family, friends, and colleagues, I needed the help of a professional psychologist. Although a lot of time has passed, the events I experienced do not go away from memory, and they continue to evoke feelings of loss and injustice. Nevertheless, the only thing you can do is to live with this, sharing your experience with others: some can be warned, and others can even be brought to a better understanding of what almost every Belarusian has been through.

When you are in a foreign country, making plans for the future appears much more difficult than it seemed before. Although I still aspire to study for a master's degree and continue working in the field of human rights, my primary goal is to see my family and friends; to feel once again, to the full extent, the connection and support that was temporarily severed. I never cease to believe that Belarus will eventually become free. When this moment comes, I will be glad to take part in its development. I also look forward to the day when those responsible for repressions and human rights abuses will be held accountable; and, as a lawyer, I will strive to achieve justice. It will be difficult to accomplish this, and, for now, I have little idea whether it will be possible to change the situation in Belarus in the near future. However, I am deeply convinced that every person, who is not indifferent, should never give up and tolerate lawlessness. We must continue to exchange information, support, and protect each other without succumbing to manipulation and propaganda, and remain true to our principles.

Bright days will come, because darkness cannot envelop reality when there is at least one spark of hope in it. Sooner or later, with no support for the current government, the regime will be shaken again, and this will be the perfect moment for good people to help it to collapse. I believe that Belarus will become a country of happy citizens; we just need not lose hope and not to forget what we have been through.

Wrocław, June 2023
hanvla@proton.me

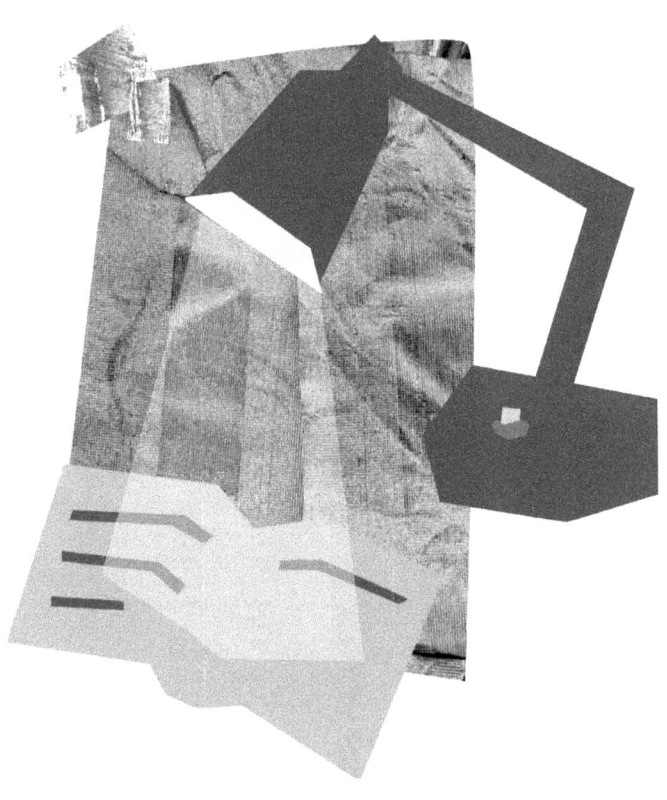

NO REGRETS

Tatiana

To my Mum and everyone who was there all that time.

The city was amazingly calm that day

My name is Tanya. I am now 21 years old. Many people say, however, that prison years do not count. In this case, we can consider that I am still 19. That's exactly how old I was when the KGB detained me. But let me start with earlier events.

I was born and raised in Minsk. At school, mathematics and physics were the easiest subjects for me, so there was almost no question about choosing a specialism.

I often brood on how certain events can radically affect our lives. A turning point in my life was enrolling at the Faculty of Mechanics and Mathematics at Belarusian State University, Minsk. As it turned out later, this is the most "incentive-driven" and active faculty of the university. I can't say that I was among the best students in the group, but I was interested in my studies, and I tried to keep up. The only subject I hated was Political Science. I remember how a teacher even kicked me out of the classroom once, because I was sleeping during his seminar! But if I hadn't slept, who knows, maybe events would have rolled out differently. At that moment, I was positively determined to complete my studies in Belarus. Moreover, after graduating from university, I was to work in the country for a couple of years. Even if I ever considered the prospect of moving somewhere abroad, it was very distant and vague.

I remember going to my first election on 9 August 2020. I thought it very important then, and I was terribly excited. After voting, my mother and I went to our favourite Minsk restaurant chain Vasilki and drank some liqueur to celebrate. The city was amazingly calm that day.

We are just at the very beginning of history

In 2020, an incredible wave of protests swept across Belarus. This statement in retrospect is hardly sufficient to fully describe the importance and character of the events that took place after the elections. The way the Belarusians rallied at that time and their daring actions were incredibly inspiring. It is obvious that students also picked up this breath of freedom. We were highly motivated!

We felt it our responsibility to bring the process that began long before us to its completion. It seemed that we were standing on the threshold of something new, something we needed to push just a little bit — and, voilà, we would live in a new and free country! Maybe from the historical point of view it was quite naive to think so, but that's how we felt. At that moment, I certainly did not suspect that my court verdict would interpret it that by singing and having tea and cookies at the university we would draw sanctions to Belarus from the European Union and the United States.

Later, while in the prison colony, the girls discussed this issue, and a woman, another political prisoner, said: "Yes, change never happens quickly. Everything takes time, during which entire generations replace one another. God grant that our children live in a new country".

Until recently, we were those very children who were supposed to live in the new Belarus! We were building our future! To spend our young years there! I thought we were already completing a long process, but it turned out that we were only standing at the very beginning of history.

It works

My detention is something that is etched into the memory like a knife and, perhaps, will never be forgotten. I can replay this day in my head hour by hour, even literally minute by minute. Now it seems funny to me, but, during the first month in the pre-trial detention centre, the moment of detention floated before my eyes in a series of terrible images every evening, and I couldn't do anything about it, I couldn't get the images out of my mind.

Ironically, I happened to be detained two weeks later than all the other defendants in the so-called students' case. Subsequently, these two weeks played a cruel joke on me. Since a day spent in a pre-trial detention centre is counted as one and a half days in terms of a prison sentence, two weeks multiplied by one and a half meant that I was released three weeks later than all my "accomplices". If I had known it would happen, I would have surrendered to the police on the same day as everyone else.

After six months spent in the pre-trial detention centre, the rest of the students finally got to know each other in the process of getting acquainted with the case materials, and my "accomplice" Hleb asked me: "Why didn't you leave the country?" I still don't have an answer to this question. I don't know why I didn't leave the country. Maybe I wasn't resolute enough. After all, until the last moment, it always seems that this will not affect you. Why? I didn't do anything illegal...

I had absolutely no premonition that something bad could happen to me. I was so confident that right in the evening before my arrest, my mother and I managed to visit a concert hall in Minsk for an organ concert for the 335th anniversary of Bach. I remember this evening very well. Most of the performers were young girls. I remember how amazed I was seeing these small and fragile girls cope with a huge and majestic organ. Olga Podgaiskaya, the organist, impressed me most. She played both Bach and her own compositions. I was surprised that there are composers who still write music for the organ.

After the concert, keeping up with our tradition, my mother and I went to Vasilki and ordered some liqueur.

About six months later, when I was already in the pre-trial detention centre, I received several letters from a certain woman. In one of them I read: "I am a musician and composer. I perform and write music for my favourite organ." Only then did I re-read the return address and the addressee's name more carefully — Olga Podgaiskaya! And the memories of the last day before the arrest flashed before my eyes again. Bach's music began to play ominously in my mind. So it happens! This is my favourite story from that period of my life. I wrote to Volha about all this, but, of course, our correspondence was immediately cut off. I still don't know if this letter was ever received.

Just a couple of days before my arrest, I was lucky enough to read an article containing instructions on how to behave during an interrogation. It was intended for anarchists, but the algorithm is in general the same for everyone. The article described various psychological techniques used by investigators during an inquiry or interrogation. The strategies suggested were like this: to pacify the interrogated person, to offer them coffee or a cigarette, to endlessly repeat the same questions until they give the desired answers, to play "good cop bad cop" — all in all, everything was in the style of traditional detective stories. When I was reading the article, it seemed terribly banal to me: "Does this work? Well, is anyone really going to be hooked up by this? They've probably come up with new tricks that are more effective now." In practice, it turned out that, indeed, nothing cooler than the bicycle has ever been invented. No need for that. Everything runs exactly as described in the article! It works.

The article helped me enormously. I quickly recognised the police agents' tricks, which exactly mimicked those suggested for anarchists described in the article. This was certainly very amusing. And it helped me remain calm and firm during all the interrogations. I must give myself credit for the fact that even when I re-read my testimony and the explanatory note later, I was completely satisfied with their content. Or rather, absolute "no-content", revealing no facts.

And here I am in the KGB pre-trial detention centre. It's strange, but I wasn't scared at that moment, I was curious. The centre has the shape of an atrium inside, so the lower levels are visible from the upper ones. On the floor where the cells are located, the central space is covered with a net, the cells are arranged in a circle and divided into sectors. It felt like in an action movie with Sylvester Stallone, where I had to escape from prison.

The first thing you have to get used to is limited space. The cells in the KGB detention centre are so narrow that two people cannot pass each other between the beds, and movement is only possible in one direction. I fully experienced that going to bed for the first time. Looking up, I realised how small the ceiling area was. Literally four steps long and two wide.

Then there was *Valadarka*. Everything there is completely different, but no less cinematic than the KGB pre-trial detention centre. You can feel the historicity of the Piščałaŭski Castle, built in the 19th century. The way to the exercise yards is through the dilapidated towers and the basement, where two-hundred-year-old vaults are preserved. And the wrought bars on the windows, three fingers thick, also seem to have been preserved from the time the castle was first built.

"Don't you see they are taking her away?"

My biggest fear in prison was that someone wouldn't be home to wait for me. It is impossible to bear the loss of relatives in that place. On the day of the arrest, besides my apartment, the KGB officers also conducted a search in the apartment of my grandparents. The security forces officers consented not to mention my arrest and to say that I was simply helping them in solving a case. I opened the door with my own keys. Naturally, they found nothing in the apartment; they just made my elderly grandparents nervous.

At last the moment comes when we must leave. I say goodbye. I leave my keys on the drawer unit. Grandma asks me if I will come back. Grandfather says: "Don't you see they are taking her away?" I wanted to hug my grandmother so much and tell her that everything would be okay. But I tried to pretend that I was leaving for a short while, and a hug would have given away the whole truth of what was happening. That is why I didn't even hug her. After the case was closed, my grandmother continued to visit me in the KGB pre-trial detention centre. I remember being amazed at how grey her hair had become. She aged a lot and changed a lot. That was the day I saw her for the last time. When in the prison colony, I learned that my grandfather had passed away. Without him, my grandmother survived for only six months.

I didn't even give them a call from the colony.

There is something mystical and karmic about it

There were also positive moments in the whole story. I will never forget Olya Syrovatko's eyes shining with pure happiness on the day before her release. You can tell a prisoner who is to be released by the look of their eyes. Straight away. This very moment makes you realise that in prison, the light fades away from people's eyes. Life literally leaves them and returns only before release. It was on the last day that I noticed what stunningly beautiful blue eyes Olya has!

I am also grateful to fate for bringing me together with many wonderful and interesting people. Obviously, there is a touch of providence in the fact that the State Security Committee linked twelve completely different people, unfamiliar with one another, into one case. Who knows, perhaps it was no coincidence that fortune brought us together and intertwined us in such difficult circumstances. I really hope that this bond between us will remain for many years, and we shall not lose touch. There is something mystical and karmic about it.

The person who became my closest friend and most important being of all the people I met in prison is my beloved Nastsia Yarashevich, with whom I still remain very close. She was my greatest support in the colony. We ate, and walked, and laughed, and cried together. And we were ready to stand up for each other to confront the cops. It so happened that Nastya was released nine months earlier than me. Absolutely unexpectedly for everyone — she was pardoned. Words cannot express how incredibly happy I was for her. Meanwhile, it felt as if the ground fell out from underneath my feet. Nastya was the only close person with whom I could cry and share all my pains.

Now she is like a real sister to me. Although we are separated by 900 kilometres, I can't wait to see her again and, like in the good old days, chat about everything in the world.

"Time multiplied by distance works wonders"

The human brain is designed in an interesting way. When I was released after two years in prison, it seemed as if these two years had never existed at all. The city hadn't changed, the people hadn't changed. Life was going on as usual.

To this day, when I tell people that in total I have spent more than two years in prison, I find it hard to believe it myself.

Have I changed during this time? Yes, definitely. My views on many things have changed and become somewhat more mature. The environment has changed. A lot of friends have fallen away, simply out of sight. But many of them have remained, too. And, in place of those who disappeared, there are many more who have become close and dear to me, whom I can call true friends. Perhaps I have become tougher and rougher. But the principal worldview still remains unchanged, of course. Rather, on the contrary, I begin to understand more clearly what I want from life. I had a lot of time to think about it. And yet, I really hope that, deep down in our souls, all twelve of us will remain youthfully daring and ambitious and retain our boundless faith in goodness and justice.

After my release, it took me a long time to cope with depersonalisation. From the very first day of my imprisonment, it always seemed as if I was not living my own life but watching some kind of art-house movie. The film is awfully interesting, for sure, but I would recommend watching it only from the outside. Oddly enough, following my release, this feeling did not disappear, but even intensified. I wanted to enjoy everything as much as possible to make up for the lost two years. I wanted to get everything at once. But this just didn't happen. My mind seemed to block out the pleasant sensations, and it took me four months before I could fully enjoy life again.

Now I have been free for six months. During this time, more things have happened to me than in my entire life. I crossed the border illegally, I started living alone in a foreign country, I enrolled for a university and chose the speciality I could only dream of. I attended many official meetings that I never thought I would attend, and, finally, I learned English. Although many of my memories of prison are still very vivid, it is becoming increasingly difficult to believe that I was really there, that all this happened to me. Time multiplied by distance works wonders. And now, looking back, I can definitely say: no regrets. I'm not afraid of anything, I don't regret anything, I wouldn't change anything. If it weren't for this experience, I would never be in the place where I am now. I would never have learned confidence in myself. I would never have learned fearlessness.

Afterword

I would like to express my deep gratitude to all those people who, throughout the difficult time of my prison term, supported me with a huge number of letters, postcards, parcels and money transfers.

I carefully stored the information so that I could contact everyone later, but some of the records were taken away from me by the penal administration, some were lost, some could not be taken out of Belarus, and it appeared simply impossible to find most people on the internet.

For obvious reasons, I cannot list the names of all those whom I would like to find, so I am attaching an email for contacting me. I will be extremely glad if one of my pen pals responds.

Long live Belarus!

Prague, January 2024
mystory.ekelchik@gmail.com

HOW TO VOTE IN ELECTIONS AND GO TO JAIL WHEN YOU ARE NINETEEN YEARS OLD?

The Thirteenth Person

Recently, I turned 22. I celebrated my previous two birthdays in prison. There I agreed with my "accomplice" N that after release we would definitely gather all our friends for one big party and celebrate all the missed birthdays. It would be fun and a blast. However, the reality turned out to be different. Some of my friends have stayed in Belarus, others, including N, have left for different countries. The big, noisy party is only in my imagination now. Everything is changed now.

Behind the prison walls you idealise a lot of things, and the desire just to go back to your previous way of life, that you have elevated to a cult, becomes a fixed idea. This is where the complexity of post-prison adaptation comes from. The world did not stand still while you were in prison.

I was born and raised in *Hrodna*. This is a regional capital in western Belarus, a calm town, with beautiful, little, two-storey buildings in the centre. I love *Hrodna*; in high school, my friends and I had the freedom of the town and roamed from end to end on our bikes. It was fun. In the summer, we made trips out of town on our two-wheeled vehicles, to the riverside and the lake. We got together and played board games on a blanket that we spread in the garden of *Hrodna* New Castle. What a great time it was to remember before lights out.

Universities

In 2018, I started my first year at university in *Hrodna*, and my major was Fine Arts and Computer Graphics. I might say, the choice of speciality was quite spontaneous, although I liked drawing all my life. By the way, my main activity right now is related to this too. I spent my first year at university trying to make sense of my capacity. At weekends, I often met with my classmates in workshops to draw and discuss various things. We made plans and dreamed. And when the year came to an end, I felt I wanted more and decided to transfer to Minsk and continue in the same speciality at Belarusian State Pedagogical University.

In my second year of studies at this new university, I was more involved in activism. It appeared much easier to find like-minded students in the capital city as well as a bunch of events, lectures, and informal education possibilities. I must admit, however, that the new university did not live up to my expectations, as it turned out much more inferior in terms of the level of education. Even some basic issues like scheduling the classes were not properly addressed, and the electronic portal did not work. No one notified us about the changes in the schedule, therefore schedule overlaps often happened. The arrangement of the educational process surprised me, to put it mildly, especially after my provincial university, where modern technologies were actively introduced into management.

Activism

During that period, among those organisational misfits, I met N. We started to attend lectures outside the university together and engage in self-education. During our second year, we completed a special volunteer student leadership programme, which focused on addressing specific social issues. I worked on a project to ensure separate waste collection in our part of the university building. Together we supported other young activists. I recall attending the court hearings for the participants of the "Youth Bloc" quite well.

I credit my family for instilling in me the habit of staying informed about current affairs and happenings in our country. My father was always interested in Belarusian culture and history, and the family often discussed the news. When I was in elementary school, my parents even took me to the polling stations. Therefore, when the 2020 election campaign unfolded, I closely followed each development.

I find it difficult to imagine myself uninterested in the political situation. So when people inquire about the past and what I would have altered if I had known about the prison ahead, I respond with a simple "nothing". I can't imagine myself as a different person. I did everything with a sincere and natural approach.

Before and after the elections

I spent the time of my first elections and the entire month of August 2020 in *Hrodna*. On 9 August, I visited the polling station during the day, and later that evening, I joined my friends in the town's main square. It was around 6 pm when people began to flock to the centre individually and in small groups. Circling slowly, the people looked hesitantly at each other, as if they anticipated something would happen. It was a strange feeling. Everyone knew why they came here, but there was uncertainty and some tension in the air. Sometimes bold spirits showed up here and there carrying insignia of the white, red, and white colour scheme. Then someone clapped, and the crowd joined in the applause.

We sat on a bench in the square and struck up a conversation with the guys sitting next to us. The atmosphere became increasingly tense as two black police vans arrived at the scene. I remember a crowd of individuals in bulletproof vests and helmets disembarking from the huge vehicles in the midst of a calm and sunny evening. There were so many of them that it was only natural to wonder: how did they all squeeze into merely two vans? They lined up and walked across the square, snatching people at random. The crowd would disperse for a time only to regroup in the square again. We were fortunate: none of my friends was detained, even though we wandered around the town centre for a long time, trying not to fall into the hands of the security forces.

During the initial days of August following the elections, the atmosphere was frightening due to the lack of information and the unreliable internet connectivity. In the evening we went into town, where we tried to dodge the "men in black", and at night we tried to find out any news about the events in Minsk. Downloading images and videos from Telegram channels was almost impossible, so we learned the news only in brief summaries. The information we received made me shiver. We didn't sleep at night, we were updating Telegram, and following the news from the streets of the capital. In the morning, anxious expectation set in again. I wanted to do something, to influence the situation in some way, and stop the violence that was happening all around. It was impossible to just sit around and do nothing. My friends and I started to put up flyers with the photographs of people injured during the protests in Minsk. The internet connection was still down, and not everyone knew how to use VPN, so we decided that at least in this way we would help spread information.

In response to inhumane violence, Belarusians arranged women's chains of solidarity. Every day, we would ride our bicycles to the central square, dressed in white, holding flowers in our hands. The protesters did not want to respond to violence with violence. The police acted so cruelly and insanely that only absolute calm could oppose them.

In *Hrodna*, participants in peaceful protests managed to compel the chairman of the city executive committee and his assistants to attend a meeting. It's amazing that this event was even filmed by the local city TV channel. The mayor promised citizens freedom of assembly and the release of political prisoners. He promised that every day he would go out to meet people in the square and report on the work done.

The communication between the local authorities and the people was short-lived: the head of the *Hrodna voblasć*, Uladzimir Krautsou, and several other officials were removed from office, and the police resumed cracking down on the rallies. This was not so easy to do, though, because the protests had taken on a mass character. I remember riding a bicycle to the next rally one of those days and seeing in front of every small or large enterprise the employees standing in rows with flowers and posters of solidarity. It seems Belarusians had never had anything like this before.

The marches of the factory workers were a powerful sight. After the shift, workers of the largest industrial enterprise, OJSC Hrodna Azot, moved in a column from the outskirts of the city to the centre for a meeting with the mayor. Imposing and formidable men dressed in work clothes walked, instilling confidence in the inevitability of victory over the regime. Workers from other enterprises — Furniture ZOV, Grodnokhimvolokno, Terrazit Plus LLC also marched to the centre.

I remember how we created an impromptu memorial after learning about the first two victims of the suppression of peaceful protests. We printed their photos, bought flowers, wore black, drew posters with their names, and stood under the scorching sun all day. By the evening, our memorial had grown several times larger thanks to sympathetic people who brought flowers and lit candles. Protest participants felt that they mustn't give up, mustn't remain silent and inactive any longer. Despite the authorities ordering municipal workers to periodically remove our memorial in the centre of *Hrodna*, people would restore it the next day.

Students' protest

August was drawing to a close, and I had to go back to studies, although at that time it was not even possible to think about studying. Already in early September, students from nearly all the universities began publishing open letters of appeal with specific demands:

— stop violence;
— release all political prisoners;
— hold new democratic presidential elections.

I couldn't remain on the sidelines, either. Together with like-minded people, we prepared an open letter on behalf of Belarusian State Pedagogical University students. Meanwhile, other students and even university teachers joined our demands. I can't say, however, that our university was particularly active. But caring guys couldn't just sit idle and wait.

On 1 September 2020, on Knowledge Day, students from all universities in Minsk collected signatures for petitions to submit officially to the Ministry of Education. However, the regular police and riot police did not allow us to do this. Detentions of activists began. They blocked the road in front of numerous student columns moving towards the ministry and did not let them approach it. But the students did not give up, they used already well-established tactics: they scattered and regrouped again.

In general, the outcomes of 1 September for Belarusian students from various universities were arrests and hundreds of days spent in temporary detention facilities.

Every Sunday, Belarusian State Pedagogical University students gathered for the marches; on weekdays we gathered to discuss new actions. We tried to think what else we could come up with: we distributed leaflets, drew posters, and even created our own photo project. In general, we acted as best we could.

A general strike was declared for 26 October 2020. Dozens of students gathered near their universities and ignored the studies. Following their local meetings, protesters converged in the city centre. By lunchtime, an impressive joint column had formed. This was a loud and vibrant day.

Immediately after the strike, preparations began for the next date — 17 November — International Students' Day. This was a significant date for us, so we began to discuss plans in advance, which, however, were not destined to come true.

Black Thursday

That very "special" Thursday arrived — 12 November 2020. I didn't even imagine that they could "come" for me. There were, of course, some uneasy premonitions, but I still didn't expect such an unannounced scenario. On that day, ten student activists from different Minsk universities and one lecturer were detained.

I remember visiting a pottery workshop on the evening of 11 November. I was fascinated by the process of creating all kinds of cups, plates, and containers. I practised clay modelling and then met with friends. I went to bed late and woke up to a long ring at the door. I was lucky that my grandparents, with whom I lived in Minsk, were at their dacha on that day. I can't imagine how scared they would have been of such "guests".

Now I barely remember the details of that day. But by 11 pm, I ended up in my first prison cell in the KGB pre-trial detention centre, known as the *Amierykanka*. The experience of staying in a pre-trial detention centre is, of course, unique. Now, after comparing it to imprisonment in a correctional colony, it even seems less traumatic to me. By coincidence, my time in detention consisted of constant transfers from cell to cell. Initially, this was very difficult psychologically, but after the third time it became easier and simpler. Over the eleven months I spent in the pre-trial detention centre, I "moved" nine times. This helped me better understand the internal workings of the prison and its daily life, and introduced me to different cells and people. During my imprisonment, I met many interesting Belarusians, most of whom were also political convicts. It was thanks to their support and mutual help that we were able to endure these two years.

Now I remember the pre-trial detention centre as a useful time spent with good people. Perhaps this is a peculiarity of the mind — to remember the good things.

A tale of court hearing

I was very much looking forward to the court hearing. Firstly, it gave me a chance to see my relatives, and, secondly, to spend time in the good company of other students.

Every time we were driven from the pre-trial detention centre to the "justice" building in two police vans, there was a convoy of the riot police detachment. Each of us was handcuffed as if we were especially dangerous criminals (defendants in "non-political" cases were transported without handcuffs). The fact of being transported in such a large group really encouraged me. It enabled us to stand up for each other in case of conflict situations with the convoy, or just to joke and support each other.

I'd like to note that being transferred to court hearings, which began on 14 May 2021, was physically challenging for me. During the time spent in the pre-trial detention centre, I developed vertigo, and the dark and cramped "glasses" in the police vans did not contribute to my recovery at all. And how stuffy it was there in the summer!

Each of us had our own lawyer. There were twelve defendants and twelve lawyers. From the prosecution side, there were two representatives of the prosecutor's office, Raman Chabatarou and Anastasiya Maliko, who were rather young, just slightly older than us.

For most of the trial the interrogation of witnesses went on, almost all of them represented the prosecution. These were university teachers, deans, vice-rectors of various Minsk universities, there were also police officers who came to meetings wearing masks and baseball caps, trying to hide their faces (I even have a sketch of one of them).

From the first questionings of witnesses, it became clear that most of them did not understand altogether the significance of their testimonies. The wording used in their interrogation reports was apparently compiled by the investigators. During testimony, witnesses blindly signed these reports filled with dry legal terminology, and then read them out in court. But the most absurd thing was to see among the witnesses those who were not even present at the events they were questioned about. It turned out that the investigator simply showed them videos, asked them to describe what they saw, and based on that drew up an interrogation report. Exchanges like "Were you a witness?" — "No, but I watched the video" were common during court hearings.

The charges contained the accusation stating that our entire group of twelve people provoked the EU and US sanctions against Belarus and, by prior conspiracy, we organised all unauthorised mass events at Minsk universities.

At the stage of witness testimony and the following debates, it was obvious that the accusations crumbled with each question raised by the defence lawyers. I can't say it was reassuring in any way. We knew that the absence of logic in the accusation would not affect our sentence at all, and we would get the verdict which the court would receive from above. It was clear that, in essence, all these trials, the speeches of lawyers, witnesses, and prosecutors had nothing to do with real justice. Everything happened as expected. Our "young prosecutors" pleaded for two and a half years in prison for us out of a maximum of three years. The minimum penalties of Article 342 start with a fine. The court "listened" to the opinion of the so-called prosecutors.

On the day the verdict was announced, 16 July 2021, we agreed with the guys about our last student action, the essence of which was to appear at the final court proceeding with the element of fire in our clothes. This was our appeal to the feat of the famous Jan Palach, who became a symbol of the student movement. Among the suitable clothes, I had "fiery" socks! We listened to the verdict in handcuffs: we were sentenced to two and a half years. For some reason, they were afraid to take the handcuffs off from our wrists in the courtroom, even in the "cage". Of course, it was morally difficult. It is not easy to realise that after almost a year in a pre-trial detention centre, you will have to spend even more time in the correctional colony.

In my final statement in court, I tried to express everything I thought about the trial and the events in Belarus. Since the trial was open, excerpts from our speeches, including mine, were recorded and published in independent media: "The last eight months have significantly changed my life. I have seen all the flaws in our society. It seems to me that our society is afraid of problems, turning a blind eye to them and thinking that they will resolve themselves. Therefore, I feel bitter about everything that is happening in our country; about the fact that the most promising and deserving students among us are forced to leave or go to prison... But I love Belarus with all its pluses and minuses — even after eight months in prison." Even today, I can subscribe to these words.

Women's correctional colony no. 4

The colony became a waking nightmare for me. It might be because I was assigned to the "press squad", where I witnessed psychological and physical violence, where no one trusted anyone else, where people constantly informed on each other, and where the squad's operational officer liked to stage punishment shows. For instance, he could come to his victim's section, turn over all the beds, scatter the bedding (not only of his target, but of all her roommates as well). He enjoyed building a "Leaning Tower of Pisa" out of bedside tables, stacking them on top of each other. Beforehand, all personal belongings were thrown onto the floor. When the victim returned from work, the storekeeper would hand her the operational officer's instructions, telling her she had to clean up the room alone, and, if anyone dared to help her, they would also be punished.

I spent a month in this detachment, yet until the end of my term, the operational officer of this detachment periodically found me and used the preventive measures I described. Why did this happen? No one spoke to you or explained anything. And this is only a small part of the "entertainment" and abuse of prisoners in the colony, primarily political ones.

Of course, you need to understand that the life of a political prisoner in a penal colony differs from the life of an ordinary prisoner. Let me give you a few examples. Basically, political prisoners are subject to special supervision, and special compliance with internal regulations is required. For example, even having one undone button on a quilted jacket can result in a disciplinary report for violating the uniform dress code. Situations often occur where regular inmates are severely punished for friendly relations or simply communicating with political prisoners. The administration constantly hints that such communication is undesirable and that political prisoners should be avoided. This rhetoric is used by the administration all the time.

They mark political prisoners with yellow tags calling this a preventive accounting for extremism and other destructive activities. Additional checks and searches become commonplace for political prisoners. Colonial staff often resort to various provocations and create fake violations for political prisoners. You become a hostage to the situation; it is impossible to prove your innocence either in court or in the colony. Women can be sent to a punishment cell only for the simple fact of treating another convict to a candy or an apple.

The madness of colony life, which never ceases for a moment, severely affects one's mental state. If it weren't for the silent, internal support we gave each other, I don't think I could have coped with such challenges. Of course, the colony administration strove to eliminate the solidarity and mutual support among prisoners, but we still tried to maintain contact and communication with each other at all costs. This gave me a last drop of hope that I preserved throughout all that time.

During the time I spent behind bars, many things changed in the world. The pandemic was replaced by the war in Ukraine, and at some point, it seemed we would be released only to step into complete ruins. We were in an information vacuum, nevertheless, we tried to find out the news through relatives during prison visits. We constantly exchanged the information we received, passing it on through word of mouth.

In any case, when you are released, you step into the unknown.

What next?

I am very grateful to my parents, who, on the second day after my release, managed to evacuate from Belarus to a safe place. I am trying to recover, slowly and with care, to restore my physical and psychological state. I am coping with emigration and want to continue my studies to become a graphic designer.

I am constantly reflecting, trying to live my life. "Thanks to" prison, at the age of 19, I have grey hair, as well as problems with my vestibular system. For some reason I find it difficult to ride public transport. I always try to sit facing the direction of movement so that I don't get sick. I am not prepared to talk about flying at the moment; my body is not ready to cope with turbulence.

Things have changed a lot, and I have changed, too. I'm free now. I have turned 22 years old. I celebrated my previous two birthdays in prison, just like other political prisoners celebrate theirs now, and many of those are women. Mine is a story about being lucky, because a sentence of two and a half years seems meagre now compared to sentences of ten to fifteen years. I don't know how I can help them. Letters do not reach political prisoners (they are accepted only from relatives), neither can I come and release them. It seems that I have no tools whatsoever to help. All I can do is talk about them and remind others. While you and I can walk freely here, our friends are going through occupational checks, suffering in punishment cells, existing on the verge of life and death. I don't know if any words can describe the scale of this tragedy.

I am now 22 years old, and I spent two of those years in prison.

City N, June 2023
poz000r13@gmail.com

A COUNTRY UNDER TWO FLAGS

Hleb

> For my wish is to walk the earth –
> The most faithful, beloved of sons.
> *Hienadź Buraŭkin (1936-2014)*

The unbounded space of Belarusian political life opened up for me when I was still at school. I remember a postcard on the fridge with Uładzimir Niaklajeŭ's pre-election slogan "I have come to help you win", and new issues of the Narodnaja Vola newspaper appearing at home. I literally devoured developments about the events of the 2010 election race, which I unsuccessfully tried to discuss in high school with teachers and classmates. The latter were not interested, they were very busy with "Dota" and "Counter-Strike", while the teachers were either afraid to say something extracurricular or, perhaps, they really cared more about their vegetable gardens and removing the leaves from the school ground. Then I enrolled in the Belarusian State University Lyceum, where I found myself surrounded by people who loved their country and were very concerned about its future. In the lyceum, we discussed everything openly: the Maidan, the Crimea and Donbas, the presidential campaign, as well as such bright personalities as Mikalai Ulakhovich and Tatsiana Karatkievich. The songs of the Liapis and NRM bands were played loud in the corridor. We organised the days of the Belarusian Language and Culture. The lyceum lived its own life and was not a typical educational institution for Belarus, which I am very grateful for, and I especially appreciate its incredible teachers.

The Faculty of International Relations maintained its image as an island of liberalism on the planet called Belarusian State University. However, one always had to pay attention to what you said and who was your interlocutor. A distinctive feature of The Faculty of International Relations was its administration — they were loyal and empathetic. At the same time, there were people who could easily ruin your life. In short, these educational institutions gave me an understanding of dignity and right actions. We were brought up to love our Motherland and were ready to work for its further development. We dreamed and aspired to become Belarusian diplomats. It is regrettable that many graduates of Belarusian State University understood this in their own way and betrayed the values instilled in them.

After graduating from The Faculty of International Relations, I was invited to undergo training at the Linguistic University in order to continue working at the Ministry of Foreign Affairs. Nourished by the romantic ideas from the memoirs of Piotr Krauchanka, inspired by the multi-vector foreign policy of Belarus, and the improving relations with Western countries, following my dream, I signed the document next to *Uladzimir Makei*'s name. I was fascinated by the very idea of a state institution that was "non-typical" for Belarus, a ministry that promoted the Belarusian economic and cultural agenda and increased the interest in our country abroad. During my internship at the Ministry of Foreign Affairs, I had a feeling that most of the employees understood the existing problems. They laughed at the gaffes of their president and hoped that Belarus would be a better country. I sincerely believed in patriotism and the ability of young diplomats and officials to influence the generally corrupt system and change it from the inside. It turned out that there were few such romantics, and in 2020, only a small part managed to tell the truth. The rest lowered their faces to the table and easily gave up their strife to achieve the best for the country. Instead of being an example for the young, a Belarusian diplomat started posting ignominious TikTok videos and making statements that incited hostility towards other countries.

Apart from Belarusian history and culture, I was also interested in football and passionately cheered for the national team. I had never missed a single match before, even if the win rate was zero. In October 2020, I decided to go to a football match at the Dynamo arena with two Belarusian flags — to demonstrate that now they would not manage to divide the people and that we all stood together against the authoritarian regime and violence of the "security forces". Whether we like it or not, we have to admit that our unique country lives under two flags: the national one, or the historical white-red-white, and the other that symbolises the authoritarian state and the socialist past. I was born, earned a university degree, and started work when the country was dominated by the red and green flag. At the same time, the white-red-white always hung in my room. This did not bother anyone at the time. This is our Belarusian historical dualism: continuously living in two realities, two historical truths, with two languages, two presidents, and under two flags.

I was detained in the stands of the football stadium. During the arrest, a group of riot police tried to lecture me on history, which made me stare at them in surprise when I heard that Poland once occupied our territory and that the Statute of the Grand Duchy of Lithuania was adopted in 1918. As it turned out later, I was arrested for holding a solitary picket and expressing my disagreement with the results of fair elections, Article 23.34. Then I found out that Dzmitry Balaba had been watching the match with me in another sector, and he did not appreciate my initiative very much. The policeman who brought me to *Akrescina*, before saying goodbye, asked me what I was detained for. "For the flag" — "What, just for the flag? Is that sufficient to go to *Akrescina*?" — "Yes." — "That's rough". What followed was the standard practice of undressing and squatting in front of everyone present, a couple of hours in the "glass", and then a day of waiting for the trial.

It is difficult to call that trial a trial, because it was held on Skype on the second floor of the same building where people were imprisoned in cells. A judge of the *Leninski* district whose surname was Shut came online wearing a mask. Apparently, she was afraid that people participating in rallies could transmit the coronavirus to her via Skype. She spoke very quickly, I only heard half of what she was saying. After relating her version of the situation, she connected a witness to the call, a policeman in a balaclava, who simply read out the version from the detention report. I felt both amused and scared. Amused because of the absurdity of the situation, and scared because this situation was real. The witness could not answer my questions about my clothes, me having a backpack, the sector of the stadium where I was detained. The judge retired to make a "difficult decision" that took Ms Shut only a minute and a half. One might call this her mastery and years of valuable experience. I was looking at the wall of the court building of the *Leninski* district on the laptop screen and could only hear a voiceover announcing twelve days of arrest.

I spent the next night in the Detention Centre for Offenders, where there were thieves and alcoholics, together with the people who had stood on the street with flags of their country. I well remember the words of one of the cellmates, an alcoholic guy with a hoarse voice: "What about you, did you study at The Faculty of International Relations? I actually built it." After chatting with the guys, receiving *Akrescina* bread in unlimited quantities, being inspected by the notorious iron woman with a wooden mallet, I was transported in an uncomfortable police van to the town of *Žodzina*, where I spent the most memorable nine days of my life. We were escorted out of *Akrescina* with the words: "We'll see you soon, but in a criminal case, if you don't manage to fuck away to Poland." Many of us took this as a call to action.

We were in a cell for "permies" (permanent inmates). There were ten people and double-decked iron beds, and mould, 24-hour electric light, cold water, and cramped space. It was impossible to sleep because of the small uncomfortable bunks and the light. We called it torture by the light. There was no bed linen, and my pillow had "328" written on it. When we went to sleep, we would say to each other: "Good night, incredible!"

Those days became an interesting social experiment for me of how to maintain relationships with ten people in a fifteen square metre cell. We chatted, joked, even sometimes sang, played dominoes made of bread, solved crosswords, read books, among them were Eden by Stanisław Lem, Didier Drogba's autobiography, a book about Columbus, one about Australia and even Bradbury's Fahrenheit 451. I am almost grateful to the authorities of my country for the chance to read the books that I hadn't had time for until then.

Another torture was Russian pop and chanson all day long. It seems to me that the prison administration specifically used it in order to kill all pro-Belarusian thoughts in the protesting inmates and to support the immortal limitations of its employees. I can't find any other explanation, because it is impossible simply to enjoy this kind of music.

It is amusing to recall the "fights" between our "house" and policemen. When they didn't let us wash, we pressed the button to call the attendant, and the sound could be heard throughout the corridor. For punishment, they forbade us to sit on the beds, but we intentionally lay on them in response. They started bringing us four aluminium mugs with compote instead of ten. In protest, we carved the inscriptions "Long live Belarus!" and "Send police vans behind the bars" on these mugs, after which we were generally left without a drink for the rest of the day. And on top of that, they turned off the water for a whole day, and the cell had such a strong smell of floating faeces. We did not win, but these fights cheered us up and inspired our new "feats". Thanks to these exploits, we received cigarettes, letters and parcels in our cell, because the policemen got tired of messing up with us.

The epitome of my entire prison journey was the national anthem of the Republic of Belarus, which was played with honour every morning in all the cells of *Žodzina* Prison no. 8, instilling in erring citizens a sense of patriotism and love for the motherland. After Sakalouski's music and Karyzna's lyrics of the anthem about the "ever-living" and "blooming" Belarus, Alexander Lukashenka's sparkling speech was broadcast in the prison speakers, where he said that Belarusians cannot survive without their leader, neither can he without Belarus. The prison staff reaffirmed this thesis every day through their actions.

The day after the end of my "excursion" to *Žodzina*, I was called for a talk at the Ministry of Foreign Affairs, where we had a pleasant conversation with the Ministry's top officials and an invited guest from the KGB. Summing up the results of this conversation, they told me that the whole problem was that I supported the Belarusian national football team, which plays like sh*t. I wonder what team they support?

I said goodbye to the Belarusian diplomatic service, and the fate of my flag remains unknown. Having been in my bedroom for ten years, now it is probably in the collection of Belarusian symbols at Correctional Facility no. 8 in *Žodzina* or, perhaps, some policeman has long since burned it. Or maybe he didn't burn it, but secretly hung it in his room, where the flag continues its dignified existence.

During my short experience in a Belarusian prison, I became even more confident in my optimistic approach to life. Only thanks to optimism and a sense of humour can one survive in such a surreal reality. You can despair, abandon all hope and motivation, but it won't do any good to anyone. I really appreciate Belarusian ahimsa: non-violent resistance. A peaceful, long and difficult path to a victorious end is our self-identity, the visiting card of the Belarusian protest, and not the reason for defeat. Thoughts about deviating from the peaceful plan, the need for revenge and killings, were often voiced in the prison. But is this the path to a civilised world we strive for? Can killing criminals solve current problems?

Among the reasons why the path to the new Belarus we dream of has dragged on so long is the firm desire of people for change with a simultaneous lack of willingness to change themselves. The majority of Belarusians want to have a new way of life, but are not eager to accept the norms of a developed social community: human rights, gender equality, respect for sexual, ethnic, and racial minorities. People are accustomed to waiting for orders from above on how to behave, but fundamental changes in their worldview can be made right at the micro level. Even in a toxic authoritarian environment.

Over the three years following the 2020 elections, the polarisation of society in Belarus has reached an all-time high. Belarusians have never been so divided as they are now. The chasm between the zmahary (fighters, protesters) and the *jabaćki* ("I-paters", president supporters) is massive, and the process of building the New Belarus depends solely on how soon we start bridging it. National maturity and the success of national development lie in broad dialogue involving the entire nation, without exception. Without national unity and attempts at common dialogue, the project of a New Belarus will not survive, because it is impossible to erase a whole part of the nation, even if that part is disliked by some.

We often like to shift responsibility to others and are reluctant to acknowledge our mistakes, seeking scapegoats. Lack of initiative and criticism with no alternatives are distracting us from building the New Belarus. Many miss out on so many fascinating things when they fail to venture beyond their personal boundaries and comfort zones. The path to change can only begin when ordinary

Belarusians who wake up at six o'clock in the morning, take their children to school, and go to work, start changing their approach to everyday life. We must do this ourselves, without orders from above, without relying on the European Union, the USA, Russia or God.

We must start changing with our own selves. According to my childhood plan, I have returned to the field of international relations and work in a humanitarian organisation, helping refugees from Ukraine to feel safe and comfortable in a new country. Despite the fact that my aspirations for the Belarusian diplomatic service have died, I feel at home, aiming to bring benefits and assistance to the world. I am convinced that good deeds return to you in life. I hope that the future of Belarus will belong to people who dedicate themselves to self-development, do the right things, and are ready to change themselves and the world around them. Among them are political prisoners and those who lost their prime in Belarusian prisons for wanting to be an honest person. I take my hat off to all the political prisoners. You are the heroes of Belarus. And the question under which single flag our country will continue its life will soon be resolved, and this time historical justice should not bypass Belarus.

Warsaw, June 2023

THE ONLY THING WE HAD WAS HOPE

Michaś A.

Picking a path

As a historian, I possess a deep understanding of the profound hardships and adversities endured by generations of Belarusians. The formative years and entire lifetimes of my fellow citizens were disrupted by the World Wars, the terror of revolutions, the brutal forced collectivisation, and the widespread political persecutions of the 1930s.

I was born in Minsk during a calm and peaceful time. The life of a child in the Belarusian capital in the 2000s was marked by happiness. I was not yet bothered by politics. I only knew that Lukashenka was the president and that the national flag was a red-green combination. I was unfamiliar with the meaning of the white-red-white flag. I did not know how the relative well-being of Belarusians was linked to the price of Russian oil. My family had enough money to go on holiday to the Crimea or travel to Kyiv every summer. What could have gone wrong?

My awareness started to grow following the events of the Square 2010. By then, I was mature enough, perhaps, to comprehend why Belarusians carried white-red-white flags and why the government opposed them. I listened to the revolutionary songs of Siarhei Mikhalok. I learned that in 1999, when I was just a year old, opposition politicians in Belarus went missing.

Nevertheless, life in Belarus in the 2010s cannot be compared to what occurred after 2020. In high school, I wore a white-red-white band and couldn't have imagined that even white and red socks would later become the pretext for criminal cases. I witnessed the annexation of the Crimea, but I wouldn't have believed that my beloved Kyiv would be bombed from my country.

I had no intention of leaving Belarus, and I was making plans for the future in my homeland. Like many children, I was initially captivated by aviation, and I also took part in the mathematics olympiad and attended a specialist school for physics and mathematics. However, as I progressed in my studies, I discovered that history was my true passion. The History Faculty at Belarusian State University quickly became a part of my future plans. I didn't even consider other alternatives, except for one thing: as I watched the Russian intellectual TV game during that period "Clever boys and Girls", I became mildly intrigued by the prospect of studying at Moscow State University of International Relations. However, I still decided to stay in Minsk, where I enrolled for the History Faculty. My resolve was reinforced by the fact that in the eleventh grade I earned a diploma at the Republican Olympiad in History, allowing me to enrol at the History Faculty without taking exams. This is precisely what I did during the summer of 2015.

Alma mater. The attitude of a Belarusian

As I started to wonder whether I had made the right choice in selecting my university, my answer was always a resounding yes. I found studying there to be engaging. The Faculty of History lived up to my expectations in terms of higher education. It was no longer sufficient to simply acquire knowledge; I had to analyse it and identify cause-and-effect relationships. Although science appeared challenging, it was worthy of a lifetime dedication. Belarusian State University was well-equipped for research. I felt a sense of pride for my alma mater when Belarusian State University ranked higher than Moscow State University of International Relations in the QS world ranking.

The most significant advantage that higher education arguably provides to students, especially in the humanities, is the development of critical thinking. It is something that is lacking in Belarusian schools. Something the authorities are trying to replace by the vaguely formulated "state ideology". I feel fortunate to have had the opportunity to study at the History Faculty before the repressive measures of the 2020s. It was with pride and pleasure that I would mention studying at the most oppositional faculty at the Belarusian State University. Not only because the students wore tee shirts with the *Pahonia* emblem to classes, but also because the university lecturers really fostered critical thinking, which was a departure from the official norm of the established one-sided positive interpretation of the Imperial and Soviet periods, and critical of any propaganda. My time at the History Faculty was marked by a profound transformation of first-year students, who initially held imperialist views, into committed participants in the 2020 protests. I am thankful to the faculty for this influence.

Looking back on my education, the goal I had envisioned even before joining the History Faculty was to become a university lecturer. This path required master's and doctoral degrees. However, initially, there was a question of distribution — a feature of post-Soviet Belarus that is incompatible with modern Europe. For a resident of Minsk, this was not a major concern: you are more likely to be hired if you do not need housing provided at the expense of the institution. That's how I got a job in a Minsk school, following a competition with my fellow student from another city. It was during my employment in the school that I encountered the protests of August 2020.

Why we took to the streets

Working as a teacher in a state school, studying at a state university — did this fact pose specific limitations on my engagement in civic activism? Not after 2020. You can lose your career, but you can't lose the chance to live in a free country. A chance that seemed real, and freedom — so close. Therefore, though I hadn't dared to join the protests before, in 2020 I joined hundreds of thousands of Belarusians.

What aim was I pursuing when I went out to protest? I believe my thoughts align with the intentions of the Belarusians who participated in the protests, which were centred around the resignation of the dictator, holding new elections, and releasing political prisoners. These fundamental issues, if left unaddressed, risked exacerbating the socio-economic and political crisis that had engulfed the country. As a student of history and someone deeply attuned to the lessons of the past, I felt a profound sense of responsibility to shape the future of my homeland. Belarus has suffered under a dictatorship for far too long. We have had enough.

By spring 2020, changes were in the air. Lukashenka's ineffective, almost non-existent fight against the coronavirus infuriated Belarusians. The authorities demonstrated efficiency only in their ability to manipulate and falsify statistical data — something they excelled in. We were unaware of the exact number of the infected and deceased, but the scale of the disaster was impossible to conceal. I witnessed cases in classrooms, where several children were already infected, yet schooling continued as usual. Later a colleague at the school also died of this disease. Even the school staff, who had long been part of the ideological education system, began voicing their discontent with the president in private conversations. Something was changing in Belarusians.

Another crucial aspect was the emergence of fresh faces who responded to society's call for transformation. The traditional leaders of the opposition were replaced by new people who did not depend on party infighting. The lofty idea of national revival could not resonate with the majority of the population until the issue of quality of life was addressed. That is precisely how Lukashenka secured victory in the 1994 elections. In 2020, the situation was reversed. It was Lukashenka's failure to enhance the living standards of Belarusians; instead, he offered them nothing better than the idea of "stability". A stability that could not be present at the onset of the crisis. In contrast, *Viktar Babaryka*, *Valery Tsepkalo* and *Siarhei Tsikhanouski* demonstrated an ability to listen to the people and instil hope.

Ultimately, Belarusians began to identify themselves as a civil society. This was evident as early as June 2020 when half of Minsk was left without water due to an accident, and the other half stepped up to help on their own initiative, in the face of the government's helplessness. On 30 July, we witnessed tens of thousands of Minsk residents gather for what was probably the largest rally in support of the democratic forces at that time. On 6 August, a rally took place without the authorities' permission. Belarusians did not need permission to show solidarity.

The black days of August

The events of 9-10 August angered us even more. Through a near-total internet blackout, news gradually began to circulate about *Sviatlana Tsikhanouskaya*'s victory being stolen, and the brutal tortures perpetrated by "law enforcement" against people who came out to defend this victory. On the morning of 9 August 2020, I was present at the polling station situated in the school where I worked. My responsibility was to guide voters to the appropriate ballot boxes. I refused to participate in the work of the commission to distance myself from any falsification efforts, as I would not be able to stop them anyway. Interestingly, the authorities permitted independent observers from Hołas (Voice) to monitor the voter turnout at the site. A pro-government chemistry teacher made efforts to expel the observers, but I was able to shield them from removal by referencing the school principal's granted permission. The election commission's reported results were quite remarkable, indicating a voter turnout exceeding 100%! This incident revealed the falsification of early voting turnout, which occurred without any observers present. Later that evening, I saw that my colleagues were not involved in the "ballot counting" process, as it was being carried out by different individuals. The most striking picture was that of the police officer's refusal to permit independent observers at the ballot count, resorting to threats with a firearm. Quote: "I've got eight bullets in my Makarov, enough for all of you." Then the teachers were forced to leave the building, and as I later found out, the riot police were called on the independent observers.

The dispersal of the rally in front of my eyes on 9 August made me cautious about joining the front line of the barricades on 10 August. We were a short distance from the place where the riot police killed Aliaksandr Taraikouski that day. I wanted to maintain my freedom and join the rally later, knowing that such an opportunity would arise soon. At that time, similar to many, I subscribed to the notion of peaceful protest. I earnestly aspired to take part. Fear was naturally present, too. During the crackdown, one could easily become a victim of circumstance. My friend had such bad luck — he simply went to the polling station on 9 August to check the election results. He was subsequently detained, beaten, and confined to a cell so overcrowded that there was no room even for sitting down, and a clichéd detention report was prepared indicating that he was apprehended at the rally on Pieramožcaŭ Avenue.

Our highest expectations were pinned on the strikes: the workers of major factories are the driving force without which the country's economy would grind to a halt. And we knew that the workers were in that particular frame of mind. That's why we decided to post leaflets calling for a strike. Then the most perilous moment for me arrived: we were spotted by a man holding a phone, who might have been recording our actions. Fortunately, we were spared: we managed to convince the stranger that we were posting flyers with employment opportunities.

The strike threat proved effective, as Lukashenka released the detainees who had been taken during the rallies on 9-10 August. Grateful to the workers, we joined rallies to show our support of them in front of the factories. Yet, what could the support rallies achieve, when the workers were threatened with dismissal as the minimum consequence, while they had children in their care? Once the strikes ceased, our hopes started to diminish. It's not that we had completely lost hope. Otherwise, hundreds of thousands of people would not have taken to the streets of Minsk on Sundays for several consecutive months. Yet, I am convinced that the end of the strikes had become a crucial factor.

As long as there is hope

I had kept my belief up to the last moment. I took to the streets nearly every day until I was arrested in Independence Square on 27 August. It happened the day after the dispersal of the rally in the square, when the "security forces" locked people inside the Red Church. The image of people confined in a church evoked harrowing associations from Belarus' past, so when I became aware of this atrocity, the question whether to participate or not no longer presented itself to me. During my detention, I was fortunate once more: on that day, the protesters were spared physical violence, and for the most part, they were not even charged with arrest. The penalty imposed on me was the highest fine permitted at that time, totalling 30 base units (810 roubles, about 300 euros).

Upon my detention, I was consumed by numerous thoughts about what would happen next. I was concerned about the potential impact on my employment and studies. During the interrogation, I disclosed my workplace in response to the officer's inquiry, as it was the specific question posed. I did not discuss my studies then, but my university later became informed anyway. My detention did not cause any disruptions to my studies; even within a state institution aligned with the authorities, collective solidarity remained influential. I might have lost my job, but the school was not informed of my detention; it was already nighttime when I was detained, and the police likely forgot to inform them.

Afterwards, I witnessed the continued protests in the avenues on Sundays, including the crackdown on the student march on 1 September. Perhaps, if I had not been detained on 27 August, I would have joined my fellow students on 1st September. The August protest inspired me so much that I maintained hope for a quick victory for a long time. If not in 2020, then in 2021. My inspiration came from the people: "The protest will die down when the dictator dies" — this slogan reflected the unwavering confidence of the Belarusian people. It was incredible that, following months of brutal crackdowns, Belarusians persisted in their protests.

I can hardly remember when the understanding hit me that this was the finale: we had no hope of winning. We had certain expectations from specific events: speeches against Lukashenka's inauguration, *Tsikhanouskaya*'s ultimatum, Freedom Day 2021. However, I had already come to the realisation that it was futile to hold onto such hopes. I had begun contemplating how to navigate life in a post-protest Belarus. I was not prepared to leave just yet. The desire to stay in my home country, no matter what, continued to drive me. Moreover, I was earning a good income in a school in Minsk, studying for a master's degree, and had plans for the future. I considered the possibility of leaving only in the case of the threat of annexation of Belarus by Russia, which grew more imminent after 2020, or if I were left without a job due to my political biography.

Life after the revolution

Subsequently, I came to realise that life in Belarus after 2020 was not solely defined by these threats. The revolution had ended, and repression had begun — I understood that. However, I was only able to fully acknowledge this, when, in September 2021, they started the mass arrests of people based on photos from the protests. Additionally, people were threatened not with fines or brief detentions, but with the possibility of actual imprisonment on criminal charges. At that point, I began to think of leaving the country, but my plans required significant time to materialise, so I decided to remain in Minsk. I saw that the peak of detentions had passed and assumed that I still had time for my departure. In 2022, I decided to enrol in postgraduate studies and ultimately put off my plans to emigrate.

Everything changed abruptly. In April 2022, my sister was detained. This is what the tragic destiny of a Belarusian looks like: she participated in a protest only once, but a single photo was sufficient to trigger a criminal case! I immediately grasped that I would be the next target. It was not difficult to identify my photos after searching my sister's phone. There was no other choice, so I bought a one-way ticket. I left my homeland, which I had promised to never abandon throughout my life.

My new life presented moments of fascination, uniqueness, and thrill. Challenges arose with language, employment, and adaptation. After the Russian invasion of Ukraine, the international community's attitude towards Belarusians shifted negatively. They started to see us as accomplices in the aggression, neglecting the distinction between us and the Russians, and forgetting about our protests against the authoritarian government. Belarusians abroad continue to support one another. I hope that the international community will still pay attention to the people who yearn for freedom.

P.S.

It has been three years since the August protests and a year since I was forced to leave Belarus. I frequently ponder whether we were doing everything correctly back then. It is disturbing to admit that the relatively mild authoritarian regime of the liberalisation period from 2015 to 2019 has been replaced by a regime that has adopted almost Stalinist-like terror tactics. Yet, it was not us who falsified the election results. It was not us who turned a blind eye to the pandemic's toll on Belarusians. It was not us who arrested the leaders chosen by the people. All this was done by one person. Not resisting him would have been akin to not opposing Hitler on the eve of World War II. We did not aim to "appease the aggressor"; rather, we sought to stop the aggression against our people. After all, an honest person would have no other option. Belarusians have been dying in wars with invaders for centuries. We had to take to the streets and try to fight, if there was any chance that our efforts would be successful. We continued to fight even when there was no hope. Although our dream did not come to fruition, I believe that Belarusians proved that they are worthy of their dream. In my opinion, 2020 was a turning point that highlighted Belarus' capacity for resilience and hope. Someday it will definitely come true!

City N, January 2024

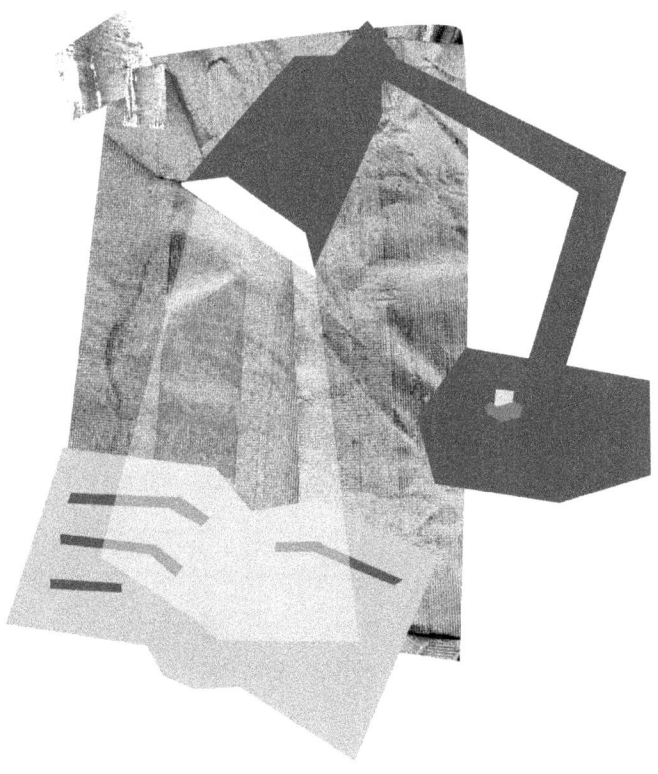

A REVOLUTION OF UNFULFILLED HOPES

Rym Antuan

I have always identified as a Belarusian

I have been interested in history since childhood. History fascinated me, inspired and excited my imagination with images of the past, which often captivated me more than typical childhood pursuits. I avidly read about a wide range of topics, including the ancient pyramids of Egypt, the Athenian democracy, the military campaigns of Alexander the Great, the Middle Ages, the great geographical discoveries, and numerous other subjects, deriving immense pleasure from these readings. It so happened that my parents and I did not reside in Belarus, which meant I did not have the chance to study Belarusian language and literature in elementary school. My family spoke Russian, and the Belarusian national idea was not a notable part of my early education. My family identified with Belarus, but this association was more civic in nature than national or ethnic. At the same time, studying in junior school in a predominantly Russian and Ukrainian cultural environment, I consistently referred to myself as a Belarusian. I found it appealing that I was distinct from some of my peers who did not comprehend the Belarusian words I had learned, such as malavać (to draw) and šufladka (a drawer). Additionally, within my family, there are Belarusian Poles, which fostered my specific fascination with Roman Catholicism and the intertwined history of Belarusian-Polish heritage. Later on, in my adolescent years, I came to identify as a Belarusian of Polish descent, and these dual identities coexisted harmoniously, enriching each other without conflict.

Schooling in Belarus, the Belarusian language, and interest in politics

By the time I began high school, my family had finally returned to Belarus. I perceived this circumstance as a very positive event in my life. I regarded Belarus with a degree of youthful idealism, and did not contemplate the various aspects of my future life and personal growth in the Motherland. All in all, despite some challenges, I successfully adapted to new social situations. However, the most daunting aspect was to grasp the "culture of silence" that was deeply ingrained in schoolchildren — you must simply listen and follow the instructions of elders and teachers without posing extra questions. Initially, I faced challenges in learning the Belarusian language, which was further complicated by the fact that my classmates universally regarded Belarusian language and literature as the most uninteresting subjects in school. In my case, fascination with history led me to the in-depth exploration of my country's past, which in turn bolstered my Belarusian identity. I yearned to take pride in my nation and my connection to a people with such a rich and interesting history. Therefore, I sought to master the Belarusian language to reinforce my national identity. However, it was only later that I became aware that the school curriculum in Belarusian language and literature was not designed to foster national self-awareness among young Belarusians, but rather to undermine it. In comparison, Russian literature was fascinating, rich in diverse imagery and complex meanings, delving into themes such as love, friendship, and other compelling plot lines. Meanwhile, Belarusian literature primarily focused on "backward peasants" and the Great Patriotic War — a significant topic as such, yet not entirely comprehensible or relevant for schoolchildren in grades 5-7. The gradual development of my interest in history, Belarusian national identity, and language inevitably sparked a curiosity about the political landscape in Belarus, along with an instinctive scepticism towards Russia.

I first encountered the "culture of silence" in December 2010, when Lukashenka violently suppressed a protest against the rigged results of the presidential election. I remember discussing this topic with my classmates, who held varying opinions and assessments, often reflecting the positions of their families. However, for some reason, we all felt an unspoken fear of inquiring about this subject with our class teacher, a very good pedagogue, as well as with other teachers. I posed the question to her with the innocence of a child: "Why did Lukashenka order the beating of people who merely wanted to say that he did not win the election?" She was very confused, but then answered: "Who told you that? All the people voted for Lukashenka, and only idle onlookers gathered in the square, so they got what they deserved. There was no need for them to be there in the first place." Her reaction astonished me, as well as the fact that my classmates, who mentioned their parents voting against Lukashenka, did not back me up in any way.

Later, my youthful idealism compounded my opposition to Lukashenka's policies. I viewed Belarus as an integral part of the European and Western sphere, believed in the value of democracy and was sure that Belarusians needed to develop their language and national idea, while Lukashenka's vision of a "Motherland from Brest to Vladivostok" stood diametrically opposed to my ideals.

University life, and observation of the development of civil society in Belarus in 2015–2020

In 2014 my understanding of the Belarusian system of government underwent a significant transformation. Belarusian society was deeply divided by the events unfolding in Ukraine. I remember how a significant number of my acquaintances would say: "Maidan is bad, and the Crimea is good." It was astounding to me, because I took a firm pro-Ukrainian stance, as I struggled to comprehend how my peers failed to acknowledge such obvious things as the illegitimate Crimea referendum and the covert involvement of Russian mercenaries and troops in the Donbas conflict. At the same time, Belarus maintained a neutral stance towards the events in Ukraine, with Lukashenka playing a certain role in the signing of the Minsk agreements in 2015, leading to a period when our nation asserted itself as a "donor of regional security". Domestically, a transformation also took place: one couldn't say that the government promoted liberalisation, but neither did it hinder the development — mainly in Minsk — of civil society and contacts with the West. Over time, it became increasingly "fashionable" among young people in Minsk to speak Belarusian and to engage with Belarusian culture and history. When I travelled from Minsk to visit my relatives in a small Belarusian town, I spoke Belarusian with my acquaintances, who were not yet influenced by the latest trends. Their astonishment was evident: they were accustomed to mimicking the manners of the capital city, and they found it hard to believe that speaking Belarusian was now seen as "trendy" in Minsk, as previously it was thought to be a language associated with rural areas.

This period coincided with a boom in the IT industry, the appearance of high-paying jobs, and a number of Belarusian companies, such as Wargaming, which became world-famous. Cultural life also flourished: many recreation spots with a national flavour opened in Minsk, international sports competitions were held. I felt that the country was progressing in the right direction. In the context of my life, significant events also unfolded, such as studying in senior classes at the lyceum, where I gained a deeper understanding of the diversity of Belarusian culture and history, and subsequently enrolling at one of the top higher educational institutions in Belarus. By disposition, I have always been more of a person who tends to find compromises than a radical, so the presence of excellent teachers at the university influenced my perception of Lukashenka and the Belarusian government. Against the backdrop of the Ukrainian events of 2014 and Russia's efforts to revive the "Union State" project, the trends in Belarus were encouraging: Lukashenka showed no signs of relinquishing sovereignty, there was a marked increase in dialogue with the EU and the USA, which made the narrative of the traditional Belarusian opposition about a "bloody pro-Moscow regime" less relevant. The notion of Belarus' political system gradually evolving towards the West resonated with me: several high-ranking officials (*Makei, Rumas, Matsiusheuski, Latushka*, etc.) seemed to support the idea of Belarus' independence and gradual transformation towards greater democracy and openness.

Hence, as a student, I believed that young people with a national orientation should play by the rules of the system to integrate into it gradually and influence positive changes in the country. I became the leader of the student self-government and put these principles into action — for instance, I delivered public speeches in Belarusian, and organised cultural events. My enthusiasm for

Europe and knowledge of foreign languages enabled me to take part in diverse educational initiatives with the EU. Throughout my senior years at university, I participated in conferences, seminars, and student exchanges on a nearly monthly basis. In general, the notion of Belarus' evolution was not entirely a utopian one: during this period, I often met people aged 20-30 who either worked in state agencies or aimed to build a career there. Almost all of them were well-educated and recognised the significance of our country's independence. Of course, there were career-oriented individuals among them, but even they were not blind believers in the Russian world. My worldview at that time was summarised in a private conversation where I said, "I will protest only if Russia occupies Belarus." It took less than a year to disprove it.

2020

2020 began quietly for me, marking the end of my student life. I was content with the time spent at the university, the skills I acquired, and especially the valuable connections I made. As a student whose education was financed from the state budget, I was subject to mandatory job assignment to a government organisation. However, I knew that I could find self-realisation in various fields, including business, and bring benefits to myself, my family, and my country. I had no motivation to emigrate within the next 5-7 years. The events that followed, affecting me, my acquaintances, and our nation, resembled a movie plot. During that period, I often felt a sense of unreality surrounding the situation.

Covid-19

The coronavirus pandemic reached Belarus in March 2020. While other countries introduced restrictions to combat the virus, Lukashenka opted to act as if nothing was happening. Not being a virologist, I cannot definitively assess the actual danger of the coronavirus, but it is clear that the authorities were mistaken in their claim that it was no more serious than a "common cold." Whatever it was — the threat to the Belarusian economy from implementing isolation measures, or simply Lukashenka's obstinacy — it led to a significant mistrust towards the government in society. In my view, the authoritarian government's typical emphasis on "averting panic" led to a situation where the government failed to react adequately to a real crisis. The peculiarity of the Belarusian government system is its strict vertical organisation. Officials will be sooner punished for extra initiative than for complete inaction. Therefore, the absence of Lukashenka's clear and univocal response to the pandemic led to disorientation of the government apparatus. The Ministry of Health artificially downplayed the number of the infected and deceased amidst the overcrowded hospitals in Belarus. Moreover, many university rectors forced students to attend face-to-face classes, threatening them with expulsion if they did not comply.

During this period, a notable shift in public perception of Lukashenka occurred. The liberal-minded Belarusians, including myself and my milieu in Minsk and major cities, who regularly read independent media online and viewed Lukashenka as a "necessary evil that somehow safeguarded Belarus' sovereignty", had no particular illusions about him as a politician. However, a profound shock came in the regions, especially for older people, who traditionally watched more Russian media. In Russia, all the media highlighted the pandemic's dangers, whereas in Belarus, Lukashenka was seen recklessly playing hockey and said that "a tractor and a sauna are the best remedies." For these Belarusians, the "Chernobyl syndrome" re-emerged, rooted in the suspicion that the authorities were concealing a real, yet invisible, threat. As a result, mistrust in Lukashenka intensified, and what's more, the unwritten social contract between him and a large segment of the previously passive Belarusian society was broken. The Belarusian dictatorship was seen as capable of providing security and economic stability, in exchange for which it expected the population to refrain from involvement in the political life of the country. This contract was violated by the Belarusian government. People took the initiative to raise money for healthcare workers, observed the mask-wearing regime and social distancing guidelines, while the government remained passive and even obstructive. Economically, the Belarusian regions experienced palpable signs of crisis following the cessation of Russian subsidies in 2019.

Participation in politics, collection of signatures for Viktar Babaryka as part of the initiative group

Lukashenka's inadequate response to the crisis highlighted the vulnerabilities inherent in Belarus' system of governance. He was no longer perceived as a "guarantor of stability". It became evident to me that in times of crisis, Lukashenka's priority would not be the fate of Belarus and the well-being of its people, but rather the preservation of his own power, even if it came at the expense of Belarusian lives. To make matters worse, Lukashenka gave the impression of someone disconnected from reality. At this point, I could almost tangibly sense the growing discontent with his regime coming from different people.

Right then the presidential election campaign began, which was expected to proceed in a commonplace manner, like it was in 2015. It appeared that even the most ardent segment of Belarusian society was willing to tolerate Lukashenka's regime to avoid the possibility of Belarus being annexed by Russia, similar to the annexation of the Crimea. However, in the context of general fatigue from 26 years of unchanged leadership, the regime's perplexing reaction to the pandemic, and the sense that negotiating with Russia to uphold Belarus' sovereignty without Lukashenka would be feasible, a strong demand for change within the nation became pronounced. This demand was personified by the three most influential alternative candidates who declared their presidential ambitions: *Viktar Babaryka, Valery Tsepkalo,* and *Siarhei Tsikhanouski.* Although the blogger *Tsikhanouski* seemed a populist to me, he managed to gain the support of Belarus' regions by vigorously criticising the dictator and his vertical power structure, echoing in many ways Lukashenka's own rhetoric from the 1994 election. I made a decision to support the head of *Belgazprombank, Viktar Babaryka,* who announced the recruitment of activists to join his initiative group via Facebook in May 2020. Following the completion of my state exams at the time, just as I was preparing to defend my diploma thesis at the university, my friend called to inform me about a compelling new presidential candidate. We had followed prominent figures in Belarus in the media prior to this, including *Babaryka,* who had supported an educational initiative at our university focused on promoting Belarusian culture. I chose to join *Babaryka's* initiative group and saw that he was a capable manager who shared Belarusian national values (as described by acquaintances who had interacted with him during the university project). *Babaryka's* employment history at a Russian bank did not raise my concerns, as I believed that under proper conditions, he would secure Russia's support, thereby fulfilling my aspiration for Belarus to undergo evolutionary transformations. Moreover, *Babaryka* was utterly prudent in assessing Lukashenka. This gave me confidence that my participation in the initiative group would not result in persecution by the authorities; at most, I risked missing out on career opportunities in the state administration system, which was not my sole aim in terms of employment and personal growth.

So, my close friend and I joined *Babaryka*'s initiative group and started collecting signatures to endorse his candidacy for the presidency. We were not afraid. My rejection of the "culture of silence" at school may have contributed to this. Additionally, I felt that I had a good grasp of the "rules of the game" in the Belarusian system and was confident that if I followed the law and did not participate in direct protests, then I would be under minimal threat. Finally, the scale of the movement in support of alternative presidential candidates was impressive: in less than a week, approximately 10,000 people joined *Babaryka*'s initiative group — an extraordinary number for Belarus. It felt like seismic changes in Belarusian history were in motion.

The collection of signatures took place during the pandemic, so I sent a message to friends and acquaintances on social media inviting them to sign up for the presidential candidate. Interestingly, many of those I contacted said they had already signed for *Babaryka* at other collection sites, while some confessed their fear, but the majority responded with enthusiasm and even brought their relatives to sign as well. My personal observations during the signature collection process testify that young Belarusian women were more interested in the political campaign than young men. Within two weeks, I had collected over 100 signatures. I collected signatures before the diploma defence, which displeased the commission chairman. Meanwhile, some collectors I know managed to gather thirty to fifty signatures in just three hours. Entire housing blocks in Minsk signed up for *Babaryka*. This was extraordinary, particularly given the potential risks that public sector employees faced by signing up, including work-related issues or even dismissal. Yet, this did not deter the Belarusians.

In general, the student self-government bodies at the leading universities in Minsk, which included representatives from organisations perceived as being aligned with the government, such as the *Belarusian Republican Youth Union*, actively participated in the process of collecting signatures for alternative presidential candidates. At that time, I was convinced that active and nationally-minded people in public bodies would back changes in the country. The arrest of *Tsikhanouski* and *Babaryka* in May-June 2020 crushed my expectations for system reform and extinguished any optimism that the 2020 elections would spur changes in the Belarusian political landscape. Of all the options, Lukashenka selected the worst course of action. Rather than choosing to engage in a dialogue with society, he imprisoned popular presidential candidates. He visited one military unit after another, threatened to gun down anyone who would come out to protest against the election results, and gave the impression of being profoundly terrified. Meanwhile, some critical statements of Russian officials provided grounds for optimism: it seemed that in the event of mass falsifications during the elections, Western countries would apply pressure on Lukashenka, and Russia could bet on representatives of the Belarusian political and business elite closest to people.

9 August 2020, or what is the price of lies

Sviatlana Tsikhanouskaya's registration as a presidential candidate in Belarus in July 2020 and her successful campaign instilled renewed hope for change. Despite Lukashenka's public hysteria, I witnessed a huge number of people who wanted change. It was an incredible time when everyone felt they were part of history in the making. I will never forget the long lines of people wearing white bands on their wrists (a symbol of their support for change) at polling stations across Minsk and the entire country. After a mere half day, my polling station had run out of ballots, while more and more people continued to arrive. I will never forget the scenes of thousands of people gathering at polling stations and Belarus' city centres on 9 August , demanding a fair count of votes. Lukashenka did not just lose the election; he was crushed, but he declared himself the winner. This lie led to the suffering of thousands of people.

Even the complete blackout of the internet on 9 August did not faze me. Intuitively, however, I sensed a growing threat. I remember the ordinary people who gathered for peaceful protests in different parts of Minsk, including those who took a casual walk near their homes on a summer evening. These unsuspecting individuals, without any protest insignia or political slogans, were among the first to be detained and subjected to torture in the most inhumane conditions. I remember stun grenades, explosions and barricades on the streets of Belarusian cities. However, Belarusians did not want bloodshed, and it was only the complete breakdown of law and order that compelled them to resort to such measures. The scream of a woman in the centre of Minsk near one of the offices echoes in my memory; bruises on her face, a broken arm. She was saying something about her husband whom they had taken away, and her father having a gun, but she did not know how to use it. I remember blood stains on the streets of Minsk. An atmosphere of fear and hatred. Then there were strikes. Hundreds of thousands of peaceful protesters flooded the streets of Belarusian cities, the white-red-white national flags began appearing in the windows of houses, instilling a renewed sense of hope. I was surprised to learn that some acquaintances I had never considered to be honest citizens were actually worthy, while some teachers at my high school, whom I had always respected, were involved in election fraud. There were many disappointments, yet these were vastly overshadowed by the admiration and love I felt for my people. I have never seen so much support, solidarity, rejection of evil and violence that I saw in those days of August-December 2020 in Belarus. I saw e thousands of worthy people, patriots of their country. And I was proud to be among them.

No one has forgotten anything

The defeat of the movement for change in Belarus is still a painful subject for me and, I suspect, for numerous Belarusians. It is crucial that these events are not forgotten and are openly talked about. The Revolution of Unfulfilled Hopes exemplified the remarkable heroism and resilience of many Belarusians, and on the other hand, it clearly demonstrated the cowardice of the Belarusian vertical power structure, which was too afraid to support a peaceful protest after receiving a signal from Moscow to back Lukashenka. The expectation that the Kremlin could act adequately turned out to be a myth. Russia sided with Lukashenka, sending an "armed reserve" to the borders of Belarus in August 2020, likely as a safeguard in case someone from the Belarusian "security forces" were to have a conscience. By the way, in the autumn of 2020, during the height of the protests, Secretary of the Russian Security Council, Nikolai Patrushev, visited Minsk, followed by a trip to the Homieĺ region, at the border with Ukraine, where he was accompanied by a delegation of Russian and Belarusian military personnel (according to independent sources). By a curious coincidence: the assault on the

Kyiv region by Russian forces originated from the Homieĺ region of Belarus in February 2022. If this was not by chance, it suggests that Lukashenka consented to engage in the war even during the protests in Minsk. Russia's support for Lukashenka's regime came at a price. Perhaps, had the West taken a firmer stance in defending fundamental human rights and freedoms in Belarus in 2020, the invasion of Ukraine in 2022 might not have occurred. But these are only speculations.

However, I am convinced that the Belarusian people embarked on a peaceful revolution (albeit an unsuccessful one) for a profound reason. In my opinion, in 2020, Belarusians finally developed as a nation and showed that they have dignity and values for which they are prepared to fight. Commitment to peace is both the greatness and the tragedy of our people.

Ukraine has demonstrated to the world that authoritarian regimes like those in Belarus and Russia are only receptive to the language of force. If they are not deterred, they will commit atrocities with impunity, devoid of any remorse. I hope that sooner or later the leaders of the free world will embrace this simple axiom. History has taught us that the people's desire alone is not sufficient to bring about change; a successful convergence of external factors is also necessary, which, unfortunately, was not in our favour in 2020.

I left Belarus in 2021. Lukashenka's speech at the so-called All-Belarusian People's Assembly, where he vowed to find everyone who opposed him during the elections, the direct support of his regime by Russia, and insufficient pressure from the West led me to consider emigration. I no longer saw a positive scenario for Belarus, only a repetition of 1937. I must admit, I was equally certain that Lukashenka would lead Belarus to war — it almost materialised. The remark of a knowledgeable person hastened my departure: "Do you know who I am?", he said. "Friendly advice — leave if you don't want to be imprisoned for a couple of years." The choice was obvious. I ultimately decided that I would not return to Belarus under the current government, when the Polish military burials in Belarus began to be destroyed. I have two great-grandfathers who fought in the Polish army, and to return to Belarus and remain silent would mean betraying their memory.

At the same time, I remain a cautious optimist and am convinced that time is working in favour of the young generation of Belarusians committed to the values of the free world. And I am certain that history will give us another opportunity to remind the world that we are Belarusians.

Nobody has forgotten anything.

Long live Belarus!

City N, January 2024
antuan.rim@gmail.com

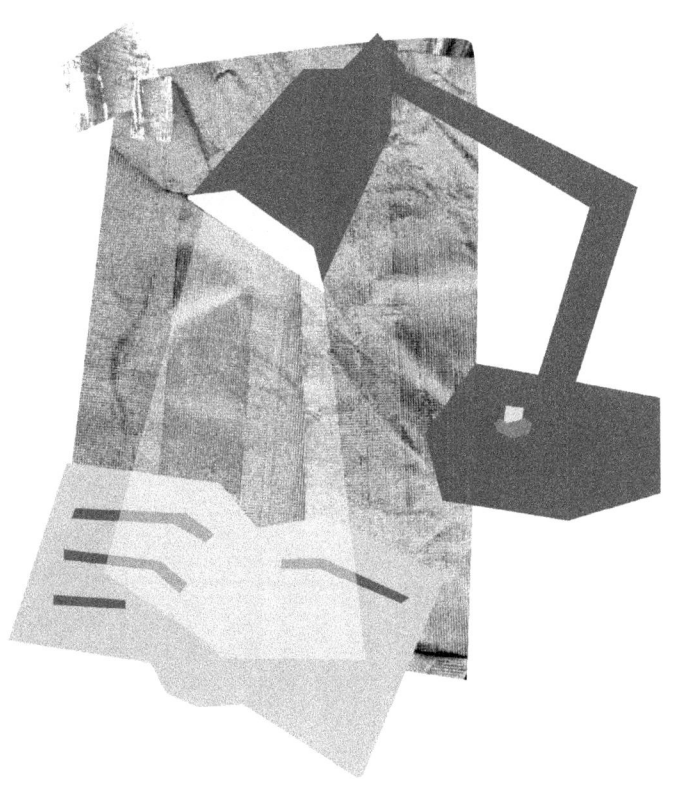

A BELARUSIAN IS BELARUSIAN TO ANOTHER BELARUSIAN

Jan Katkov

Studying in Belarus

In 2018 I enrolled for the Belarusian National Technical University (BNTU) in the Faculty of Information Technology and Robotics, and moved to Minsk.

I chose Programming as my speciality because I think it is a highly dynamic and developing area. The world today is unimaginable without modern information technologies, which I see as a driving force for global progress. Technologies are always advancing, the world is in a state of perpetual change, and specialists solve an ever-increasing number of digital challenges every day. Judging by the huge leap in technological progress that has occurred over the past fifty years, it is even hard to imagine what will happen in the next decades. Therefore, I would like to be a part of this progress. In my opinion, studying programming gives me a good opportunity to turn my ideas into reality.

I can't say that I didn't enjoy studying at BNTU. In my studies, as in all aspects of life, there were both positive and negative moments. Some subjects appeared and still appear completely unnecessary, including some directly related to my speciality. Sometimes it seemed that BNTU was frozen in time. While technology advanced rapidly, we were still taught about outdated concepts. It was quite amusing to listen to lectures about computers with punched cards.

In terms of teaching, very much depended on the specific lecturer. Some teachers still read from their notes during lectures, while others were leading engaging classes and were open to interesting discussions. The problem of biased or unfair treatment of individual students deserves special attention. This can also include sexism fail them on exams. Alternatively, they could make concessions to simplify things for women and merely granted them credit. Another example includes the existence of a category of students, so-called favourites, who were given high grades without any clear basis.

In general, the quality of education left much to be desired. Frequently, we were removed from classes and taken to various "socially significant" events on a voluntary-compulsory basis. I should also mention that part of the studies were online because of the coronavirus. The quality of these online classes did not align with the needs and expectations of all those involved in the educational process. On the other hand, that's what higher education is like: those who want to study, they go and study, those who don't — stay idle. Here is an amusing fact: coming back to the classroom after online classes, we ran into students from the voluntary squad standing near all the entrances to the campus, checking student IDs. Failure to show them denied access onto university property. This was attributed to the "fight against coronavirus".

Participation in protests

Initially, I joined peaceful protests in my hometown. I think one of the reasons the protests were so promptly suppressed in small towns was the strategy of redeploying police forces from one small settlement to another. Consequently, the "enforcers" became less concerned about being identified, and they started to act with increased cruelty. I believed that a nationwide strike, however, would be the most powerful form of protest.

As we know, after the presidential election results were blatantly falsified in August 2020, widespread student protests broke out. Mass arrests of students took place, and some universities "invited" the riot police. The most severe repressive actions were taken by university administrations after 26 October 2020, the date the nationwide strike was scheduled.

On that day, I came out to the university courtyard, where I joined other students in a march from building to building, carrying flags and urging people to join the strike. All the while, the first vice-rector was closely watching us. When we assembled at the main building, he attempted to intervene and halt our action. After that, we decided to leave the campus and march towards Independence Avenue, aiming to reach other universities and join forces with other students. Within minutes, the entire avenue was swarmed by police, who began to arrest students. It turned out that the university gates were locked from the inside to prevent students from seeking refuge within the campus. As a result, I was detained and escorted to a van that proceeded to the Belarusian State University of Informatics and Radioelectronics (BSUIR) for a full "refill." We were then transported to the *Partyzanski* district police department, where we remained until late in the evening, before being moved to *Žodzina*. The cell with four beds accommodated sixteen people, leaving us to sleep sitting on benches and the floor. The next day, we had a court hearing. I was fined, and after returning to Minsk, I went back to my classes. However, on 28 October, I found out that, by an order issued on 27th October, I had been expelled, along with more than forty other students. While I was in the police department, I initially thought that missing classes on 26th October might lead to a reprimand or warning, but at that moment, I did not anticipate expulsion. We only joked about it.

As later became known, on the day following the declared nationwide strike, Lukashenka convened a meeting with officials, during which he harshly criticised students involved in protests:

> "Students who are here to study, go and study. Whoever wants to — let them study. Those who engage in unauthorised actions and violate the law forfeit their right to be students. Dispatch them, some to the army, and some — out into the street. Let them walk the streets. Anyway, they must be expelled from university. The same applies to teachers. They are a minority, those who misbehave in universities. I repeat, do not plead or persuade them — it is futile. In the best case, we will push them under the carpet, and they will re-emerge again. So, let them choose where they want to live, how they want to live, and what they want to do."

Following these words of the illegitimate ruler, a surge of expulsions swept through Minsk universities. On 29 October, I and other students were called to a meeting at the dean's office, where we were informed about our unfortunate situation. The dean announced that a special commission would be set up to deal with our case. There was no mention of expulsion. After the dean's office, the next meeting was at the university rector's office. Students were summoned for a "talk" with the vice-rector, and ultimately, they were simply informed about the expulsion order, which cited "systematic failure to fulfil student duties" as the grounds. There we also received summons to the military commissariat. I attempted to clarify the reasons for my expulsion, requesting to see the text of the order. However, I was only able to view the document's content several months later, during a court hearing.

When I learned about my expulsion, my initial thought was, "This is some kind of joke." Later, when I left the office, I was informed about Lukashenka's statements. The notion that a few words from Lukashenka could lead to the expulsion of students was hard to comprehend. The thought of challenging this injustice, including via a Belarusian court, began to take shape.

With the assistance of my lawyer, we lodged a complaint with the Ministry of Education regarding my illegal expulsion, but it was met with inaction, and the ministry sent our complaint back to BNTU. Meanwhile, we started preparing the necessary documents for a lawsuit against the university. Of course, I considered the expulsion order to be illegal. As I listened to the arguments of both sides in court, I became convinced once again that the expulsion order was flawed due to numerous violations. Until the last minute, I clung to the hope that the court would invalidate the expulsion order. Unfortunately, it happened as it happened. Along with all other expelled students who filed a lawsuit against BNTU, I was denied restoration, and the expulsion decision remained in force. I attempted to appeal this court decision, but I achieved nothing.

The impact mass protests had on my life

The protests of 2020 served as a defining moment that delineated my conventional life into the before and the after. I always had a good history of academic excellence, including finishing school with a gold medal and securing free admission to university and a bonus scholarship. Upon moving from a small town to Minsk, I started thinking about my long-term plans. After completing my third year, I intended to look for a job in my field of specialisation. Perhaps, over time, I could get a job online in a foreign IT company. These were typical aspirations and ambitions of an ordinary student.

When the protests began, I started paying more attention to the events unfolding around me. After the first arrests of peaceful action participants, I realised that everything was much more serious and frightening than it seemed. Right before the election, I reached the age of eighteen, marking my first opportunity to participate in the electoral process. I was concerned that expressing an opinion without fear of repression in our country was impossible. And the more time passed, the more I came to realise that a change was necessary. It turned out many people shared my concerns.

Following my expulsion from the university, I didn't know what to do next. Pursuing my studies at BNTU was no longer possible, so my plans were shattered. Since I still wanted to get an education, one of the options was to continue studying abroad. Departing the country, despite the circumstances, was a challenging choice.

The developments in Belarus were a psychological blow for me. This was not only due to my personal experiences, but also the overall climate in the country after the suppression of mass protests. My participation in the protests stemmed from a desire to express my personal dissatisfaction with the authorities' actions, and I genuinely hoped that we could achieve some form of appropriate response to everything that had happened. However, the outcome fell far short of even minimally fulfilling my hopes. At that time, I desperately wished that everything would change, even though the realisation that this might not come to pass was gradually taking root in my mind.

Despite the negative outcome, I still believe that many positive things happened in Belarus, too. Thanks to what happened, we were able to gain a deeper understanding of many things. Throughout the protests and their aftermath, I witnessed the remarkable unity that emerged among Belarusians. "A Belarusian is Belarusian to another Belarusian" is a short and simple expression that actually means a lot. Mutual aid among people undoubtedly intensified, including emotional and financial support, as well as psychological assistance; aid was also crucial in particular circumstances and had a broader positive impact on the mind. After all, everyone knew they were not alone. We felt that those around us were not indifferent to the situation in Belarus. Even small things helped us fight and move forward.

About the present and the future

After the protests, I relocated to Poland and started a language course through the *Kalinoŭski programme*. I found it more engaging than I had expected thanks to the excellent teachers and classmates, some of whom had been compelled to leave Belarus after participating in the protests. A substantial community of Belarusians has emerged in Poland, united in their willingness to provide support and aid to their compatriots.

However, I also grappled with some difficulties in Poland. This could be attributed to my departure from Belarus at such a young age. While I had not yet seriously confronted this problem in our country, in my opinion, Poland is plagued by terrible bureaucracy. This is compounded by the fact that all documentation is in a language which is foreign to me. Moreover, I faced recurring housing problems. Renting an apartment often requires having an alternative address in Poland, where you can be evicted to if you fail to pay rent. Nevertheless, the Polish authorities are making efforts to support Belarusians.

In 2022 I enrolled in a polytechnic university in Poland. While studying here presents additional challenges, particularly due to the language barrier, it is also more engaging. To add to that, the main difference I observed between the Polish and Belarusian universities is the treatment of students. In Europe, there is a greater sense of mutual respect, and teachers do not harbour prejudices against students. Additionally, the evaluation process is more transparent and equitable.

Overall, the quality of education in Poland is quite high, giving young people the opportunity to find a good job in their field in the future. So, my primary objective is to determine the specific field of study that aligns with my interests and goals in university education.

Besides, I have a strong desire to contribute to the future development of Belarus. I am confident that nothing lasts forever, and the current situation will eventually come to an end, but the crucial questions are how and when this will occur. We must prepare for this moment now, without wasting time. The course of future events largely depends on us. Our actions will determine whether the status quo in Belarus persists, or if we can steer the country towards positive change and democratic progress.

I believe we possess the necessary potential for this development. A growing number of people have begun to engage with and follow the events unfolding in the country, indicating that many have come to recognise the significance of their actions and the ability to shape their own future as well as that of the nation as a whole.

This will not be easy, of course. It may take a lot of time before we achieve the desired result. But the main thing, in my opinion, is to take action. There are numerous examples of other nations where people fought and ultimately achieved their goals. I believe that each of us can contribute to this future, and I hope that we can achieve it in the shortest time possible.

Warsaw, July 2023
polemipl@proton.me

FEELING LOVE, OR THE EVENTS OF 2020 IN MY LIFE

Alexander

I was born in the city of *Homieĺ*, situated near the border with Ukraine and Russia. I used to consider my hometown small and boring. However, after moving to Germany, I realised that *Homieĺ* is comparable in size to Hanover or Nuremberg and, by European standards, is quite a large city. I grew up in a private house on the outskirts of *Homieĺ* and attended an ordinary school. I might have followed in the steps of most of my classmates (to end up in a factory or get involved in criminal activity), but I was saved... by my passion for history. I did not notice how history became a part of my life. From the fifth grade onwards, I started winning prizes at regional and later republican olympiads.

Participating in history olympiads brought me numerous benefits, including admission to Belarus' most prestigious university without exams, trips to *Polack* and *Hrodna* (as the final stages of the olympiads were held there), and valuable prizes such as a tablet, a phone from the school administration, and bonuses from the district administration. What's more, the olympiads substantially expanded my knowledge, heightened my enthusiasm for history, and brought me into contact with a lot of interesting people, with some of whom I still keep in touch. Of course, educational competitions were not my only hobby, nor did they consume much of my time. In addition, I had a passion for long-distance cycling (riding to places like Rečica and back). During the summer, I would pick and sell berries, and I also enjoyed fishing and occasionally playing computer games. However, it was the olympiads that ultimately guided me to a pivotal moment in my life — enrolling at university.

I moved to Minsk, and it was a very important moment in my life. During my school years, I had an ambition to become a psychologist and to help people. I realised that the only way to settle in Minsk was by enrolling at the History Department at Belarusian State University. I fell in love with Minsk, much like a young man who had never seen his beloved and communicated with her by correspondence. I was intoxicated by Minsk, and I can't explain why. Minsk is a city where I always feel at home.

My desire becomes reality

At the beginning of my university studies, I was haunted by the feeling that I had entered the wrong place. The reality did not meet my expectations, and I found classes quite monotonous. We studied the early periods of history, which did not captivate me. The constant emphasis on reading extensive literature was overwhelming and led me to consider withdrawing my documents and enrolling on the Psychology programme instead. However, I mustered the courage to overcome my doubts: I was diligent in attending lectures and seminars. Perhaps I just needed time to adjust. Now, I can confidently say that I am proud of myself, and recall this period with a warmth in my heart.

In my third year, things changed. It could be that I had simply resigned myself to the situation, or it may be that I had developed a genuine interest in learning. Most likely, it was both. I approached my studies primarily viewing them as a social elevator, focusing on the opportunities for new connections and broadening my horizons. When the time came to choose a career, I didn't even have the opportunity to think about my options, as my future workplace had already been decided for me — either a school or a museum. The prospect of a future job in a school was not appealing to me, nor was it for many of my fellow students. I vividly recall the first year: when asked if we wanted to work in a school, only five out of sixty students responded positively. However, by the fourth year, it was evident that securing a teaching position in a Minsk school was great luck. I have no idea what the remaining fifty-five, including myself, were thinking about. Perhaps they mentally pictured themselves in a building near the History Department, such as the Presidential Administration, or in the German and US embassies. I occasionally had such thoughts. I was also drawn to journalism, attempting to write articles, besides, I couldn't fully suppress my thoughts about psychology.

I strived to be an active student, trying to gain as much experience as possible, both through volunteer work and in my daily life. However, not everything could be achieved. I wanted to improve my English skills and participate in an exchange programme in Europe.

In my final years at university, I truly enjoyed studying at the History Department. During my fourth year, I worked extensively, taking on various jobs such as working in a restaurant and picking berries in the summer. After graduating, I got a job at a branch of the National Art Museum, a respectable institution (not a school). To get accepted, I had to go through three rounds of selection. I wanted to pursue a master's degree (for the benefit of living in a dormitory), and I managed to achieve that. I remember I learned about my admission into the master's programme while I was in the forest. Isn't it amazing?

My 2020 in Homieĺ and Minsk

Of course, like many of my fellow students in the History Department, I was interested in politics, but I was unable to imagine my active involvement in it, nor the turbulent events that were about to unfold in Belarus. Before 2020, I merely observed protests as a bystander. In 2020, I felt a powerful urge to alter the situation in the country. The realisation that I was not alone in this desire led me to consider taking action. Most crucially, I came to understand that it was possible to make a difference.

During the summer of 2020, I was in *Homieĺ*, where I participated in my first protests in support of new political figures. Initially, I supported *Viktar Babaryka* (by the way, he hosted an event that I attended during my university years), then *Sviatlana Tsikhanouskaya*. I sensed that many people were driven by a desire to improve the quality of life in our country. I clearly realised that this was achievable. The energy behind this sentiment propelled me to participate in protests in *Homieĺ* and later in Minsk.

I am a passionate and emotional person, often unable to explain my actions. I recall how, after the official announcement that Lukashenka had secured eighty percent of the vote, I reacted instinctively and rushed to the city centre to join the protest without much thought. It was an event that turned my world upside down. Nervous and apprehensive about the possibility of being detained, I sensed I had crossed the line between a "good boy" and a romantic who was ready to confront his fears. At a protest rally, I saw a harrowing scene where four policemen were dragging a man along the pavement, and people were murmuring among themselves that he had been killed.... This sight filled me with rage and further solidified my conviction that we need to ensure a change in power in Belarus. I really hoped that the situation in the country would change. I didn't have any special expectations, I just had faith. I attended nearly every rally, and I was certain that Belarus would never be the same again. During the second half of August, I felt that the government was poised to either relinquish power or engage in talks. The sentiment of post-Soviet doom and gloom was about to become a relic of the past.

I have no regrets about anything in my life, and I definitely don't regret my participation in protests. I believe that I did everything right. An armed protest wouldn't be an option for me even now — I do believe the Belarusians did everything they could and even more. What Europeans know about the events of 2020 in Belarus is the merit of the people who came out to protest.

The Belarusians inspired me greatly. I saw so many beautiful, brave, romantic, and worthy people on the protesting streets that I couldn't help but be drawn to their faces! I experienced a sense of love and admiration for my people that was both pleasant and unusual. This feeling still lingers. It's not just a fleeting rush of adrenaline and hormones. As to adrenaline — I almost became addicted to the thrill of it all: when you're running away from the police, it makes you want to repeat it again.

In the autumn of 2020, I started a master's programme and worked at a museum in Minsk. I resided in a comfortable dormitory, and also took up a job as a watchman at a church, which still fills me with trepidation. As I look back on this period, I am drawn to its memories.

Every weekend, I took part in protest actions. I vividly recall meeting a woman at a protest next to the museum where I worked on 1 September. I liked her. We stayed together in the "interlocked chain", but the riot police forced us to scatter in different directions. The danger increased with each passing weekend, yet I couldn't resist going out because I felt an incredible sense of strength within myself and the people who joined the protests.

My love for Minsk grew stronger with each passing day. I continued attending protests until mid-October 2020, when I was first detained. That time I managed to escape with minimal consequences — just a night in *Žodzina* and a fine of five *basic units*. However, following that experience, I began to express my discontent with the situation in the country, particularly the seizure of power, differently: I became a student activist who assisted in defending rights. I communicated with undergraduates and masters students, writing posts and doing everything I could. Even the museum where I worked became the makeshift headquarters of my organisation. I would fall in love, meet people, work and study… I lived and I loved. What would I prefer to bring back from that time? Certainly, the sense that everything can change at any moment.

A series of arrests and life in anticipation of big problems

At that time, I lived the life of a student, a museum employee, a believer, and an activist. This continued until March 2021, when the *GUBOPiK* burst into my room and took me to the *Maskoŭski* district police department. I realise now that if I had been more vigilant about information hygiene, I would not have been detained or would have been detained later (my friends with whom I was supposed to meet were detained a few days after that). This changed my life dramatically. I spent fifteen days behind bars. The imprisonment was undoubtedly a difficult ordeal, yet the solidarity of my colleagues enabled me to endure it with greater ease. I met a great many interesting people, a few of whom I maintain regular communication with even now.

After my arrest, I was fired from my job, where I was to work for a certain period since it was an official assignment. I ended up in a "case under development" of the special services. But I withstood, and I coped with it — of course, not without difficulty and not without the support of friends and colleagues. I toughened up, but my romantic side remained intact. My affection for my people and conviction that change was inevitable remained unwavering. These events, for which I am deeply thankful, directed my course, like a river's journey culminating in the Amazon delta, to where I stand today.

Throughout 2021, as well as lots of other people, I experienced a persistent feeling like "the screws were tightening": the space for living was shrinking. The yearning for change and my pride in my nation were tempered by the fear and heartache I felt for those whose lives were turned upside down by arrest, humiliation, and the theft of their future.

The atmosphere at the History Department was deteriorating. The administration increasingly emphasised the faculty's integration into the system. I was unable to present my master's thesis, as I did not meet the tailored formal requirements set specifically for me. Although the experience was unpleasant and painful, I do not regret it. By the way, in my first year, I would not have been able to survive such humiliation.

In August 2021, I found myself back in jail for fifteen days again. It so happened that I arrived at my arrest by taxi. Amazing, isn't it? I contracted Covid in the cell, and kept drawing comparisons between the cell and a concentration camp. After my release, I started seriously to consider leaving the country. I realised that the situation was unlikely to improve, and the likelihood of avoiding a criminal charge was becoming less and less.

Despite feeling bitter about the state of my country, my pride in it remains boundless. The atmosphere of Minsk still resonates with me. I hold dear the lifestyle I embraced in this city. Mentally transporting myself to Minsk evokes a feeling of kinship, as if I am with my close ones, my dear ones. It was a source of genuine support for me back then. I got help in finding another place for job assignment, and I continued working as a church watchman. I discovered love in human incarnation.

Forced migration and thoughts about Belarus

My situation could have continued, but, by the winter of 2022, the relentless pressure from the security services made my life simply unbearable. With tears in my eyes, I was forced to part ways with my loved ones, colleagues, and financial savings. I had to abandon my stable lifestyle and adopt the lifestyle of a nomadic emigrant. Over the course of a year and a half, I found myself living in Georgia, Lithuania, Germany, and briefly visiting Switzerland and Armenia. As I faced the need for drastic life changes, my emotional state began to unravel. Emigration turned out to be a more daunting challenge than repression. Forced emigration gave me a feeling of uncertainty about the future. I started to feel like I was always on the verge of running out of time. In Germany, my life became even more stressful. I realised with bitterness that my knowledge of English alone was insufficient. Frustration overshadowed many things. I found myself in a state of perpetual survival. I understood that my life in Minsk had also been lived in survival mode. The world was harsh back then as well, but I was unaware of it and a little naïve.

My expat experience is very versatile. While in Batumi, I awaited a visa and collaborated on texts for the team of a Russian politician. In Lithuania, I undertook various jobs in construction, delivery services, and text editing. I am pursuing a master's degree in Germany (sweet destiny), and despite the challenges I face, I want to stay here. I have been studying German, enhancing my English skills, making German friends, and exploring many cities in Germany. I'm happy. I want to embark on a new path — guiding tours throughout Germany. This links me with my past, my studies in the History Department; well, I like it. In the future, within a free Belarus, my ambition is to conduct tours for foreigners, understanding their passion for travel and the appeal that Belarus could hold for them. I recognise the feasibility of pursuing this profession, and I aim to set realistic goals that I can attain. I have found my vocation; this is probably one of my most important achievements of this period. To pursue this, I enhance my German skills, engage in continuous learning, study exemplary tours, and explore different cities. And I like it.

At the same time, my Belarusian identity becomes increasingly defined. In the countries where I have lived, and I am living now, I frequently meet Belarusians, and I am filled with pride and joy when interacting with them. Of course, I miss Belarus, Minsk, and my family. I am very pained by what is happening to Belarus now. And it's even more painful to realise that while I am focused on surviving in Europe, there are limited opportunities for me to help my country. Yes, I am still a member of the same organisation, and we have started a project to help repressed students. I also try to engage with it actively. However, it is very difficult for me to do so due to my heavy workload. I am confident that Belarus will become a democratic nation, where citizens can freely express their opinions. I believe that once Belarus achieves true freedom, foreigners will be able to visit Belarus easily, as well as Belarusians. This is my dream, and I pray for its realisation. How to achieve it? I don't know, actually, very few know this. Certainly, the sentiment that prevailed three years ago, when the atmosphere was charged with the potential for change, is not present now.

In addition to the pain of being able to do little for my country, I am also frustratedly dealing with everyday issues that are significantly more difficult to cope with than in my homeland (for example, getting a haircut or going to the pharmacy are really stressful for me). However, I am resolute in my determination to endure all the hardships and misfortunes that come with living in exile. I am certain that this is a necessary phase in my life's journey. I hope to return to a democratic Belarus one day — not because I dislike living in Europe (on the contrary, I enjoy it), but because love compels me. What would life be without it? It is difficult to thrive without love in our time. I am pleased with my life as it is now; it simply requires time to overcome new difficulties, which is part of the process called "growing up". I have become more mature. I am nearing my 25th birthday. I have no regrets whatsoever.

In lieu of an epilogue

I found great ease in writing this essay. I feel a pressing need to discuss that particular period. Giving interviews and engaging with others brings me joy, even though I could have hardly repeated my previous experiences now. I definitely miss the rhythm of life from that time. Without it, my story does not seem bright or fascinating to me. Memories hold significance for me as they allow me to reflect on myself once more and recollect that simultaneously terrible and marvellous period. When I was writing this, I was anxious about having enough space. Now I see it is quite enough. There is enough space for everyone where we are needed. I was able to spot my own place within the space of life. There is, was, and always will be a lot of space for Belarus in my world.

Somewhere in Germany, July 2023

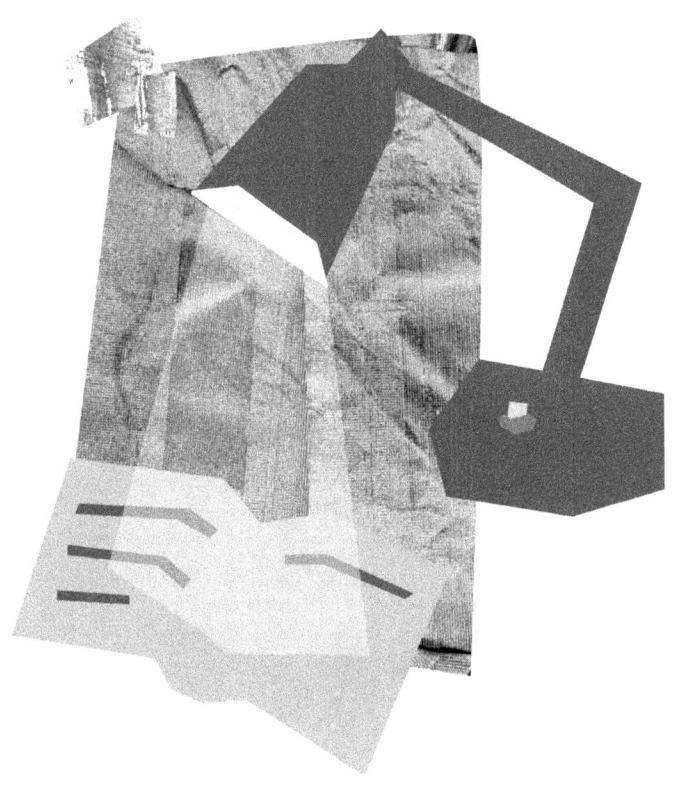

HOW TO LOOK HAPPY

Kasia

> This day will become the beginning
> For new desires and better ideas.
> *Artsiom Lukyanenka (NaviBand),*
> *The Story of My Life*

Life before the protests

I was born in Minsk and spent nearly my entire life in this city. I completed eleven grades at one and the same school without any transfers or relocations. At most, my family travelled only to our village in the Brest region, the place where I learned to fish, play football with the neighbourhood boys, and treat wounds by myself after such games. But that was not all to it. Recalling that time, I realise that even as a young girl, I already loved my country. Why? Because in a Belarusian village, the air has the sweetest scent when you, a wet and dirty girlie with dishevelled hair, make your way home in the evening after a hot day. This air carries the gentle murmur of the river behind my house, the sweet scent of wildflowers, and the beauty that eluded my childish understanding back then. And even the barking of my city dog, who sees a hedgehog for the first time in his life, sounds sweet. And then comes supper — mum has cooked potatoes, of course, and added dill from our vegetable garden; there is also a salad of cucumbers, young leeks and sour cream of the Brest Litovskiy brand. After supper, my dad would come to my bedside and tell the most captivating stories about the little wolf that lived in our forest, about other forest inhabitants and their adventures. It was magnificent. But I still believe that I am a city dweller. University brought a new chapter in my life, with new people and new interests to explore. In the first year, I was fascinated by everything except studying itself — and there was nothing surprising about it, because I did not know why I needed it and what I wanted to do next. I joined the student theatre club and dedicated most of my time to it. Prospects were nil! However, we staged a play about Belarus. I enjoyed it. Over the course of three years in the theatre, there were many engaging events, but ultimately everyone started to pursue their own interests and attended the rehearsals less and less. Around that time, I found my studies to be more interesting. I started attending almost all of my classes, but most significant was the appearance of second language courses. French! Well, how could one not be enamoured with it? Step by step — and here I was, planning my move to France. It is a whole new country, and it promised to be anything but boring, as I imagined it.

Belarusian protest

For me, everything began with the arrest of *Viktar Babaryka*. On this day, my friend and I found ourselves in the centre of Minsk. It was incredible: everything was buzzing, cars honking, and people were waving "peace" signs to each other. Well, I showed it, too, openly, at the windscreen of the riot police minibus. Who would know what they looked like back then? It happened at a small crossing near the Centralny supermarket. The vehicle suddenly started driving towards us at the red light, and we had to jump back. It turned, and something like a black cloud jumped out of it, which in a flash seized a young man who had been the first to approach, lifting him by his arms and legs. We ran, not knowing where to hide. It was a terrifying moment, but I yearned for only one thing then — to shout to the whole world about such injustice.

On the night of 9 August, no one knew what was happening, but our feet carried us towards the Stella monument. Streams of people floated out from the dark alleys, merged into a single procession, and moved forward, even as everything rumbled, and the air was filled with the sounds of screams and explosions. They continued walking until objects started striking the crowd. Or until a black, foreboding block began hurtling towards us. And then one had no choice but to run in the same direction as this block, only your goal was to outpace it. The next few nights were no different, only becoming more dire.

I saw the light at the end of the tunnel on the morning of 12 August. I needed to put on white clothes urgently, find flowers, and run to the Kamaroŭka market before the opportunity slipped away. But the end was not in sight, as we stood for hours, finding joy in this act.

I was surrounded by the very essence of beauty. I saw this phenomenon only during women's protests; I don't know whether this beauty exists anywhere else. The white nymphs emerged from the canvas. Did the ancient Greeks know who they were painting? Following that day, I tried to join all the women's actions: marches with flowers, chains of solidarity, and processions near the Red Church. It seemed that we had claimed the city as our own, and the most enjoyable aspect was that you could look in the eye of the riot police without fear. For a certain time. And then the arrests resumed, starting with the men. We made every effort to protect them, shield them, encircle them. At times, it worked. But then they started detaining the women as well. When we could assemble, stand together, the fear lessened. The true fear arose when it was time to disband, because you never knew what would happen next. I used to go with my friend, we were always together. And we were never arrested. We never got arrested, and I'm not sure what our secret was — perhaps it was prudence, plain good luck, or our long legs, but I prefer the latter. One day, we were walking back down the avenue, both wrapped in flags. A policeman suddenly jumped up from somewhere (God knows where they appear from) and told us to hide our flags, because fifty metres ahead we would be detained. We hid them, and I felt ashamed of this.

My friend and I attended even the most violent protests. We would hide wherever we could — at the *Domino's*, the *Veterans' House*, and a construction site at *Niamiha*. We marched, ran away, but we were never detained. At some point, I developed a complex of feeling inferior as a Belarusian. It seemed that if I was never arrested, then I must have failed to protest, and in general, I did little to contribute to the cause of our victory.

However, one day, my involvement in the protests did not go unnoticed. Towards the end of one of the marches, a thunderstorm began, causing people to seek shelter and flee. Yet, many remained standing in front of the barricade of armed vehicles and riot police. On this march, I had arranged to meet one of my friends, as we had planned to take a photograph together. At that time, she and I cultivated a kind of tradition — marking significant events with a kiss in photographs. In the pouring rain, we searched for each other for a long time in the crowd. Once reunited, we promptly began taking photos against the backdrop of the armed riot police and beneath the white-red-white flag I had sewn, water streaming in all directions. My other friend who accompanied me on the marches, was taking pictures of us. Holding the umbrella with one hand, battling the wind and a hundred droplets of water on her fogged glasses, she managed to press the camera button where it was supposed to be. You know, the photos turned out to be very good, but the internet never got to see them. As soon as we started taking pictures, a woman in a vest ran up to us with a camera in her hands. Many journalists were present, but only this woman was drawn to us. In a brief moment, she took several photographs, two of which were featured in the news, and only one of them captured the world's attention and began to spread farther. The post with this photo generated a lot of comments, with the audience divided into two distinct camps. The first group consisted of those who disliked the image, expressing their disapproval with comments like "We do not need such freedom." The second camp responded with a different perspective: "If you limit the freedom of others, then please explain how you differ from the current government." Interestingly, I didn't feel like I was being condemned or supported by dozens of people; instead, I was just an interested observer of the comments unfolding before me, unaware that they were actually about me. I was still a little pleased nevertheless.

Then someone made a drawing of this photo and displayed it in an exhibition, and, eventually, the police took an interest in me, sending a summons. Although they made a mistake with my birthdate by ten years, I still went to the police station. I was seated at a table and asked if I knew why I was invited there. I replied that I didn't know, and I really didn't know. Then huge photos of me with a kiss printed on paper were placed in front of me. I even laughed, and was not penalised for that. A young policeman was talking to me, he was also joking and did not take me seriously at all. In the room, there was another protester who was slated for another arrest, with images picturing him on some march. He had a broken cheekbone, and when he asked if anyone would be responsible for it, they offered to break his other cheekbone. It was said in a harsh tone, but they spoke to me in quite a gentle manner at the same time. However, the conversation ended instantly when I began reading the paper they handed me to sign. "Do you want to read it? You have fifteen days to do so." My testimony was already written on that piece of paper. It would be intriguing to find out what I said there. This is what they call an "explanatory conversation". The only thing I learned from this visit was that the employees of the Central Police Department have a very peculiar mentality, which changes the mood of the policemen every two minutes, and I find it frightening.

Life afterwards

During the protests, my intention to move to France was put into question, as it was then that I truly realised my belonging to Belarus for the first time. I recognised this and did not wish to be abroad. After my visit to the police station, I realised that I needed a contingency plan. In the autumn of 2020, I had many drawings, but there was only one Polish university that was still accepting applications. The pictures were well-received, and a unique period of distance learning during the coronavirus pandemic began. After the crackdown on the protest, I was overcome with sadness, and nothing seemed to help. I applied to a programme in France from a Polish university and travelled there to seek new opportunities. The dream came true. However, living in France in my dreams and living there in reality proved to be vastly different experiences. The land of France taught me a great deal. I got to know a variety of people. But you see, while being there, I could no longer listen to French music in my headphones, as there were too many foreign things around, while I craved something that made me feel myself. I was unable to express many things to the French or emphasise something in my own intonation, as they simply did not understand it. I knew what I had to say to make it clear to them, but their phrases and their intonations were artificial to me. I did not regret it when I had to leave after the programme completed, because I had a network of Belarusian friends in Warsaw. I started working and continued my studies. In Poland, I've found a sense of ease, for I feel a connection to Belarus. Did you know that there's a Belarusian children's art school in Warsaw? We've already done a lot of interesting things with these children. A week ago, my friend who was with me at the protests said: "Well, at least now you look happy." Today, Warsaw is filled with new ideas, Belarusian children sing songs in Belarusian, and in a small room I adorned with paper flowers, *Malavanyč* brings his puppet theatre to life.

Warsaw, July 2023

MUFFLED VOICES: A STUDENT'S PERSONAL STORY ABOUT THE EVENTS OF 2020

Virus

My name is Virus, I am a young man. My roots are a blend of origins: my father is an ethnic Russian, my mother is of Belarusian and Polish ancestry, plus there are proven French traces in my family's genealogy. Despite this diverse ethnic background, I identify strongly as Belarusian.

I was born and raised in the city of M., where I spent the majority of my life, including my school and university years. In this essay, I will not delve into the details of my school experience, as I consider that period to be relatively ordinary, not differing significantly from the school days of other Belarusian students. I will just mention that I excelled academically, consistently earning high marks and participating in school olympiads and conferences. History and computer science were the subjects that particularly piqued my interest. Additionally, throughout my school years, I was actively involved in sports attending several sports clubs concurrently. However, I did not demonstrate any notable political engagement during that period.

As I approached the final stage of school education, I started contemplating my future profession and university admission. Primarily, I relied on my abilities in history and computer science, but there were certain problems. On the one hand, although I held history in high esteem, I did not envision a career as a historian. On the other hand, I struggled with my confidence to pass entrance exams in mathematics and physics, which would enable me to enrol for Computer Science. Therefore, I had to seek an alternative that would align with my interests, abilities, and opportunities. Fortunately, I found such an option.

Faculty of International Relations at BSU: first meeting and study

I first encountered the faculty during my 11th grade at the annual Day of Meeting Applicants. The event featured an assembly between applicants, their parents, and the administration of the Faculty of International Relations (FIR), led by Dean Victor Shadurski and the teaching staff. This provided an opportunity for the applicants and their parents to ask questions of the faculty representatives, gather information about the educational process, and learn about the admission criteria.

Following the event, I gave serious thought to enrolling at this faculty, as I discovered relevant reasons for my decision. Firstly, I believed it was feasible to pass the entrance exams and achieve the required points for admission in native and foreign languages, as well as social studies. Secondly, the atmosphere at the FIR on the Day of Meeting Applicants impressed me with its high level of communication culture and respect shown by university representatives towards applicants. At school, I was used to a more administrative and command-oriented approach to students, but at FIR, I experienced a different, more democratic atmosphere. Thirdly, I was drawn to the opportunities that awaited me at the FIR: studying in Minsk at one of the country's most esteemed faculties, learning two or more foreign languages, participating in international projects, and interning at renowned global universities, ultimately leading to a career as a professional diplomat. Considering all the factors, the FIR stood out as the top choice among the available options at that time. Consequently, after passing exams, the only place to which I submitted my documents was the Faculty of International Relations at the Belarusian State University.

I consider studying at FIR a very progressive period in my life. During my school years, I had been more focused on my personal goals and aspirations. Consequently, I showed little interest in the school's social life. At the university, my life took a dramatic turn. In my second year, I joined multiple student organisations and initiatives, devoting my time and energy to them. I organised events for students, led a club for English language and Anglo-Saxon culture enthusiasts, moderated meetings with European political figures, was engaged in research, and took part in academic conferences. I was actively involved in the UN simulation organisation at the faculty, dedicating a significant amount of time to it. Additionally, I worked in various companies, balancing extracurricular activities with academic responsibilities. To be honest, the academic process was not always my top priority, however, I never struggled with it. As a result, I graduated from the university with honours.

If I had to highlight what I loved most about studying at FIR, it was the welcoming atmosphere for students fostered by the dean's office and the faculty departments. Of course, not everything was always ideal. Some teachers were surprisingly resistant to updating their courses or adhered to scrupulous compliance with formalities. Nevertheless, there was generally a sense of mutual respect and trust between students and faculty. The atmosphere was marked by a spirit of student unity and cohesion, as well as an openness from the faculty leadership to constructive criticism. This created an impression of respect for individual opinions, and a motivation to study diligently and actively to contribute to the advancement of the faculty and its prestige, instilling a sense of pride.

Our dean was instrumental in shaping the FIR into a respected European faculty. Notwithstanding his authority, this man was and remains approachable, friendly, and attentive to student and staff concerns. I am convinced that without his unique approach the FIR would not have maintained its image over the years.

Finally, reflecting on my university studies, I would like to point out that I have never regretted choosing the FIR as my alma mater, even though my current profession requires some different knowledge. However, the faculty has played a significant role in my development, and I am grateful to all those who contributed to this.

2020: plans, prospects and their transformation

The year 2020 started with a sense of foreboding for many of us. Beginning in January, people began to actively monitor the spread of the threat of what later would be called SARS-CoV-2 or Covid-19. If I were to say that I felt the fateful events approaching, I would be misleading, but the year ahead was certain to be a tense one. In the summer of 2020, I was scheduled to graduate from the university, and, that semester from January to June, I intended to focus on preparing for state exams and defending my diploma thesis. As part of the graduation requirements at that time, each student was mandated to complete an internship before presenting their diploma thesis. I seized the opportunity offered by the faculty and was sent to a state institution for my internship in February.

My internship did not even last a few weeks, as the first cases of Covid-19 infection emerged in Belarus around the time. By internal order of the university, all students were recalled from their internships. People all around began to take serious measures to protect their health and safety, including maintaining social distancing, working remotely when possible, and avoiding large gatherings. Our university also responded by shifting classes to an online format, a decision initiated by the faculty management. I should emphasise that, in the face of an alarming situation, people were anxious to protect themselves, but the state was reluctant to take decisive action to support the normal epidemiological situation in the country. The mask-wearing regime was not introduced at that time, most institutions continued to operate without switching to a remote regime, and normal testing for the disease was not deployed, nor were numerous other measures. Accordingly, in the initial weeks, sceptics emerged who doubted the official infection statistics reported by the Ministry of Health and openly criticised the state's shoddy preparation for the emergency situation. We can recall the words of the head of state, who declared that he "did not see any viruses" at all.

In response, I chose not to risk my health by exposing myself to the virus, so I adhered to the self-isolation rules as closely as possible. I used the time freed from internship to focus on research for my diploma thesis and preparing for state exams. During this period, I also began actively to explore my professional prospects and potential employment opportunities. Given my prior experience in official employment in Belarus, I maintained connections with former colleagues in case I decided to return to my previous field of work. Additionally, I considered employment options in my speciality, including government institutions.

Beyond these professional pursuits, I was particularly interested in the possibility of continuing my studies to obtain an academic master's degree. My motivation stemmed from the increasing competition among graduates in the job market and my own desire to expand my knowledge. My objective was to enrol at an institution with an economic profile to earn a degree in economics and enhance my employability in private international companies. To achieve this, I considered both Belarusian and foreign universities, but I was more inclined towards the latter. During the epidemic, I had a clear plan to enrol at one of China's top universities to pursue a master's degree in business administration. However, due to the circumstances of that year, I was unable to execute this plan.

I considered several economic programmes in Belarusian universities, but when my plan to study abroad failed, I chose to delay my admission to the university for a period of time and wait for more information about the epidemic. Therefore, when I had the chance to get a job again, I decided to take it and wait out the epidemic in a more stable financial position.

Protests 2020: the beginning

The tension in society and dissatisfaction with the authorities had been escalating for some time before the elections, but the culmination of popular discontent was the widespread falsification of the 2020 election campaign. It is well-known that many popular opposition politicians were arrested shortly before the candidate registration or prevented from registering as candidates for dubious reasons. The authorities' move to eliminate popular opposition politicians, coupled with the official lack of action in combating the epidemic, led to a sharp response from society. As summer approached, the first protests erupted, with people gathering at spontaneous rallies and forming chains of solidarity along main streets in support of the detained politicians.

The first time I experienced the current law enforcement system in Belarus was when my friend was detained in Minsk in July. In short, he was returning from a walk near the site of a peaceful protest when he inadvertently got caught by the police in an indiscriminate "snatch raid".

My friend was detained overnight at a police station; he was convicted under *Article 23.34* the following day and was fined. Looking back on the events of those days, I can say the sentence was humane, considering the escalating brutality displayed by the "security forces" and the state apparatus towards the dissatisfied citizens since the day of the elections.

Election day and detention

The most dramatic event for me in 2020 was my detention in Minsk on the night of 9 August, while returning home from a peaceful protest. It all started when I decided to visit my polling station on the evening of 9 August to learn about the election results. Outraged by the outcome, which I believed to be invalid, I called a friend, and we arranged to walk along Independence Avenue to see what was happening in the city. I'm not sure what motivated me at that moment — human curiosity, concern for the future of my country, respect for my own choices, or possibly all of these factors combined — but my legs carried me to the city centre that night.

My friend and I met on Pieramohi Square and walked down the avenue towards Jakub Kolas Square. That night, the epicentre of events was the intersection of Bahdanoviča Street and Mašerava Avenue, where police cordons and protesters stood on opposite sides of the street. Although there were only about a hundred people present, at that moment it felt like there were many more. After our walk, we joined the protesters, who did not violate public order and did not engage in any violent behaviour towards the police. The protest was peaceful from the outset, but the situation was continually escalated by police officers who threw stun grenades into the crowd and jumped out from behind the cordon to detain individual protesters. While we were there, we were forced to flee several times from such attacks, but after the police's unsuccessful attempts to detain us, we returned to our original location. The police eventually changed their tactics and instead of making individual arrests, they launched a mass crackdown on the streets. We were lucky that time, as the policemen passed by while we were hiding in the yard of a house on Mašerava Avenue. Once the danger had passed, we headed home.

To reach my friend's house, which was closer, we had to cross the road and enter the adjacent yard. But because of exhaustion and the stress we had endured, we lost our guard and approached the crossroads without caution. A moment later, a red *Minsktrans* bus pulled up, and the riot police jumped out of it with shouts. The last thing I managed to do was to look at my watch: it was three o'clock in the morning.

Police station and detention centre

Men in black uniforms, armed with machine guns, leaped from the bus. One of them brutally knocked me down on the asphalt, threatening to shoot me if I didn't obey his orders. After that, he grabbed my arms, which were handcuffed behind my back, and dragged me onto the bus. My friend was dragged in immediately after me. I recall being punched in the head several times at the door, possibly with a baton once, and then I was ordered to sit on the floor. The bus started moving.

We arrived at the police station after about half an hour. They collected our phones on the bus. Next, they escorted us individually to the police station door, where they made us kneel with our hands behind our backs, and forced us to lower our heads to the ground. I was unfortunate: instead of the ground, I found myself on the hard concrete by the threshold. In this position, without lifting my head, I sat for about two hours. There were around forty to fifty other people, including women, in the same situation.

At the police station, they took my personal information and ordered me to wait in a room with other detainees. I was convinced that we would be released soon, but my hopes were dashed. After having their lunch, the police gathered us in the corridor and informed us that we were being taken to a detention centre, where our future would be decided.

Upon entering the detention centre, we were met with brutality. First, we were forced to run along the corridors, where the internal troops were lined up by the walls and beating the detainees. Then, we found ourselves in a wide corridor of a residential block, where the cells were located. We were called individually for an inspection, where we were stripped and some of our belongings were confiscated, the ones we could use to harm ourselves or others. After that, we were divided into groups of eight and escorted to our cells. I was placed in a cell designed for eight people, but, with the new arrivals, it was soon overcrowded with twenty-four individuals. The conditions were dire: there was a catastrophic lack of ventilation, water droplets from breathing formed on the walls, and there was not enough space on the bunks to even sit down. Additionally, my friend was placed in a different cell, which meant I lost contact with him for several days. However, twelve people were transferred out of our cell at night, so there were twelve of us left. We spent the next few days in isolation, disconnected from the outside world.

Late in the evening on 13 August, the cell door suddenly opened, and the staff called one of our cellmates into the corridor. Shortly after, a few others were called out. Outside the door, the noise gradually increased. Then all the voices fell silent, as if someone of importance had turned their attention. It was indeed so: in the corridor, a man, likely a duty officer, began to deliver instructions to the gathered detainees in a low voice, detailing how they should behave upon release. After the officer finished speaking, the sound of shuffling soles on the concrete floor filled the corridor. After a few minutes, the corridor was once again quiet. However, after ten or twenty minutes, the staff began calling people out of their cells again, and, this time, they called my name. I waited for a while in the corridor before being sent to collect my belongings. Then, I was escorted to the office of a person who was presented to me as the local prosecutor, to sign the papers. My conversation with this man was short. All he said was: "If I see you again, I'll kill you." I don't know if it was a figure of speech or if he really threatened me, but I took that short phrase very seriously. I silently signed the commitment to appear in court and then rejoined the group of people waiting to be released in the corridor. Seeing my friend among them provided consolation. After a few more minutes, we were grouped into columns and escorted to the exit.

I didn't expect to be met, given that I had vanished without warning. However, I was mistaken: a crowd of approximately 600 to 700 people had gathered right outside the institution's gate. Journalists were at the forefront and rushed to us eager to ask questions and get comments. I politely refused. Parents were standing a bit farther away showing photos of their detained children. I tried to look at every face in these pictures, but I didn't recognise anyone in them. Suddenly, someone in the crowd called out to me, "We're here!" It was my father standing a little behind with his wife and my friends. A second later, I was hugging my loved ones tightly. This moment became my triumph of freedom. Afterwards, I quickly said goodbye to my friend, who was also met, and promptly got into the car. As we drove home, my father and friends discussed the events that had unfolded in the country since 9 August. At that moment, my only thought was: "How will we live on?"

The present time

After returning home, my mental state began gradually to deteriorate. During this mid-August period, the protests were still heating up, while the level of violence perpetrated by the state was increasing. The videos I saw of the crackdowns from 9-13 August had a severe impact on my emotional state. I was shocked to see the true face of my country, and I began to fear for my safety. I need to add that my trial could theoretically start on any given day. My sentence could become the state's revenge, including for all the resistance that people demonstrated in Belarusian cities at that time. I did not count on mercy or "forgiveness" at all, nor did I rule out the possibility that if I stayed, I might risk ending up behind bars again. This led me seriously to consider emigration.

One day in late August, my friend, who had been detained with me, called me as he wanted to say goodbye because he was leaving for Poland. We met and he told me about his strategy and future plans. He departed a few days later. I decided to follow my friend to Poland and make further plans there. I typically take my time to think through the potential outcomes of my actions, but at that moment I was overwhelmed by a sense of anxiety and danger. After a quick discussion of details, I said goodbye to my family and left the country.

I am in Poland now. I have been living here for almost three and a half years. During this period, I have had the opportunity to live in both small villages and picturesque Polish cities. Currently, I live with my girlfriend and I have a fulfilling job in an IT company. I recently completed a master's degree in quality management, realising a lifelong ambition for a second higher education qualification. Unfortunately, since 2020, I have not had the opportunity to see anyone from my family except my mother. Throughout this time, I have not visited Belarus either. Although living abroad is not at all easy, I feel calm and stable here, which allows me to work normally and envision my future. However, the most significant outcome of my move was the sense of genuine freedom I experienced, which was starkly absent during my final months in Belarus.

Although I miss my home very much, I am currently unable to return until certain changes take place.

Motivation, conclusions and the future

My acquaintances often ask about my personal motivation for participating in the events of 2020. As I mentioned earlier, at the most critical moment, I was guided not so much by my civic position, but by the interest of a young person in the unfolding events, a sense of not being indifferent to my own life, my choices, and the world around me. Additionally, I believe that if you allow others to tell you lies, it means you do not respect yourself.

Of course, besides my personal circumstances, there were other, more significant reasons for being at the heart of the events in August. It seemed that the indomitable spirit of the Belarusian people, which had been held captive for more than a century until that moment, had finally broken free and united us into an invincible force. To be honest, I have never witnessed Belarusians as resolute and united in their spiritual yearning for freedom as they were during those days, which inspired me and many others around to make certain choices. Unfortunately, we did not succeed in attaining our goals of creating a fair Belarus in those days, but I am certain that in the future we will have such an opportunity again. Although the open protest has long ended, we saw each other in a new light and recognised our capacity for remarkable deeds and victories.

Many Belarusians are now abroad, with some peacefully pursuing education or working and contributing to diaspora efforts on the ground, others actively promoting our culture and values, and still others — focused on shaping the future of our country and securing support for Belarusians both abroad and at home. Despite these various "tasks", the most important thing is that we are working for the common cause together, protecting our collective identity, and remain Belarusians for each other. If someone asks what we should do in these dark times, I would respond poetically by saying "To be called people", and then I would advise joining local Belarusian diaspora groups and associations, donating money to open Belarusian schools and publishing Belarusian literature, participating in peaceful marches and holding concerts in support of our compatriots, creating Belarusian art, and protecting ourselves and our loved ones. In my view, all this ultimately leads us closer to a Belarus where peace and justice prevail, where equality and sincerity are valued, where dictatorship is recognised as a crime rather than a brand. To a truly free and independent Belarus.

To sum up my story, I would like to emphasise that unity and support are our most reliable allies today. It matters not whether you are a student or professor, an IT specialist or doctor, a labourer or artist. Mutual support can change the course of history. On my entire path, my family and friends have been my constant source of support, my colleagues and various foundations have provided aid, and compassionate Belarusians both in Poland and even overseas have offered their help. And this is just my single example, so you can imagine how vast and dense our community is worldwide. The events of 2020 apparently changed my life, as well as the lives of millions of Belarusians, but I believe that these changes were for our benefit. Personally, I have become more compassionate and kind towards people, but what is most significant is that I have felt myself even more of a Belarusian. I intend to preserve this feeling and the self-identification that has developed over the years of trials, and pass it on to my descendants.

Warsaw, June 2023
essaycontact2023@gmail.com

(NO) DREAMS OF BELARUSIAN STUDENTS

Kacia

My name is Kacia, I graduated from university in 2021. I was born in Minsk and studied in Minsk. Despite the opportunity to get an education abroad and the solid knowledge base that the lyceum provided me, I decided to move forward in my development and study alongside my school friends, making the most of Belarusian higher education.

Memories of the university

The absurdity of the situation that unfolded during my final year at university is difficult to convey in words. Online learning, strikes together with lecturers in our online chats, the "students' case", termination checklists and expulsions — probably these phrases can best describe the events of that period. At first we were possessed by the spirit of freedom, unlimited opportunities, true studentship, and self-organisation, but then everything changed to depression and fear. Even those who protested began to pretend that nothing had happened.

I opted for the Faculty of Humanities to pursue my studies. My interest in social sciences was a major factor in this decision, and I was also drawn to the opportunity to focus on marketing statistics. Well, to be honest, my best friend had already applied there. I don't remember much from my student years, but a few moments come to mind instantly as I reflect on my time at university.

First, it was very boring. This was particularly noticeable after attending the lyceum. However, considering that the lyceum, like all other academic institutions, was subjected to repression, it was actually one of the best educational facilities. Until my third year, I didn't feel like I was gaining new knowledge, except for a few specific subjects. To be honest, my enthusiasm for studying at university faded rapidly. However, from my first year, I became involved in activism. But more on that later.

Secondly, it was very difficult to motivate Belarusian students to participate in political-ideological and pro-Belarusian activities, and songs or skits with an overly ideological meaning were dismissed and not accepted at the events. The system strongly suppressed such initiatives. My student activism projects turned into a real fight against the system. Starting from my second year, I was overseeing a creative student initiative. We organised Mother Tongue Days and educational events, which became a novelty for everyone. Meanwhile, other loyal student organisations staged amateur concerts, contests like Mr and Miss Faculty, in short, that was just entertainment. In the end, we were left to dream of the number of people who attended those "fun events", as each of ours was a struggle, involving negotiations with the dean and securing the endorsement of each guest. However, the administration was always present at our parties, watching. On the Mother Tongue Day, for example, we hosted an acoustic concert by a Belarusian musician. Despite our best efforts to publicise the event through active advertising and announcements, people did not gather. I had to ask our lecturer to cancel the evening class and persuade fellow students to attend the concert to create a crowd. It is worth mentioning that before the Mother Tongue Day, we faced a threat from the dean. We hadn't got the endorsement from him for the invited guests, so we held the event "under personal responsibility". The following year, we did not give up, and we held the Mother Tongue Day again. As a result, more people attended, as they got more engaged, and we became more effective in promoting and fighting for our cause.

And thirdly, what I recall quite vividly from my student years until 2020 is the censorship and political partiality of the faculty administration, as well as the complete political apathy of my fellow students. Here are some examples.

The deputy dean used to invite my friend and me to tea, approving our actions as the right thing and expressing her full support. However, in 2020, she became a witness for the prosecution in my friend's trial related to the so-called students' case.

On the Mother Tongue Days, the administration would visit our stands, where we displayed gifts, and inspect whether we had Belarusian symbols there. They would ask us to remove certain stickers and badges.

We were repeatedly called in for talks to the dean's office concerning the guest lists for our educational events and concerts. They would demand that we not invite certain individuals, and they would make threats.

Expressing pro-Belarusian ideas in our university was challenging and often unrewarding. We created performances with ideological undertones, but they never made it to the finals of competitions. Despite this, there were some positive moments, too. During classes, we had the opportunity to discuss social projects and hold national events. It's worth noting that there was at least some relative freedom. However, since 2020, this possibility has disappeared.

Future plans and activities until 2020

When I enrolled in the university, I envisioned pursuing a career in marketing or PR management, being interested in studying economics, psychology, and methodology. I actively sought out internships in communication and PR companies to explore my interests in business. I also made it a point to volunteer wherever possible. My goal was to build a strong network of useful contacts. I thought it was very important, although I was not entirely sure why.

Initially, my civic activism was a spare-time activity. I volunteered at "Live Libraries" events, handled tasks such as chair delivery and guest registration. It was a fortunate encounter that introduced me to sincere, open-minded people with robust principles and values. I gained knowledge about new things and developed the ability to communicate effectively with different people who had different needs. Through these interactions, I developed a strong sense of non-discrimination and tolerance, which constituted the core values in my life. I realised that activism can be a lifelong commitment and a driving force in one's life. Once or twice a week, after classes, I would hurry to a briefing in a non-profit organisation where I got a job. These meetings became more significant to me than attending lectures. Simultaneously, I was exploring my professional interests in the commercial sector, and I got a qualification in nail tech. I was a typical student trying to find my place.

Now I realise that my life was transformed by the Belarusian Summer School in Human Rights, which I completed between my second and third years. I gained an understanding of human rights, and this concept became meaningful for me. I wanted to shout out loud about human rights! It seemed that this knowledge could revolutionise everything. I no longer understood how one could seek employment in advertising or marketing. The most pressing thought in my mind in 2020 was the question: "How can one devise strategies of marketing sour cream when the streets of the country are grappling with human rights issues?" So, that summer school in human rights marked a turning point in my life, shaping my destiny and guiding me towards where I am now.

About 2020

In the first half of 2020, when the "turbulence" began, I instantly joined a human rights organisation as a volunteer, where I assisted people whose rights had been infringed. I had to learn everything quickly. By mid-August, I was surprised to find myself proficient in administrative and criminal law. My grandfather would likely have been delighted (if I hadn't kept my activities a secret), as he had always hoped that I would become a lawyer. I was available to answer calls from 9am to 9pm, and I heard stories about violence, about loss, about pain.

It was impossible to believe that in less than a month, I would be back on a student bench, with the academic year starting as if nothing had happened, despite the level of repression in the country. Of course, studying at a Belarusian university never resonated with my dream. From the uncomfortable seats in the auditorium, designed for the fictional Pinocchio (two boards: one for the seat, the other for the desk), to the educational curricula and syllabi, everything seemed to have been tailored to meet the needs of an authoritarian system.

Only in 2020 did I finally experience the authentic spirit of studentship. A closer examination of student actions and activities in that year reveals several notable features.

Strikes

Of course, they looked a little specific, since the Belarusian students had scarce chances to obtain such expertise. The element of online education was also a factor. That academic year was partly online, seemingly because of Covid. I cannot say that I believe it. In Belarus at that time, Covid only existed when it was convenient for the dictatorship. We immediately realised that the online learning was done to prevent us from protesting. Our strikes resembled a vocal refusal to participate in classes. At the beginning of the class, we would write in a chat with the teacher that we did not agree with what was happening in the country, and therefore did not find it conceivable to continue studying as before, and refused to participate in the educational process.

Now I realise that our actions were more about our conscience than actually causing any systemic changes. Systemic changes could have occurred if the entire group or, rather, the faculty and university had refused to have classes. In fact, initially only 5 to 7 people turned down the classes, but then fewer and fewer did. After two or three months, perhaps, we stopped this action because it affected neither lecturers nor classes. If you are curious about the teachers' reaction — I can answer: it was nil.

Marches

This is my fondest memory from the student protest, because the first general student march was truly powerful. I was more thrilled than ever to walk alongside other people. I felt a sense of unity and our collective strength. I didn't usually feel like a student, and it was difficult for me to associate myself with the university (perhaps due to the difference of opinion, or the unpopularity of our events among students). But at the first general student march, I felt more vividly than ever that I belonged to this group of people. I was laughing and shouting various student slogans, watching other people as if I had known them personally long before. I felt regret and pain that this march, like many others, ended with police violence, detentions, fines and arrests. Such an event did not happen again due to repression. Eventually, they began to intimidate students, give warnings and expel them.

Being a student is highly esteemed among Belarusians, including young people. In our culture, it's uncommon for students to drop out of university if they're not satisfied with their chosen major. Parents often insist on higher education, making it difficult to dispute with them.

It can be argued that the Belarusian student was non-politicised. Most likely, this and other factors influenced the suspension of large-scale actions and major protests. However, the way of struggle that has always been and will continue to exist for Belarusian people is partisan activity.

Partisan struggle

I cannot speak about partisan actions as I did not participate in them, but I think this was an important moment in the struggle of our students. Student initiatives and organisations were creative in drawing attention to repressions, election falsification, and the situation of Belarusian students. I think that without their active involvement, the situation for expelled and repressed students would likely have been even more severe.

Rallies and actions

I took part in several large-scale actions near the main entrance of the university. It was on the day of the actions that the repairs near the rector's office would suddenly start and we were unable to meet with anyone from the administration. Despite this, we sang songs, hugged, and held placards with political appeals. We expected justice and we yearned for it.

Quite a few rallies were held on the steps of my faculty building. There were usually five people there, but occasionally dozens gathered. At such actions, the administration threatened us, and even if they did not threaten us, they stood on the sidelines, watching us closely. The police were called on us, forcing us to leave quickly. The security guards on duty approached and swore at us. We were filmed on the "narks'" cameras. However, I was glad it did not stop us in the first couple of months. We stood our ground, spoke out, and demanded change.

For participating in one of these rallies, I received a summons to the prosecutor's office, which was handed to me by a methodology specialist from the dean's office. This fact is also worth remembering, because the university staff began to perform the functions of postmen, assistant prosecutors, police, draft officers, and so on. I was summoned to the prosecutor's office without knowing the specific reason, as the summons didn't provide any details. I was extremely worried, fearing I might be sent to a colony for five years. However, it turned out to be a standard warning that participation in unauthorised mass gatherings is illegal and would result in administrative action. Given my background in human rights work and familiarity with international standards for regulating peaceful assemblies, I appealed this warning with a sort of pleasure.

Cancellation of mandatory (i.e. forced) student association membership

Indeed, in 2020, there was a widespread student cancellation of trade union and *Belarusian Republican Youth Union (BRYU)* membership. I could still understand the trade union, but *BRYU* was always a quango — a government-sponsored institution, exerting pressure on independent youth associations and councils in the university. When my friend and I submitted our applications to cancel our memberships in these organisations, I recall being berated and accused of being brainwashed, with the implication that we were acting at the behest of some unknown people. They attempted to persuade us that these organisations exist solely for the benefit of students and bring only good. In essence, there was no autonomy of action to speak about.

I remember this period as a time of solidarity, even from those I didn't expect would do anything. It was then that people's true nature was revealed through their actions and inactions. Each person chose their allegiance.

Then two pivotal moments transformed my activity from the student movement to human rights. The first was 12 November, known as "Black Thursday", the beginning of the so-called students' case process, when twelve people were detained and sentenced to terms of two to two and a half years in July 2021. My best friend was among those people. Next, I remember countless trials, parcels, and court meetings with the teaching staff (unfortunately, more often as part of the prosecution). Even after November, it was hard to encourage fellow students to attend open court sessions to show solidarity and support. This was a moment of final disappointment and acceptance of reality. The second defining moment that changed my perspective was the home searches of human rights defenders on 16 December.

I have a hazy recollection of the final months of my fourth year of studying. Sometimes, I even question whether I was there at all. I have no clear memory of the subjects we studied, whether we had face-to-face classes or online sessions. Even the exam session passed me by. I didn't feel the urge to write a diploma thesis until the last minute. I would often ask myself: "What's the point of all this?" I even considered dropping out of university altogether. However, the prospect of having nowhere to go made it difficult. I cleared all my academic debts and defended my diploma thesis. I decided that having this qualification could be useful, just in case. By that point, I had fully immersed myself in activism and human rights work. For nearly the entire fourth year, my friend was kept in detention in a pre-trial facility, followed by a two-year term in a women's prison colony. Occasionally, when her name was called out during attendance checks, I replied in a rude tone that she was in prison. I was angry about this disconnect from reality. I have never been able to fully understand how the conscience and consciousness of indifferent people work. Though I vaguely remember it, the second half of the 2020-2021 academic year was not so bright. The students' case, expulsions, arrests, and fines frightened people (and I understand them well). As a result, public activism declined and emigration began. In my soul, there was a deep sense of loneliness and a realisation of the futility of the educational process.

Towards the end of the academic year, just before receiving my certificate, I took the final steps in my fight against the system. I then refused to complete the departure check-list, and I didn't even come to collect it for a very long time. The departure check-list is a document where you must obtain signatures from the library, the trade union office, and the *Belarusian Republican Youth Union* confirming that you don't owe them any items. According to Belarusian law, the completion of the departure check-list should not have any effect on the issuance of one's diploma. However, in practice, I was not even invited to the graduation ceremony, and was told that my name would not be announced there. Seeing the photos from the event filled me with great sadness, not because I wished I had been there, but because I yearned for the repression to stop. I now understand that even during wartime, there may still be social events like balls, and perhaps that is necessary, but I was mortified then.

My refusal to fill out the departure check-list was my final chance of dissent within the university walls. In June and July 2021, with the assistance of a lawyer, I attempted to collect my diploma certificate without the check-list, printing out and citing relevant legal excerpts and visiting the ethics officer and the dean. The final blow was the dean's remark that I should not "find a cover in the law." I was taken aback, as I was not prepared for such words — that the law would be viewed as a "cover" rather than a set of norms and rules that must be followed.

I must admit that at that moment I gave up. My friend was under trial, the dean told me not to hide behind the law, and all my fellow students had already received their diplomas and forgot about the university. I gave up and fell asleep on 13 July, thinking that the next day I would fill out the departure check-list. But on the morning of 14 July, they came to me with a search warrant.

Studying at a Belarusian university is nothing like a student's dream. There is no freedom in selecting courses, the administration censors any activities, and membership in student associations is coerced. If you are a Belarusian student, you risk expulsion for your views or arrest for political involvement. The events of 2020 were a very positive shock for the Belarusian universities. I believe we were able to frighten many people and demonstrate our collective strength. Belarusian history lacks significant open and political solidarity action at the university level, so this experience was definitely valuable for everyone who participated. Valuable, yet often tinged with sadness. Currently, I reside in Europe and interact with people here. These people are familiar with the practical application of human rights and the potential for democratic change. I believe that the knowledge and experiences we gained in 2020 have instilled in us a strong appreciation for the most fundamental rights and freedoms. This understanding is not something that can be easily acquired.

Currently, my aspiration is to continue my education. If I succeed in collecting my diploma certificate, I plan to pursue a master's degree. I hope to do this not only to gain more knowledge, but also to experience what a truly free university can be like. Occasionally, I feel a deep sense of sadness that I did not have the opportunity to experience student life as depicted in American movies (excluding those about protests). I yearn to know what it feels like to have a carefree youth, without the constant need to fight against an oppressive and heartless system. I sincerely hope that this chance will come again, as I envision a future for Belarus that is free, democratic, and governed by the rule of law and that belongs to us. We must be prepared for such a country — to understand the fundamentals of human rights, to be able to exercise and assert them, and truly to comprehend and embrace freedom. This knowledge and mind-set must be cultivated within ourselves, because, when the regime eventually changes, these essential qualities will not simply materialise on their own. To introduce new practices to the country, we need to accumulate knowledge, study them, and select the best that would work for us. I found myself in exile and have come to realise that it is in these activities that the significance of my time away from home lies.

Throughout my involvement in student solidarity actions, I was driven by the hope for change and the conviction that there is no alternative. Violence, pressure, and injustice cannot be tolerated, cannot be ignored, cannot be silenced — otherwise it will never stop. Only by voicing our discontent and disagreement can we effect change. Although we did not succeed in changing the system in 2020, I am certain that we have changed ourselves profoundly; we have become stronger and confident in our identities and aspirations. These transformations will serve as the foundation for the creation of a future Belarus.

City N, January 2024

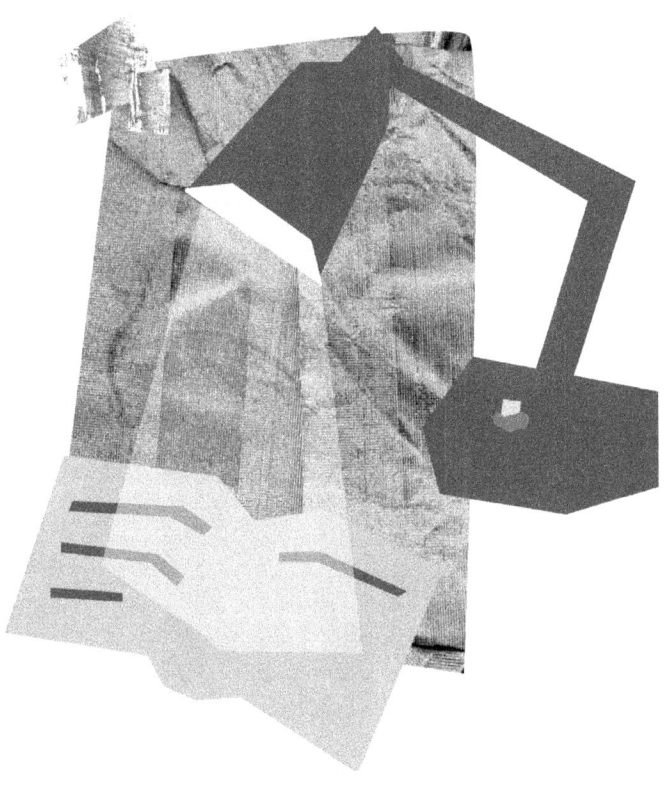

I AM DETERMINED NOT TO GIVE UP

Asia

My name is Anastasiya. I am 22 years old. I was born in Mahilioŭ city, and I studied at an art school. After graduating, I attended the regional lyceum, specialising in English, history, and social studies. I finished the 11th grade in a class for the in-depth study of language and literature at Minsk Lyceum no. 2.

My mother, grandmother, and aunt all studied technical specialities in their time, so I decided to explore this field, despite my passion for creative and humanitarian pursuits. I was curious about my ability to handle technical sciences. This led me to enrol at Belarusian National Technical University. I chose the Faculty of Mechanical Engineering, focusing on technological equipment for mechanical engineering production.

I only had the opportunity to complete one year of studies, so I didn't have the chance to fully grasp the intricacies of the speciality. Our curriculum included materials science, engineering graphics, physics, and higher mathematics, as well as general subjects like history, chemistry, English, and physical education. In materials science laboratory work, I consistently volunteered for various experiments. This subject, despite the dense volumes of theory, was engaging and captivating due to the dynamic nature of practical classes. My studies were progressing well. In general, learning things was easy for me, I had no retakes. Being the only female in the group, I was also the group leader and an activist.

Recalling my university experience, I would like to highlight some of the drawbacks in this sphere. We were trained using outdated syllabi, and the equipment was antiquated. I remember a particular situation during the "Introduction to Mechanical Engineering" course where the head of the department showed us old machines that were no longer used in Belarus, while there was no functional model available. I would also characterise the educational system as outdated, with students spending most of their day in a classroom. Distance learning during the Covid-19 pandemic revealed that nearly 50 per cent of information is available for self-study.

The first year curriculum was quite general. Moreover, I was among the second generation of students to be admitted to the four-year curriculum (the previous curriculum was designed for five years in my speciality). At the start of the academic year, they told us: "We can't foresee your exact future professions upon graduation." Facing these circumstances made it difficult to stay motivated and formulate specific goals. Although, as I already noted, my studies were progressing without problems, I didn't find them particularly engaging, so by the end of the first year, I decided to explore more creative options in my life. In my view, the Belarusian education system is in need of a modern approach, particularly in terms of giving both students and teachers more freedom.

In the summer of 2020, I was just 18 years old. I attended my first protest in June, following the arrest of the presidential candidate *Viktar Babaryka*. This fact led me to take a more active interest in current events, read independent Belarusian media, and engage in various political discussions with friends. This, in turn, helped me shape my personal opinion about events in the country.

On 9 August, I attended my first presidential elections in Mahilioŭ, wearing a white band on my wrist. The following day, I returned to Minsk and witnessed the events near the Puškinskaja metro station. What I saw there changed me totally, and I returned home a "different" person. Prior to that, I had only witnessed violations of the law and, as I believe, dishonest elections, but such atrocities against peaceful Belarusians were beyond my understanding. The world as I knew it was turned upside down. From that day on, I participated in women's solidarity chains every day and in Sunday marches. I also joined the student protest movement.

When the academic year began, I thought, "How can I go to classes when these things are happening in the country?" On 1 September, I joined the student march. I wanted to demonstrate, as a student, that I did not support the actions of the authorities. I thought it was essential to protest as a student, because students are a vital and active part of society. In a sense, students are its driving force, having their own voice and the right to exercise it. I still believe that we should be heard.

On that day, a student column from BNTU and other universities organised a march to the Ministry of Education with a petition to support students in three main demands: new elections, an end to violence, and the release of political prisoners. However, we were unable to reach the ministry, just as we were unable to get a reasoned answer from representatives of the authorities to the question of why our demands were incorrect. Why were we dispersed on the way to the ministry? Why didn't the ministry provide a public comment on our petition and student march?

Later students from my and other universities continued to gather for protests, without violating university regulations. We gathered during our free time from studying and carried out peaceful actions without using insignia, as this was prohibited on university territory. However, we still faced repressions from the university administration. Following the national strike alone, more than fifty students were expelled from my university. I was one of them. I was expelled and served an administrative arrest for taking part in the students' march.

After being released and expelled, I was once again detained by KGB officers as a suspect under Article 342 of the Criminal Code of Belarus and became a defendant in the so-called students' case. This case involved eleven students and one professor, who were accused of organising student protests across Belarus, grossly violating public order, and even provoking sanctions from the EU and USA (even though the sanctions were not imposed until April 2021). We were ultimately sentenced to two and a half years in prison.

The real moral test we faced was seeing our teachers, deans, and rectors acting as witnesses for the prosecution during the trial. Those few who tried to stand up for us and told the truth, did not remain at the university for long, as far as I know. The majority of the witnesses tried to remain neutral, but under the judge's slightest pressure, they agreed with absolutely identical written statements they had signed several months prior to the trials. It was a terrible scene. My dean claimed that he did not know me, although back in 2019 he had sent my mother a thank-you note for her daughter's upbringing.

My worldview was turned upside down. When you do something right, honest, and end up in prison for it, you have to re-evaluate all your principles and ideals, and your outlook on life. When people who are supposed to teach you something and to help you defend your rights brazenly lie in court, and you sit in a cage, you realise that not everything in this world is as it should be.

While in prison, I came across thieves, swindlers, and murderers. I tried to view this experience as an amazing opportunity, being innocent, to understand how this whole punitive system operates. It was a frightening experience.

Throughout the first year of my imprisonment, I clung to the hope that we would all be released soon, that justice would prevail, and that the nightmare would come to an end, but this did not happen. In 2020, at the start of the protests, most people believed in a swift victory over the dictatorship, but as each month passed, this belief gradually faded away. I know that many people now have lost faith in rapid changes and do not expect anything positive from the future. It is also clear to me that the process of liberating Belarus from a brutal dictatorship will take years, yet, I still believe that the terrible lawlessness in the country will come to an end. After all, history is cyclical.

After witnessing such cruelty, violence, and obvious injustice in 2020, I had to reassess my views. I believed that the role of a university went beyond just teaching you professional skills, but also included helping students develop as a person, supporting initiative, and nurturing aspirations. However, to my disappointment, I discovered that reality is far from what I imagined. I always believed that people are drawn to light; therefore, it was difficult for me to acknowledge that there are such malevolent and cruel individuals in the world. Previously, it seemed to me that only criminals were imprisoned, but I ended up there myself, being innocent. I spent a lot of time brooding about life and the things happening around. In my closing statement, before hearing the verdict, I said that I no longer believed people, but I would never stop believing in people.

Now, there is more barbed wire everywhere, not just in pre-trial detention centres, colonies, and prisons. The entirety of Belarus is surrounded by barbed wire, making it a prison for all its citizens. Many thousands of people remain imprisoned. Some have been released, but many are still in captivity. Many thousands of people have suffered and do not know how to continue living. That's why I haven't left the past behind, that's why I don't want to forget what happened to me and my family.

After being released, I received a ban on leaving Belarus. Reinstatement at the university was out of the question, as my expulsion order lacked the standard phrase "with the possibility of reinstatement" found in most such orders (in any case, I saw this phrase in other orders given by my university). During those five months in Belarus, I worked, studied the language, and took up dancing.

To lift the travel ban, I took my case to court, but the outcome was a thirty-day prison sentence. After that, I was able to leave for Lithuania.

For this academic year, I have not had the chance to enrol in any courses. I am now a twenty-two-year-old woman with no qualifications from higher education or specialist skills, which is making my situation very difficult. Despite this, I refuse to give up. Currently, I am pursuing my creative interests: painting, making jewellery from epoxy resin, dancing, and taking social media marketing courses. I am about to start graphic design training. While I am unsure about returning to mechanical engineering in the future, I am certain that, in my life, I am determined not to give up!

Lithuania, January 2024
ogurchikovaa@gmail.com

BURN TO SHINE THE LIGHT!

Angelina

> In helping others, we shall help ourselves, for whatever good we give out completes the circle and comes back to us.
> Flora Edwards

A troublesome story with a good start

My name is Angelina, I was born in a small village. I was often bullied at school. My classmates tried to humiliate me because my clothes were not as fashionable as those of other children. Restricted by modest financial conditions, my family was focused on keeping our clothes clean and untorn. Everything they earned was spent on food and our education. Therefore, we would pick berries and mushrooms in the forest during the summer to save money for school supplies and personal expenses. From a young age, the importance of hard work was instilled in us, and there was a firm rule: if you want to buy something, you can earn money for it.

Bullying at school taught me another crucial lesson: no one will help you except yourself. I began to stand up for myself and other children who were weaker. Most likely, this moment marked a turning point in my life and shaped my core principles. I also came to understand that violence in any form is unacceptable. If you witness violence and do nothing, you are silently condoning it, but this is not my way. Furthermore, I developed a strong conviction that every person has the right to freedom of speech.

High expectations

When I enrolled in university, I felt extremely happy, because I had put so much effort into preparing for it. I had been working long and hard towards this result.

I had to take off my rose-tinted glasses when my studies began. At university, I was disappointed not to find the anticipated atmosphere of community between students and teachers. I had to rely on self-study, constantly seeking out contemporary educational resources to enhance and expand my knowledge. As the twenty-first century moved forward, some lecturers still continued to teach students using outdated textbooks from Soviet times.

The approach adopted by certain lecturers towards students was highly demanding, as they expected the students to already possess some knowledge. I used to respond by saying that my purpose in attending university was to acquire new knowledge and skills. Ultimately, I proved to my critics as well as to myself that I am capable of accomplishing more, driven by my ambition and determination to achieve outstanding results. I quickly adapted to student life, started writing research papers, exploring foreign practices, studying diligently, and achieving excellent results in exams. Overall, I exhibited great determination and tenacity in pursuing my aspirations.

I would like to express my gratitude to my lecturers, who not only motivated students to work diligently, but also taught their subjects in an engaging manner and consistently introduced us to various web pages containing useful resources. Unfortunately, after 2020, many talented teachers left or were fired, because they could no longer work in a system where students were arrested and colleagues were terminated. This is a sad and unfair reality.

I had always aspired to complete my university education and become a competent specialist, with the intention to work in our country for the benefit of society. Unfortunately, in the autumn of 2020, along with 124 other students from different universities, I was expelled for political reasons.

No to violence and injustice

It all started on 18 June 2020, when *Viktar Babaryka* was detained. For me this was the most outrageous thing. It was difficult to comprehend how someone so kind and good could be put behind bars. Or, say, how can someone be detained on the street for simply passing by? Not to mention the violence against civilians. I am a pacifist by nature and always condemn violence and war. I find it difficult to understand how one person can hit another, or how someone can mock or humiliate another human being.

Soon the authorities began arresting students and imprisoning them for several days, and the university administration failed to intervene. Instead, they stressed the need for these arrests. Besides, they threatened the protesting students with expulsion; and the teachers were also affected by repressive measures, many were forced to leave before the start of the academic year.

At first, I felt depressed: witnessing everything that was happening, I didn't know how I could help the victims. I longed to make a difference, so I gathered my resolve and decided to act as a mediator between the administration and students, drawing on my experience as an active student.

I started checking the lists from the temporary detention centre for students of the technical university and informing relatives that their child had been detained. Next, other concerned students and I tried to reach out to the administration, arguing that students should not be expelled for their opinions or their unfair detention.

I began to receive more and more threats from the university administration, but I was at a loss then, as well as now, how to respond to them appropriately. On Knowledge Day, like many students, I was detained. This is what happens when you are unwelcome at your university. Subsequently, the university administration provided crucial evidence against me. In September, I was detained for seven days and tried under Article 23.34 of the Administrative Code (for participating in an unauthorised event). The indictment claimed that I chanted "Long live Belarus!" and "Disgrace!" (Hańba) while waving a flag, although this was not captured on the video of my arrest. It became clear that it is difficult to combat a system where everyone blatantly lies.

Following my release, I returned to my studies. My detention became a powerful motivator for other supporters; they started to perceive me as a symbol of freedom and truth at the university. Many students began to recognise me and ask questions. This led to the emergence of more like-minded people, and it became clear that my actions had inspired them, although I didn't want it to happen. After all, I decided to take the inevitable risks myself. These were my principles and ideas, and I did not intend to impose them on anyone. The students provided a lot of support, attention, and care. Then, it all went beyond the university; parents of other students started contacting me. They brought various goodies to the university, provided financial assistance, and wrote posts about me. There was a great wave of solidarity!

In addition to the university actions, I also recall the events that unfolded on the streets of Minsk. I felt a sense of joy when I saw people participating in peaceful protests and bringing their children with them. There was a sea of flowers, smiles, and positivity. During those three months (August to October) of 2020, I had the opportunity to meet many kind and compassionate people from various walks of life. It was heart-warming to experience the affection, mutual understanding and support around you when you went out. Many participants in the peaceful demonstrations brought water or sweet treats to share. There were also those who prepared and distributed snacks like soups or salads during the marches. But it's not just about treats. People also tried to shield and protect fellow demonstrators from police violence. Girls shielded boys, grandmothers shielded the young. These moments were showcasing the profound unity and solidarity among Belarusians – when you start thinking about and caring for one another, rather than just yourself.

At such moments, I felt a burning passion within me. People were finally demonstrating genuine kindness towards one another, which was exactly what I had always yearned for. I think that we were united by a common misfortune and a shared hope for a free life. Of course, as a Belarusian, like many others, I thought that people could change and solve everything, because this is our country and our life. However, everything turned out differently than we had expected.

On 28 October 2020, I was expelled from the university. That day, there were many expulsions from all educational institutions. I was the first to know about my expulsion, as I received a call from the dean's office, asking me to come and collect my documents. I was not upset, as I had anticipated this outcome and had already started exploring options to study abroad. To make the most of my time, I decided to start working, as I could not imagine living without personal development.

"Things could have been worse!"

I would repeat this phrase throughout my imprisonment. Many people didn't understand how I could smile so much at everyone, from the pre-trial detention centre staff to the convoy and the colony staff. At that time, this was my instinctive defence mechanism against all the troubles I faced. It was also my natural reaction in stressful situations.

On that fateful Tuesday, 12 November 2020, which would later be referred to as the "Black Thursday of Belarusian students," I was returning from work with my colleague around 6pm. I had a sense of foreboding, and it turned out to be true. As we walked through a dark alley, two men in black approached us. They showed their documents and asked us to get into the car, and my colleague protested. I didn't even have time to get scared, as these strangers were polite and treated me differently than the people from *GUBOPiK*. Once we were in the car, I discovered that they were KGB officers. When the car started moving, I thought they were taking me to the *Vaładarka* pre-trial detention centre. At that moment, I did not yet know that the KGB had its own pre-trial detention centre, popularly dubbed the "American" (*Amierykanka*) facility. As we drove through one of the streets, I realised we were heading to my home. Upon arrival, a search began, followed by the first interrogation, and then the transfer to *Amierykanka*. The most striking thing was that these officers didn't search for or confiscate anything significant in my home. They weren't even bothered by my flag on the wall, my talk about violence, or my appeal to them with the question of why people behave so horribly. It seemed to me that they understood everything. And this realisation made my heart ache even more. These men understood, but did nothing to change the situation. One of the officers even showed concern for me in his own way. As I was arrested immediately after work, they knew I had not yet had time to eat. Since I was not likely to get my prison dinner, they suggested I either take food with me or eat at home. However, there are also bad recollections. That day, a cat in my apartment had been on IV for a month due to a blood virus, and I was worried that she might get another infection. Since the cat was sick, I asked these officers to remove their shoes, but they refused.

After the search of the apartment, we went to the KGB office, and once all the details had been ascertained, I was taken to *Amierykanka*. This peculiar structure is cylindrical, with eighteen cells arranged in a circle. Four of these cells have a toilet (I was lucky to be in one of those), while the remaining cells only have a bucket. There are specific rules in the isolation ward. For instance, you are not allowed to laugh loudly, as this constitutes a violation of the internal regulations (IRR). You are also prohibited from sharing items with others and cannot say your last name out loud. When they escort you out of the cell and point a finger at you, you must state your name and patronymic.

Another issue was the toilet, which lacked any wall or curtain. When a prisoner is using the toilet, guards can enter the cell or look in through an open "trough" (a window for dispensing food). For a normal person, this is a significant source of stress, so for the first three days, I couldn't use the toilet during the day and waited until nightfall. The cells in *Amierykanka* are very small, approximately five to six square metres, which means everyone is very close to each other. I appeared to be an extra one, as I was the fourth person in a room designed for three. When I checked in, I was given a wooden pad on which to place a mattress. The prison building is made of concrete, so it is very cold in winter and very hot in summer. Significant amounts of condensation build up on the walls, causing it to run down in streams. From the first days, the cold caused my back to ache, and I found it difficult to sleep, worrying that the cold temperatures might affect my kidneys. I would move to an upper bunk during the day, hoping to warm up and get some sleep. To distract myself from the harsh reality, I often slept through the day. I was fortunate that the rules of the pre-trial detention centre allowed for this routine. My day began at six o'clock in the morning with cleaning, breakfast, and sleep, followed by waking up, lunch, and sleep again. In the evening, I could read something, then have dinner and sleep once more. This pattern continued for almost the entire eight days I spent there. Throughout those eight days, I constantly thought that everything would come to an end soon, and I worried about my family. I believed that everything would be clarified, and I would be allowed to return home. Even if someone had told me that my detention would last for so long, it would have been easier for me. It's more difficult when you know the beginning but don't see the end.

On 20 November 2020, our group was transferred to a pre-trial detention centre in Valadarskaha Street, where I met the people with whom we were united in a single criminal case. It was the first time we discovered who had been doing what before our arrest. An odd sense of deception and betrayal arose: we were accused of being an organised group, though we only met in the pre-trial detention centre. It was in custody that I realised there were eleven of us, representing different universities, all arrested for participating in student protests.

Then everything unfolded like a continuation of a terrible nightmare: they provided us with bedding and escorted us to a cell with our bags. There, I encountered Marfa Rabkova, a volunteer at the human rights centre, *Viasna*. I was stunned, as I had written her a letter just two weeks earlier, and now we were sharing the same cell. It was only later that I learned that Marfa had been sentenced to fourteen years and nine months in prison on fabricated charges. I didn't feel any fear; instead, I was overwhelmed by shock at the injustice I and thousands of other honest Belarusians had faced. And then – the new rules, new people, new conditions again. Two weeks later, letters started arriving from relatives and strangers, marking the beginning of a new chapter in my life.

"A few words about feelings"

In the *Vaładarka* pre-trial detention centre, I discovered the value of support. The letters I received from different people were my salvation and solace in those tumultuous times. During my investigation, I received more than 1,500 letters – a small portion of what actually reached me. Unfortunately, the rest were irretrievably lost. I don't know the reason why the letters were destroyed. Perhaps the jailers were envious that we were viewed as heroes. Or maybe they wanted to demonstrate that no one cared about us. Their favourite song was: "You've been forgotten, no one needs you". And so on in the same vein.

What struck me as remarkable was the persistence of many letter writers, with some sending me more than twenty letters. One person, in particular, wrote me twenty letters without receiving a response, yet continued to write. Later, smaller and larger packages began to arrive, containing parcels and vitamins. This was a welcome relief, as it became increasingly difficult for relatives to pack parcels due to rising prices. I am deeply grateful to all those who provided assistance, and for not leaving my family to face our misfortune alone.

Among my correspondents, there were regular pen pals, and even entire groups of people who wrote to me. For instance, several families from the same apartment building and a club of grandmothers shared their stories and experiences with me. I was particularly delighted by letters where people shared something with me, sent photos and even poems. One girl, a tour guide, took me on virtual tours through her letters. Another girl wrote that she imagined me as a "fire of lights". I was able to meet some pen pals after my release and thank them personally.

However, I also recall moments of deep sadness, which would suddenly wash over me and leave me feeling utterly drained. You'd lie there, silently weeping from the bitterness and hopelessness. But it was the warm letters and support from fellow inmates that helped me hold on to my sanity. After all, the cell had become my temporary home, and the four walls had become familiar, every bend and cavity was etched in my memory. When you are locked up, the most difficult part is reconciling with the fact that these four walls separate you from the entire world. Of course, going for walks is like a holiday in another country. Meeting new people is also a kind of journey into the outside world, with new stories and conversations. It happens, when you are transferred to a new cell, and everything starts all over again: new people, new walls, and a new story. You have to adapt to something new one more time. The blue sky is like a breath of fresh air, the sun is like the light at the end of the tunnel. Greenery or dandelions are like the story of your entire world. At such moments, you begin to appreciate everything you had in ordinary life and didn't attach much importance to before. I turned to books in order to find myself in them. I was fortunate to have a vivid imagination, which allowed me to visualise everything I read about. Afterwards, I would describe in letters to other people and my relatives what I had read, sharing my thoughts and feelings. When my heart was heavy, I found it difficult to write, not wanting to burden others with my emotions.

Simulation of a court proceeding

Then came the trials, with hearings that allowed me to meet with my relatives. In my closing statement, I aimed to convey my core sentiments: "I could not and will not put up with unjustified violence against civilians, turn a blind eye to it, or pretend that everything is fine. I still believe in the honour, dignity, and justice inherent in people. I'm not going to confess to something I didn't do."

After the trial, a transfer to the colony awaited us. Of the entire two-year imprisonment, this stage stands out as the most difficult memory. You are running from the police van to the train, weighed down by heavy bags, while around you there are people with machine guns who are shouting at you, and against this background you can hear a dog barking. You rush into a narrow carriage passage, where you are shown a place to sit.

This was a standard compartment designed for six people, but twenty prisoners were crammed in. The air was thick with the smells of tobacco, sweat, and urine, with no fresh air at all. I started crying, because I remembered similar scenes from old films and documentaries, where people were taken to camps and colonies. It was terrifying. I had never felt such intense fear, pain, humiliation, and shame for what I had to go through. When we arrived at the colony and were taken out of the police van, I was able to put my bags down and take a deep breath. My first thought was that I had survived that hell. But it had only been ten hours.

748 days

A colony is a gathering place for people from diverse social backgrounds. Compared to the pre-trial detention centre, it was more bearable for me. At least, I had some semblance of freedom. I could hear and see my loved ones. The first six months were a period of adjustment to the regime. These months flew by rather quickly. And then time appeared to have frozen in place. You even start to feel trapped in a time loop. You live from parcel to parcel, from trip to trip to the store. This cycle continues endlessly. Letters to the colony became less frequent, until only messages from relatives remained. But this was no longer so important, as you always had the support of people like you. I met different people who were imprisoned "for politics"; they became my source of strength and support within the colony walls.

A colony is a place that completely dehumanises you, erasing your identity, where they point out your shortcomings and convince you that you are the scum of society. When you first arrive there, they make you sign off on the internal regulations. One of the rules is that you cannot share anything or help other prisoners. How can this be, if all my life I have been taught to give selflessly to those in need and to assist others? Because of this, I drew attention to myself numerous times. I was constantly reprimanded for sharing candy or helping someone with their work. I still don't understand how this can happen. Over time, of course, you become accustomed to this, and you learn to ignore insults and even respond in kind. My first work group was led by a supervisor infamous for her rapidly changing moods. If she was in a foul mood, those who couldn't defend themselves were the first to face her. I stubbornly persevered through the first month, keeping my head down and my mouth shut. But eventually, my nerves frayed from it all, and I started to yell, standing up for the other girls. The situation escalated to the point where even the foreman (a civilian from the outside world) didn't dare say anything to me. I yelled that all the women here being mothers, sisters, and someone's daughters were behaving like monsters. Everyone fell silent. The conflict was over. But it only took two weeks for everything to start all over again. The hardest aspect of such negativity and emotional turmoil was preserving my own self: I cried and wrote letters home, expressing my fear of becoming aggressive and soulless, which was worse than prison itself. A week before my release, I received my first punishment. Do you know why? Yes, it was for standing up for a girl who was being yelled at and disrupted during her shift. I sat in silence for four hours, but eventually, I couldn't take it any more and spoke out. However, this was not an excuse for the administration, as I broke the rules.

A colony is also a place where you can die and no one will save you. During my term, about six people died. I also often found myself in situations where I needed emergency help, but as a prisoner, I was not due to get help. I was expected to endure. I had to deal with blood pressure of 220 over 160, terrible headaches (I suffer migraine), and even fainting from the heat. There were so many cases when girls suffered from midge bites, with severe allergies and swollen legs, and yet they were forced to continue working. In normal life, people would be hospitalised for such conditions.

You have no rights, no voice, no opinion. You are forced to follow the crowd, like in a herd. You are forbidden from praying, visiting the library, playing sports, or even relaxing. Now I understand why there are so many relapses in Belarus. Prisoners are essentially "killed" while incarcerated. After release, it is difficult for them to adjust to normal life, as they struggle to make decisions and adapt to changes in the world.

Upon my release, the hardest thing was to say goodbye to the girls. I still feel guilty to this day, like I felt then, knowing that I was free while they were still imprisoned. I've worked through this guilt with a psychologist many times, but it's like trying to heal an abscess – as soon as it starts to close, this thought begins to nag you again.

Even after my time in the colony, I remain convinced that the Belarusian people are incredibly resilient and that we must continue to fight for our freedom and the freedom of those who have been unjustly deprived of it. Two years have not changed my perspective; on the contrary, I have gained a more profound understanding of many things, including that the criminal code is merely a book with no real legislative power – court sentences are handed down based on the "telephone law".

I am currently studying in the Czech Republic, and I have a scholarship and new friends. Is it easy? I would say no. My heart and soul are drawn to home, and home is Belarus. It's still challenging to learn the language, but these are just small problems compared to what I experienced after the summer of 2020.

Prague, June 2023

AN IMPRINT OF A WORLDVIEW

Anonym

Imagine a heavy tree branch with its crooked and rough features. Paint it in your favourite colour and create an imprint on paper. What have you got?

Has everything fit on your sheet? Are all the curves of the twigs visible? Can you see all the particulars of the bark? Perhaps some paint accidentally dripped, staining a fragment of the print. Can you truly understand what the branch actually looks like from this imprint?

This is how this essay was created.

When sharing my story, I would like to be extremely sincere, without getting lost in excessive details. I want to describe what happened to me, my thoughts and dreams, and my current situation, while keeping the most intimate aspects private.

This essay was crafted amidst turbulence. I pose questions to myself, re-evaluate my personal experiences, and just start to shape my evaluation. This is not an autobiography, but rather an imprint of my recollections and experiences. I believe this is the core of my essay. And I'm very curious to see what will result from it.

I've always been keen on creativity

I had a thirst for knowledge and a desire for self-discovery. Straw weaving, fine arts, ceramics, journalism, music school, and theatre performances – I tried all these pursuits before finishing school.

Nobody created obstacles for me. There were always people around who believed in me, so I was able to keep my creative appetite alive. When it came time to choose a university, I was still figuring out my path. I determined that developing artistic skills would be beneficial, so I sought out a programme focused on fine arts.

The university I ultimately attended was not the one I had dreamed of. And it never lived up to my expectations. It felt overly ordinary. There were few people there who genuinely appreciated creativity, while nonsensical regulations abounded – likely a by-product of the former.

I frequently observed that not only did the students lack enthusiasm for their studies, but the faculty and administration also seemed to lack understanding of the need for commitment. I found this attitude, particularly among the administration, to be especially disheartening.Moreover, what can we expect from a university that does not always close admissions, thereby creating a situation where there are more available places than students interested in attending?

Many students attend this university simply because they were unable to secure a spot at another institution. My friend described it as a "cardboard university," where the name is the only thing that resembles a real university. Belarusian students will likely understand what I mean.

When I first examined the curriculum, I was looking forward to discovering a range of captivating subjects. The sculpture and painting classes truly stood out: at least the instructors were committed to teaching and guiding us. Unfortunately, the rest of the staff failed to make a meaningful impact.

I was unsure what I wanted to do or what I would become after graduation. I used to say jokingly that, as a last resort, I would consider becoming a school teacher. However, everything I had heard about working in schools suggested that it was a profession with low pay, where it was difficult for teachers to maintain a healthy psyche. The prospects were not very bright, although I liked working with children.

At a certain point, I became familiar with public initiatives. This sparked a great deal of interest in me. I appreciated the way interaction was structured within these organisations, and I enjoyed the feeling of freedom. I felt that the people around me were invested in the outcomes of our common cause and were not afraid to explore new ideas. It felt very relatable. I saw that my desire to make the world a better, more convenient and more pleasant place could be realised here. This desire turned into my resolution in 2020.

2020: then and now

It is my feeling that the extensive peaceful protests have had a positive impact on my life. I saw within them a model of behaviour, a model of courage.

I was dissatisfied with the status quo and the functioning of the system. Hoping to make a difference, I also believed that taking action was crucial. The large-scale peaceful protests provided an excellent platform for expressing one's point of view loudly and effectively. I can't imagine a better situation to change myself and the country.

The Sunday protests provided a space where I became convinced that the problems were real and that I was not alone in seeking solutions. Seeing so many people around, observing their freedom, and feeling their energy instilled me with confidence and courage.

The state's pursuit of power and apprehension of relinquishing it seems to have precipitated the 2020 protests. This served as compelling proof to me that the system required reform, and that fear should not be the driving force.

I must admit that occasionally I would have fleeting thoughts like, "Maybe I'm just imagining things? Maybe everything is fine in Belarus? Maybe it's OK not to want any changes, and maybe I'm still very young and don't understand things?" Such thoughts would arise, but any doubts swiftly dissipated when I contemplated the brutal treatment of those who held opposing views.

I remain uncertain about some actions of peaceful Belarusian protesters, their effectiveness and expediency. I am not yet prepared to offer a definitive assessment of the situation. The story appears unfinished, making it difficult for me to evaluate it objectively.

In order to see the full picture, it must be viewed from a sufficient distance. However, I hope that Belarusians managed to see each other, to realise what we have done together and individually.

The crucibles

Imprisonment was a very hard period of my life. I had to confront isolation, the deprivation of my rights, the inability to make decisions about my own life, the invasion of my personal space, the destruction of my understanding of the world at large, and of all my principles and moral guidelines.

The security forces deliberately fostered an environment that compelled prisoners to rely on their self-preservation instincts. This facilitated the process of dividing and controlling them. Such tactics evoked feelings of fear and even horror. In an attempt to withstand this destructive experience, the mind sought out ways to endure.

On the first day of my detention, I started looking for the positives. The first thought that came to my mind was: "At least I'm taking the place of someone more active." Then, I realised that isolation was beneficial because I now had time to reflect on myself and the world around me. Next, I thought that I could derive valuable insights from my observations, which would help me progress in life. In the end, I realised that in addition to the benefits of my arrest, which perhaps I had imagined, I would be able to preserve my memories. I'd like to believe that these memories can have a positive influence on Belarusian society.My observations not only helped me cope with isolation, but also enabled me to view the situation more comprehensively and accurately.

Rituals were a way to cope with the loss of autonomy and the deprivation of rights. Engaging in activities like sports, taking care of your body, writing letters, and even drinking tea together with cellmates provided a sense of control over my body and the processes as such.

Propaganda exerted a profound influence on one's worldview, attempting to convince you that everything you knew about the world was a fabrication. At times, I felt like I was descending into madness.

When I was imprisoned, I observed a sudden shift in the news narratives, emphasising dialogue and collaboration with students. I felt a pang of offence, realising I was not among those who were part of the dialogue, but rather silenced. My cellmates, however, explained that everything reported on TV required scrutiny. They revealed that the news actually signified that purges were being carried out among students.

At some point, I learned to filter the news in a way that prevented it from causing me undue distress. While it was initially difficult to watch pro-government channels, I eventually sought out content that would offer me support. Some political prisoners found solace in reading Andrei Mukavozchik's articles, as they frequently addressed some issues related to protests. These articles provided us with specific details and facts about the activities of those who were not indifferent.

Through pro-government articles, I became aware of the National Anti-crisis Management (NAM) led by Pavel Latushka and other Belarusian emigrants' initiatives. Furthermore, I discovered that a new package of sanctions had been introduced, along with the details of individuals detained during this or that month.

I also recall how advertisements and certain TV shows started vanishing from the airwaves. In the evenings, they began repeatedly airing the same films. I remember them broadcasting the same season of Ice Age three times throughout the winter.

Letters offered a vital window into real life. They slowed down the process of deterioration and made the collapse of worldviews more manageable.I received letters from my family; they were filled with stories about their daily lives, such as visits to the dacha or Easter celebrations, accompanied by photographs and drawings. I found drawings particularly endearing because they often allowed people to express themselves more freely than when conveying their thoughts verbally.For a certain period, I received letters from strangers. One woman who wrote to me left a lasting impression, as she initially sent me very good poems and later began sending photographs from exhibitions. I often asked those who corresponded with me to share similar items. I even memorised some of the poems.

I shared the paintings with my fellow inmates, organising viewings and engaging in discussions about their meanings, as well as exploring topics of art. This enabled us to explore important issues, which we might not have addressed in prison otherwise. When we viewed the drawing of bees, we discussed ecology, and when we examined the work featuring stones in a dark circle, we explored internal sensations. Without access to the internet, we attempted to comprehend the complex terminology used by artists to describe their works. It was both enjoyable and fascinating.

These memories hold great value for me. I received letters containing good poems, stories, children's drawings, recipes, and brief tales about the cities where the pen pals lived. It mattered little what was written in the letter; I knew that people were trying to support me. I wouldn't say that all these letters made my imprisonment easy, but they helped me preserve myself at least a little, serving as a lifeline that kept me going.

The future

It is my belief that in order to gain something new, one must create something new. This is why I closely observe emerging initiatives. Personally, I aspire to undertake something impactful.

I spend a lot of time thinking of how to improve the situation of those presently detained. I often reflect upon the reform of the penal system in Belarus. The current system fails to fulfil its stated function of correction and damages people instead. It is crucial that we make it more humane and effective. The Department of Corrections is responsible for the execution of sentences in Belarus, and the facilities where offenders are typically housed are referred to as correctional institutions.

Punishment presents itself to me as a rather doubtful instrument for "re-education". It also seems that no system can re-educate a person without their eagerness to change. Wasting resources on threats is a pointless activity. The focus should be on creating an environment that allows a person to live differently without compromising the freedom of others. The ideal system would involve personnel who refrain from categorising individuals as either good or bad while working with them. We need a systematic approach to correction. Changing the conditions of detention is not enough; it is essential that attitudes towards people change. This would enable people to overcome their fear, manipulative inclinations, and the desire to placate. It doesn't matter how old the beds you sleep on may be, or what kind the decorations are there, as long as you know you're safe. When I think about this, I am reminded of summer in the village.

In my milieu, we raise such issues as restoring justice, the problem of lustration, and the courts. I am concerned that Belarusian society may not be prepared to restore justice or, conversely, may become overly harsh and recreate the same horrific system.

The topic of fear and its impact on society is one that I often reflect upon. I have seen how fear can reshape a person, and have felt these changes manifesting within myself. I have also observed this phenomenon in my cellmates and in those implicated in my imprisonment.

Fear has a destructive effect on both the individual and society. It helps control people, which is a tactic employed by authoritarian regimes. However, in the long run, a society governed by fear will ultimately deteriorate.

Fear is the antithesis of progress. A system based on fear is alien to me. I hope that Belarusians in the future will never have to endure the same hardships that Belarusian political prisoners are currently facing.

Reforming the Belarusian education system is a pressing necessity. Although I do not have a concrete reform proposal, I feel our education system is deficient in both liberty and adaptability. I aspire to study in different countries and observe various approaches and methods they employ. This could empower me to develop a more comprehensive vision for the changes I would like to see implemented in Belarus.

I intend to recover, to grow, and to acquire a quality education. I believe this is the sole path through which I can exert a constructive influence on the future, not just for myself, but for the entirety of Belarus.

We have a long way to go. Even if Lukashenka were to leave office tomorrow, the public dialogue would likely progress slowly, but potentially in a more constructive direction.

I aspire for us to build a more equitable and just society – a Belarus where people will once again want to live.

City N, January 2024
ottisk637@gmail.com

I HAVE BEEN FIGHTING FIRES FOR THREE YEARS

Aliaksandr Parshankou

Looking back is not always easy, but it is necessary. I have a dark anniversary ahead of me – three years since my life changed completely and irreversibly. I am a historian, and my participation in any event never happens without primary analysis from the historical perspective. I have been keeping a diary for four years, documenting the events in my life as well as the developments in our society. By reviewing the entries from 2020-2021, I can reconstruct the entire course of events and gain a deeper personal understanding – asking the question "Why?" Why have I been fighting fires all this time, helping people find their place in the world, supporting them with my last ounce of strength, and searching for financial resources? Why do I keep finding out every month that one of my numerous friends has been convicted or detained, and every week, being horrified to see the growing number of political prisoners? Why do I have to live in forced emigration, constantly on edge like a hot pan? Not only me, of course. Why, why, why?

The events that I witnessed and participated in have their roots in centuries past. I am not the sort to deny the past's bearing on our present reality. I do not associate with those who believe that everything depends solely on them and can only be changed by their own efforts. At the same time, I cannot regard myself or our society as captives of circumstances.

The evening of 9 August 2020, in *Homieĺ* is forever seared into my mind. As a student on holiday, I participated in the protest in my hometown, of course. The not very wide central Savieckaja Street was packed with people marching forward on the pavements, chanting "LONG LIVE BELARUS!" I vividly recall an August day, when a white-red-white flag fluttered over the main square of *Homieĺ*. It was an incredible feeling! For a day it seemed as though we had achieved victory and were living in the future. I felt even happier on 1 September when I helped organise the Faculty of History column at the general student march through Minsk. We were dispersed and detained, but we managed to regroup and march through our city on OUR day.

In the first week of the protests, much later after this thought occurred to me, I wrote in my diary: "We are the people... The first fear and the first victory over fear... The first three days were terrible. This fear was squeezed out drop by drop. All of us are kin, and all of us are at the protests. We rushed in a crowd... Initially we fled just from the sound. Someone would shout 'AMAP!' [riot police] and we all would ran away... We didn't know why we were coming out, we didn't understand what it was like..." In *Homieĺ*, my goal was to lure the police forces away from Minsk, at any cost. I was determined not to let them have the opportunity to suffocate the capital, since the reality of our daily protests prevented them from relocating all the police resources to Minsk.

And conversations, conversations, conversations with everyone about everything. I was delighted to listen to those I considered to be the elite of society, expressing their disagreement with Lukashenka's dictatorship. They all spoke with one voice, claiming that new times had come. They were the people of such a high cultural level, which is very difficult to find. Veterans of the movement argued that something must happen! Something that would radically change the situation. Beyond the August protests. Beyond our revolution. I recall that even the former Minister of Education, Piotr Bryhadzin, who was our lecturer in the History of Belarus, recognised the fact of the revolution. Time passed, friends ended up behind bars, and this enigmatic "something" failed to materialise on the stage.

Rallies gave way to letters and parcels to prisons. Friends had already appeared in court. The dates of my own detentions piled up on top of one another – 18 October 2020, 3 March 2021, 5 March

2021... And the realisation that there was no room for manoeuvre on top of that. One step – and you would "survive on swill", as the "officers" at *GUBOPiK* told me.

Was it scary? It was very scary. During the last months that I stayed in my homeland, moving from apartment to apartment, waiting for a positive response from the Czech Embassy to my visa application, I started having nightmares. But I was usually scared for others. I recall seeing my friend's mother in the waiting line to pass parcels for the inmates. She was carefully sorting out the food items to pass over. At that moment, my heart froze. "This is my mother," I thought. The same could happen to my own mother! A red line cut through my soul, and I felt a sense of defeat and ruin. It wasn't the constant taunting me as a "KGB guy" at the History Faculty, nor the three detentions and threats of punishment. Nor was it the wiretapping or harassment by the university administration. It was this frail, vulnerable woman in the prison reception facility that shook me to the core.

Was it hard? It was. Constant fighting and arrests. Pressure from the administration. Threats. A biased review of my master's thesis. I barely defended it. And I was also the head of the independent trade union of students at Belarusian State University; the self-proclaimed leader I never wanted to bet I assumed the responsibility because no one else would: A person who was not ready for those events, A student without experience or training. And there were many of us like that... A legion.

Yet I had never felt more fulfilled than I did during that time, In an unending daily struggle. I learned that every day lived freely in that struggle was for the greater good. The fact that I could live and think freely in Belarus was a beneficial result, a sufficient reward. And if I could protect a student, prepare a parcel, apply stickers with a white-red-white flag, or send a letter to a prison,that was my idea of happiness!

"I don't understand your chains of solidarity", a cop told us, the detainees, at the *Frunzienski* district police department. "It makes no difference to me whether it's Lukashenka or *Tsikhanouskaya*. I'll keep working". But we knew exactly what we were fighting for and against, collectively and individually. As students, we stood together for the right to gather freely and speak the truth out loud. We have a voice!. We opposed the university's subjugation to Soviet traditions and approaches. We wanted freedom, as everyone understood it. Illusion! Utopia! Well, we didn't have a specific plan, because the possibility of achieving it seemed so unbelievable.

On the morning of 2 March 2021, I was taken out of the dormitory to *GUBOPiK*. Half a dozen people stormed into the room, ordering me to pack my things. "You communicate with us as if we were dirt under your nails," they taunted me in the infamous building in Revalucyjnaja Street. But I persevered, overcoming my fear and weakness. They were scared of students. Even *Kachanava* came to negotiate with us, the top university in the country. We were called in to the Prosecutor General's Office. The KGB closely monitored our every move. By the way, they tried to recruit me as an informant at *GUBOPiK*; perhaps that's why they hadn't detained me, hadn't forced me to breathe chlorine and survive on water, like they did to my friend and neighbour.

Student protests worldwide illuminate the path forward for society. They are a wake-up call for people, igniting the masses who cannot be stopped any more. The History Faculty staff who were hiding in the shadows during the protests told us, "We will follow you. You go, and we will provide support." But there were precious few who actually backed us. Despite some representatives of democratic forces trying to downplay the student protest, it remained strong. We organised rallies not only at the faculties but directly in front of *Akrescina*! There were even attempts to set up tents. However, all this eventually faded away, went underground, and has not resurfaced yet.

As I am writing these lines, I am turning the pages of my diaries. Five notebooks filled with travels into my past, five notebooks filled with travels into the past of my Motherland. And do I understand why?

The sleep of reason produces monsters. The sleep of a nation allows the grain of that nation to be made into flour of any coarseness. I am currently immersed in the memoirs of our Nobel Prize winner Aleś Bialiatski, eagerly absorbing the most poignant fragments of his recollections. I am learning how groups of Belarusians united around their own values: the Belarusian language, culture, and history. How a decade of a relative thaw nurtured a generation ready to embrace independence. But as they grasped it, they also let it slip away. Society as a whole, excluding individual, exceptional, and intelligent minds, was unprepared to sustain the struggle.

Many left activism for business, teaching, and a quiet, ordinary life. Yet, the fight had to continue.

Why do our adversaries label us as fighters? It is precisely because they are intimidated by the concept of fighting itself. Fighting is an idea that embodies the willingness to protect oneself and help others. However, we lacked the necessary reserves to sustain this fight. People grow weary and seek comfort, leaning, like on a cane, on the support of friends, politicians, and leaders, feeling their kindred souls close by. However, alongside these lie fear, misfortune, hard work, exile, and prison... These challenges did not arise overnight and will not vanish tomorrow. We are part of a continuous process that cannot be halted. We are a people striving to become a nation. Yet, there is a powerful enemy nearby, the immensity of whose power, when comprehended, can drive one crazy.

Nevertheless, when I analyse the reasons behind our current situation, the motivations for protest, and contemplate the future, I realise that I remain an optimist. Not because the dawn always follows the dark night – this cliché no longer resonates with someone who has endured nearly three decades of waiting. I remain an optimist because I understand that eternal values will endure. And what will be important in thirty years from now? For Belarusians? for Belarus? The key is to act now, to the best of our abilities, and we will be saved. This is how I live in Prague, amidst the challenging psychological conditions of emigration. The future Pope Paul VI was once asked what he would do if the Russians entered Rome, and he replied, "I will serve mass, as I do every day." This is not about submission in the least!

So why? Why is everything the way it is? I can provide an answer. A river that overflows its banks may return to its original course, but a person who has thrown off the yoke of slavery will rarely wish to be enslaved again. Those who have awakened will naturally change their perspective, and some may even regret that they "stepped into it". However, the fundamental truth remains: it will be impossible to go back. We are paying the price – some for their silence, and others for the silence of their relatives. While Lukashenka rose to power, who was busy building summer homes, earning a living to support their families, or tending to their personal lives? Simple Belarusians. Almost the entire society supported a man who should not have held the position he did. They believed that the struggle could be halted, that everything would be fine. But there are no prophets when we are unwilling to listen. The deputies of independence were left unprotected and unsupported. Later, the system brutally punished everyone – both those who fought and those who were merely passing by. The batons of the riot police spare no one. And they will not spare.

I am recalling my life before all these events. I was a Presidential scholarship winner, a high-achieving student, and a holder of a diploma with honours. I had published two collections of poems, enjoyed reader's meetings, staged plays, and my photo was on the board of honour at the university. These are artificial values that have never held much importance for me. They are relics of the past. All this is left behind. And what holds great significance for me are my relatives with whom I can hardly meet now, friends – already ageing – who cannot leave Belarus, whom I cannot see and who will pass away before I return to Minsk. My grandmother, who longs for my return, implores me to come back, and cannot comprehend why I do not. Everything has a price, and one who understands the cost becomes more responsible, more sincere and more honest. 2020 allowed me to cultivate my finest qualities. This also covers all the bitterness of what I had to endure, what was lost in the whirlwinds, and what will still be lost. A man must strive to be a man.

How many of our people in Europe are now reassessing and redefining their identities? We were given the opportunity, and we had to engage with the cultures of other nations, learn languages, and gain a wealth of knowledge that one could only dream of. However, this also poses a test for us: will we be able to preserve our cultural identity? Will we remain Belarusians? If so, what does that mean for us? I always find it amusing when I hear about Źmicier Lukašuk's project, the Belarusian National Idea. On the other hand, the search for a fern-flower sometimes pushes away sad thoughts and allows for more imaginative dreaming. Maybe, in the 21st century, it is necessary to ask a question that was answered in the 19th century? And this is not just an attempt at self-publicity.

I re-read my diaries and correspondence with friends who are behind bars, and I find in them the strength to carry on, and moral support. They are there, and I am "on the other side of the bars, which for some reason is called freedom" (*Alaksandr Fiaduta*). My friend Aliaksandr Fiaduta was sentenced to ten years in prison and is now in Mahilioŭ. I have received about fifty letters from him.

In a letter dated 3rd October, 2021, he wrote the following words: "By the way, as you can guess, I'm also feeling sad. The difference is that I'm about to turn fifty-seven, so I'll celebrate this in a completely 'American' way. In other aspects, my life has passed even faster. And although I have managed to do something (at least in science), I have not managed to change the world for the better. It will be your generation's task." You have to live, to live you must, as the classic once wrote. I live, including for those who are in captivity, in order to really change the world. Maybe it will work?

I have been fighting fires for three years, dedicating my life to the rhythms of my people and my country for three years. I stay by the side, in thoughts and phone conversations, of the relatives of political prisoners, who are tortured and actually killed in prisons and colonies. I stay by the side of those who study under immense pressure in Belarus, by the side of those who struggle to survive in a world where it seems impossible. I am striving to contribute to building a new system, a new Belarus, which can compete with the old one for a place under the sun. Only in this do I see salvation. There will always be disagreements, but whether our country will survive depends solely on us, who shout from all corners of the world today: "Long live Belarus!" And I believe that Belarus will endure!

Prague, June 2023
aliaksandr.parshankou@seznam.cz

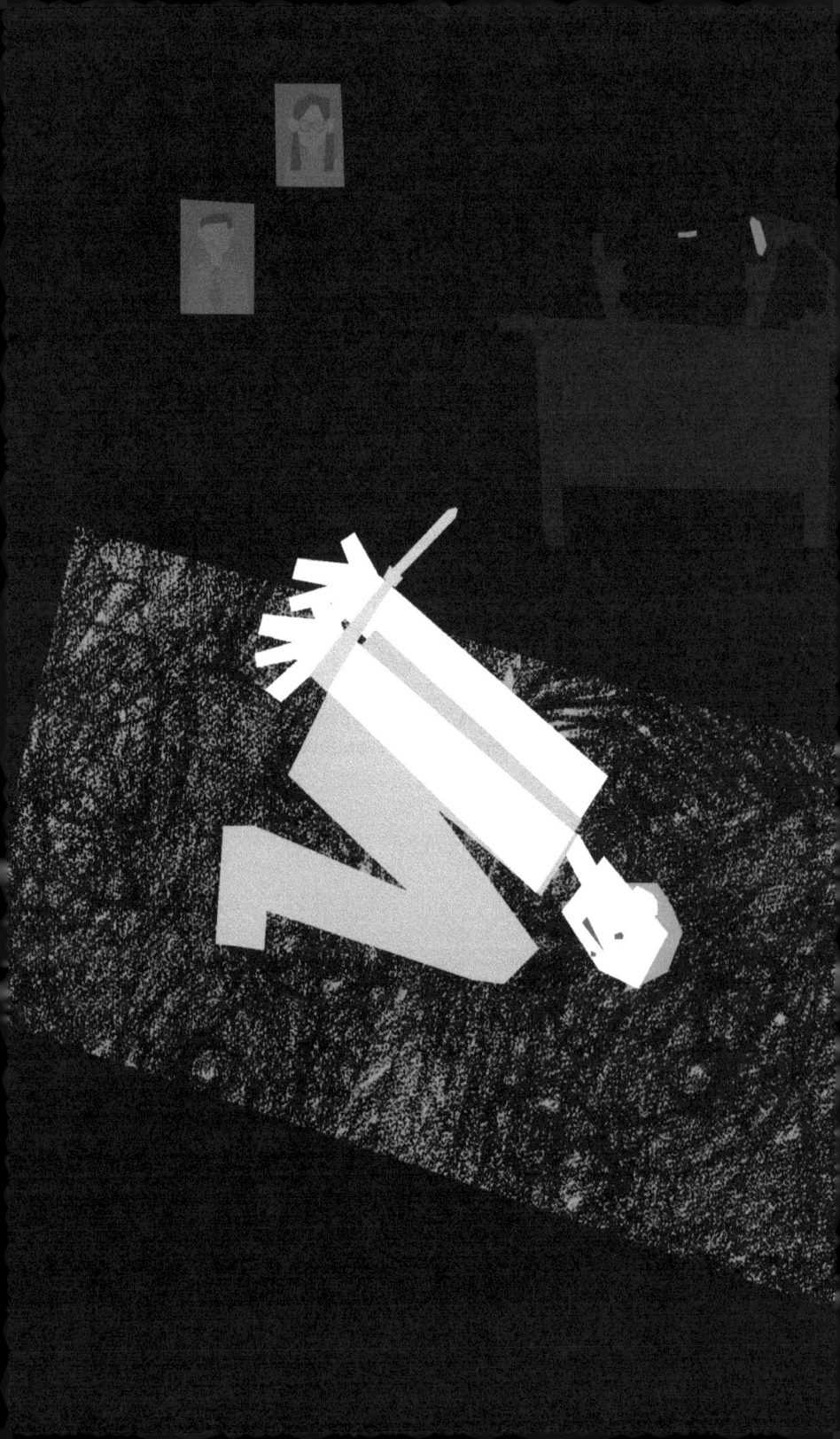

FROM THE DISTRICT HONOUR TO THE POLICE "WANTED" BOARD

Alexey C.

Firstly, I would like to apologise for writing in Russian instead of my native Belarusian. Upon graduating from the Lyceum of the Ministry for Emergency Situations, I had a strong command of the Belarusian language and could speak it fluently. I regularly read books in Belarusian. To gain admission to a higher educational institution, I had to pass a written exam in either Russian or Belarusian. Naturally enough, I opted for Belarusian. However, due to the threat of arrest, I was compelled to leave for Poland, which led to a mix-up of Polish, Belarusian, and Ukrainian words in my mind.

Here's a bit about myself: I am twenty-five years old and was born in a small town on the border with Ukraine. As a child, I was quite energetic and enjoyed meeting and communicating with different people. I loved reading and learning new things about the world I lived in, and I still do. I excelled in school and regularly participated in regional competitions across various subjects. My academic success and prizes won at olympiads earned me a place on the photo board: The School is Proud of Them.

The Lyceum

Although everything was going well in my life, I realised that my native village might not offer the best educational opportunities. After completing the sixth grade, I made a firm decision to switch schools. Since my family was not well-to-do, it was obvious that no one could financially support my life in the city. Moreover, my mother would be very worried about my safety. The most practical solution in this situation was to enrol at the Lyceum of the Ministry for Emergency Situations, where I would have a roof over my head, constant supervision from officers, and where I could study with good teachers.

I completed my five-year education at the lyceum, graduating with an excellent certificate score. During my time there, I remained committed to extracurricular activities, participating in regional and republican olympiads and attending scientific conferences throughout Belarus.

When the time came to decide on my next steps in higher education, I had two options: to follow the path of least resistance by continuing my studies at the University of the Ministry for Emergency Situations, where I could enrol without taking the centralised testing or any exams, or challenge myself by entering the top university in Belarus, Belarusian State University (BSU). I opted for BSU because my passion for learning and self-improvement outweighed the "allure" of a stable life in the security forces. I sought to develop my abilities, become a better and more informed individual, and contribute to the well-being of people, rather than report "on the carpet" to the officer why the floor was poorly washed or why I didn't point my toes well enough during drill training.

Now I am incredibly happy that I made the right choice by enrolling in a speciality that I am passionate about and where everything depends on my skills and abilities, and not on an officer who cannot write a reference for me without spelling and grammar errors.

Faculty of Philosophy and Social Sciences

Studying at BSU was an amazing journey: you are accountable for your own progress, you learn from the brightest minds (in most cases), and you are surrounded by interesting and gifted group mates. It's as if you've stepped into a heavenly realm on earth!

At university, I was no longer an outstanding student, but I still performed well academically. I devoted most of my time to the student union, participating in the organisation of various events for students of the faculty and BSU as a whole. My best friend and I worked together at the student union to secure sponsors for these events. Probably, my most significant achievement in this area in my two final years was the organisation of an amateur football tournament among BSU students. We took great care in planning every aspect of the event, from the smallest details to the cool prizes for the winners. As a result, around 150–170 people took part in the first tournament, and the next year the number of participants increased to 250 people. Foreshadowing the events in my story, I will mention that we planned to hold a third tournament, but it was thwarted: due to persecution for participating in peaceful protests, I was no longer in Belarus.

I was involved in securing sponsors and partners for student events as I had a definitive goal in sight: after graduating from university, my aim was to pursue a career in sponsorship for a professional football club. Since childhood, I have been passionate about football and other team sports, and I always wanted to work in a football club. Initially, I had no idea in what capacity, but during my studies at the university, I discovered how to effectively combine my hobbies and professional skills so that the work would be enjoyable and provide a stable income.

There were many aspects of university life that I would have liked to change. For instance, the lack of licensed software and normal computers for working with databases was unacceptable, as was the second shift for final-year students (when 90% were already working) and physical education classes on Saturdays (when students wanted to play football in the evening). While these issues might have been specific to my faculty, I suspect they were not unique. However, these drawbacks are overshadowed by the numerous advantages that my alma mater gave me.

Therefore, after completing my bachelor's degree, I intended to enrol in a master's programme at my faculty to further enhance my professional skills. Regrettably, this plan was not meant to be realised. On 9 August 2020, the authoritarian ruler chose to falsify the election results, having previously detained all his main competitors. I vehemently disagreed with this action.

Elections without a choice

In fact, prior to the presidential elections in Belarus on 9th August 2020, I was deeply pessimistic. It was widely believed that Lukashenka would once again manipulate the election results to secure the coveted 80% victory. I anticipated a small turnout of several thousand people who would come to the square only to be brutally beaten with batons by riot police, according to the well-established pattern, with many subsequently arrested and imprisoned. If you were fortunate, you'd be charged with an administrative offence: the judge would impose a few days of detention or a fine. And the less fortunate would face imprisonment for three years or more. I was convinced that everything would unfold according to this script. Many of my friends intended to protest, as the entire country knew that Lukashenka was a thief and a fraudster, and it was clear that he would not hesitate to falsify the results. I discouraged acquaintances and friends from going to protests, as I believed that it would not lead to any meaningful change and that the participants could risk losing their health or freedom.

However, on the evening of 9 August, I was genuinely shocked. I didn't anticipate that so many of my friends would gather in the centre of Minsk to protest against the falsification of the election results. For the first time in my life, I thought that our country had a chance for a normal democratic future. That evening and night, rumours spread that somewhere people had forced the security forces to lay down their shields. I felt a sense of euphoria that we were close to achieving new, fair elections in the country, and Lukashenka, following the example of Yanukovych, would fly to Rostov and never return to Belarus. However, I would like Lukashenka to be held accountable in court for all his crimes and be sentenced to life imprisonment. This would be the most honest and fair outcome.

In a state of euphoria, I began to prepare to join the protests in the square, as for the first time in my adult life, I realised that the people had woken up. As part of my people, I felt a deep sense of responsibility to support my fellow citizens. It was my duty to fight for our civil rights and express outrage at the regime's deception.

After getting dressed and gathering the essentials (water, money, and passport), I tried to call a taxi to the city centre, as I lived quite far away. However, I soon discovered that there was no mobile connection or internet. A friend who was already in the city centre managed to call and informed me that riot police and internal troops had begun to disperse and beat honest Belarusians who were not indifferent to the country's future. Later that night, reports emerged that approximately two-thousand people had been detained at *Niamiha*, but the rumour that riot police had switched sides turned out to be false.

At that moment, my hope for democratic changes in Belarus was once again shattered.

Therefore, when on 10 August Telegram channels and my friends invited me again to demonstrate my civic position, I refused, thinking that after the mass arrests, a small group of around three-hundred people would show up to protest, mostly in Minsk.

But this time I was wrong: a lot of people came out, and hope settled in me again. Then on 10th August, I made a promise to myself: no matter what happens, no matter how many people are arrested, I will definitely go out into the streets on 11 August to show that I am against the theft of election results, against widespread corruption, which was put on a conveyor belt in Belarus, and against the further crippling of the country's economy. These were not my unfounded claims, as during my graduate year, I worked in a consulting company and participated in joint projects with state enterprises. I witnessed first-hand the incredible mess going on there! If I were to say that they calculated revenue in tons of manufactured products, rather than in money, most people would likely be incredulous. Since 2016-2017, nearly 90% of open joint-stock companies (OJSCs) have ceased publishing annual financial statements, and from the same period, out of approximately 1,700 operating OJSCs, only 900 remained by the summer of 2021. This is unacceptable in my country. If I chose to stay, aware of these facts and dissatisfied with Lukashenka's dictatorship, it would mean that I condoned this situation and was a traitor to my people. I could not tolerate injustice and lawlessness. As a citizen of Belarus, my vote cannot be stolen, and I cannot be deceived!

Going out to protest

On 11 August 2020, I ventured out. I had no doubts, being firmly aware of where I was going and for what purpose. I didn't mean to engage in any violent or illegal activities; I merely wished to make an appearance and demonstrate my disagreement with what was happening. Initially, I planned to join my friends in the centre of Minsk, at *Niamiha*, with the historical flag of Belarus, and stand there to the finish. However, it turned out that my friends decided to take a break from racing bouts with the riot police and stayed at home. Then I shared my plan with another group of friends. We agreed to meet at the Puškinskaja metro station. As I mentioned earlier, our plan was straightforward: to take to the streets and stand with white-red-white flags, attracting like-minded citizens who were equally outraged by the elections. We intended to stay until our voices were heard.

As I walked through the courtyards, I noticed minibuses with tinted windows filled with people wearing masks. Riot police were dispatched to confront peaceful Belarusians. The riot police, with shields and batons, clad in uniforms that resembled space rangers, were visibly outraged that some incomprehensible citizens were forcing them to work in the evening. Obviously, the intentions of the riot police were much less pacifist than mine and other people's. Detentions of protesters began, and I spent the whole evening trying to avoid the riot police, first at Puškinskaja and then at Kamiennaja Horka.

Eventually, I was detained at night and taken to the *Frunzienski* district police department. To be honest, I assumed that if I was detained, they would beat me. But I couldn't even have imagined what would happen on the night of 11 August in the *Frunzienski* district police department! A massive crowd of people knelt on the floor, their faces pressed against the ground, with broken heads, humiliation, and stun gun shocks for no reason! You couldn't even lift your head, let alone ask for water or use the toilet. It was a terrifying and dehumanising experience. I was afraid they might kill me! Especially after the intense intimidation during our transportation to the police department. The police rejected this idea not out of humanitarian concerns, but likely because they were too lazy. I spent the entire night on my knees, with a huge bruise forming on my head. My knees hurt so badly that I can't even think of anything to compare the pain with. I hope I never have to endure something like this again.

In the morning, the guards changed, and they began preparing us for transfer. I thought we would be taken to court, where we would face fines or brief arrests, but instead, we were taken to the Isolation Centre for Offenders (ICO) in Akrescina Street. I have no desire to recall what happened there, as it was even more brutal than our experience at the police department! That evening, I came to a disturbing realisation: that some creatures who appear to be human on the outside may not possess a human mind or conscience, and that there are no limits to human cruelty. Looking ahead, I can say that my theory was confirmed when another elderly, maniacal dictator decided to start a war in Ukraine.

I spent three days at *Akrescina*. I was released under a general amnesty on 14 August. During this time, my parents and friends frantically searched for me throughout the country, but their efforts were in vain, because no one at the police could tell them anything intelligible. The company I worked for hired a lawyer and a psychologist to assist me. The psychologist didn't help much, to be honest. I think I didn't really need therapy, as, since childhood, I've always been someone who reflects on life and works through traumas on my own. However, the lawyer was helpful. After leaving the ICO, I saw a new Belarus around me. Despite the fact that the moustachioed *Škloŭ monster* still holds power, my people have awakened. Although we lost the battle, the war against dictatorship continues.

Forced emigration

It's now been three years since I left Belarus and settled in Poland. My best friend and I have started a business producing sports equipment, and we support Ukraine, morally and financially, in its fight against Russian aggression led by its bloody dictator. Unfortunately, I am unable to return to Belarus, as every month the local police visit my parents, relatives, and neighbours asking about me. My photo was removed from my school's honour board and placed on the police "Wanted" board. It turns out that all previous achievements can be erased if you do not agree with the dictator.

I retain my optimism and firmly believe that sooner or later we will emerge victorious, and the people of Belarus will live in a free country, just like the people of Ukraine.

Long live Belarus!
Glory to Ukraine!

Warsaw, 06.2023

THE LOST ONE

Todar Szpak

Both then and now, I am unsure about what I truly want. Why do I receive more and more pieces of paper, cardboard and plastic cards every year? The people I meet give me a job, a fleeting passion for themselves. Some provide shelter, some fill me with energy and warmth, but they all eventually leave. Each of us has likely grown accustomed to this since school, and perhaps even since kindergarten: only a few people remain nearby. Ignorance and loneliness are the pain of an emigrant.

My surrounding

When the events of 2020 unfolded, I was a university student, a home child, a good son and grandson, a barista, a person with a large network of acquaintances, and a clear path ahead of me, destined for an office where I would spend my days moving papers from one place to another.

After finishing a secondary school, I was eager to enter the law faculty, but God and my parents saved me from that. I enrolled in one of the country's private universities to major in the humanities and completed the first year with almost honours. In private universities it was not very hard to achieve this. Regrettably, I found that many teachers lacked the fundamental knowledge to teach, and students didn't even possess basic school knowledge. This was a fairly important observation that subsequently enabled me to break free from my bubble, where I was at the bottom of the list of smart people, and at the university, I became the smartest among the fools.

In my second year, I transferred to the Belarusian State University. I was briefly introduced to the university's workings, the proper education system, and the various activities I could participate in. This marked the beginning of an intriguing student life. However, in 2018, I couldn't have imagined that this life would transform into something straight out of a historical book. I still struggle to comprehend where I am – in a history textbook, a social experiment annotation, or a cheap action movie where the level of absurdity is off the charts.

The transition to a new university was smooth, and I was lucky to have a supportive teaching staff, the dean's office staff, and fellow students who smiled at me from the first day to the last. I am still grateful for their kindness. After retaking twelve subjects in a week, I was able to fully engage in my studies.

To understand the environment in which I studied, I will briefly describe my group mates. They represented various social backgrounds, cities and villages, as well as different countries, including China and Turkmenistan. However, judging by the attitude towards people, Belarus and these two countries are not much different from each other, with a shared love for cults, a strong vertical power structure, and a prominent presence of men in uniform on the streets.

Despite the diverse backgrounds of the group, no one took the liberty of being rude towards less affluent students; instead, everyone tried to help everybody else. Everyone, whenever possible, shared their own experiences about the world they grew up in. What is typical for the Faculty of International Relations is that there were few lagging students. Of course, there were athletes who enrolled at the faculty under a special quota. I met people who had spent years studying English, yet their reading skills were limited to syllable-by-syllable reading. Everyone understood everything, and even these individuals were fully integrated into the group. Should I say that we got along well with each other? Yes, we were very friendly to a certain extent, but friendship at the university was often built on an understanding of benefits. This was precisely what made the university so remarkable. We learned to navigate the adult world, gradually taking off our rose-coloured glasses. I was the charismatic "lost one" in this company. I was a man for everyone and for no one in particular. To walk from the smoking room to any classroom at the university, I had to hug at least ten people. I can honestly say that almost the entire university knew me, but I had no close friends.

As for the teaching staff and administration of the university, we were very fortunate: we had relative freedom and the opportunity to engage in discussions. I had a wonderful relationship with the dean's office staff. At times, I would approach these caring women for advice. They always greeted me with a smile, provided assistance, and occasionally even offered me food.

Prior to 2020, the majority of lecturers were kind, polite, with a fairly good sense of humour, and were able to set appropriate boundaries. There were also teachers that made almost all students "suffer." I must give them their due: I still remember the subjects taught by these lecturers. They were giants in their field, and this commanded respect. It was to these teachers that I was always referred first, when I was late during an exam period, or when any questions arose. They couldn't stay angry with me and always ended up smiling, which my other group mates took advantage of.

2020 brought about a lot of changes

University is a place where some people rely on their strengths to get by, while others use the strengths of others to advance their own interests. I also drew upon the strengths of my group mates.

As for politics, we thoroughly explored the topic through lectures and seminars by regularly reading the news and studying the characteristics of different political systems. However, most teachers avoided discussing internal politics, possibly due to fear. In informal settings, my group mates outlined their opinions more distinctly and clearly. However, those who were most vocal during "peacetime", often kept "under the radar" and showed little courage during elections. Like most of my classmates, I didn't have a deep understanding of how politics and economics function. Some of us were already working, while others were looking for jobs in IT or planning to move abroad. We were not particularly interested in the struggles of entrepreneurs, the wages in rural areas, we were little concerned about how the penitentiary system works in the country, or whose sphere of influence we were operating in. No, we were not fools, we perfectly comprehended the conditions we were living in, we were well aware of our autocratic system. We knew that Soviet stereotypes were passed on from generation to generation, even after the collapse of the Soviet empire. We understood that if we wanted to thrive, we had to either leave the country or strive to reach the top. One can say that while we were allowed to exist, we made the most of our time as students.

For me, student life ended with the onset of Covid

Together with fellow students, I took part in a faculty-organised competition. One of our team members fell ill, which put me officially at risk. The following day, the sanitary doctor contacted me to inquire about a suitable time for my hospitalisation. I was standing near the Kastryčnickaja metro station with a friend who tutored me in French. Actually, this was our third and final lesson, as it turned out. On that beautiful, sunny day, a haunting thought dominated our minds: "the end of everything." No one at that time had any idea of the true danger posed by Covid, its transmission dynamics, or its symptoms. Moreover, even the most basic mortality statistics were absent. In our country, the prevailing approach is to "pacify" the public's psyche. If a nuclear power plant explodes, or a revolution or a pandemic occurs, the whole truth is unlikely to be revealed. In the worst-case scenario, you might be told in places like *Vaładarka* dungeons that no one is interested in your truth. This harsh reality has become evident to our generation, particularly since the Covid pandemic.

Three hours later, an ambulance arrived to transport me, though it lacked the specialised containment unit typically used for Covid patients. While I was having my temperature taken, the paramedic, a young girl, casually stroked my cats. I was consumed by panic, just in case. When I called my parents to tell them about my hospitalisation, my mother wept into the receiver, begging me not to die! Truthfully, I had no such plans.

The dermatology and venereology unit, where I was placed along with other students and faculty members who had been in contact with the infected individual, felt more like a recreational facility than a medical institution. I was permitted to smoke in the toilet, my friends provided me with cognac in a thermos flask, and my parents brought delicious homemade meals. In the evenings, I would lean out of the window and listen to stories about China from an older faculty acquaintance. We played online games with the entire faculty. And we kept our noses to the wind.

I was discharged after five days. I was one of the first "liberated", but no one explained anything to me, they simply said: "Pack your things." And no more information.

Covid might not have directly touched me again, if not for my parents who are physicians. What happened to medicine at that time was akin to absolute hell. Replacement protective gear kits were unavailable; everything had to be washed several times. Masks were scarce, with only one or two allowed per shift. It was left up to the doctors to find a way out. The situation was the same everywhere: from hospitals to ambulances and intensive care units. On television, they claimed that everything was fine with us, that doctors had all the necessary resources and didn't need any assistance. In reality, the state had practically abandoned doctors and all Belarusians to their fate. Medical workers were putting their lives at risk. As a result, my parents got sick and spent more than 50 days in hospital with double pneumonia. For this reason, I had to be in home quarantine for 14 days, unable to visit them and constantly fearing I might lose them.

It was then that I began to hate propaganda, the government, the police, judges, prosecutors, and all the other self-proclaimed servants of the people. Officials from various levels of the power structure were afraid to cause panic and thus forced everyone around to die or lose their health with a "gag in their mouth." For the first time in my life, I wished death upon the nonentities who, out of fear for their own skin, did everything to make people suffer.

All the previous events began to converge into another dystopian incident – the election race. Drawing from the experiences of elections, I knew there would be little to be pleased about, but this time the public internet, a strong discontent and pandemic-induced fatigue, seemed to be on the side of the good.

Everyone realised that a game without rules was about to begin. It was intriguing to see how the authorities would handle the opposition, what they would do with people this time, and whether the situation would resemble the events of 2010.

The description of the election process is worthy of a separate book

To quickly go over the key points, the first arrests of the opposition leaders were predictable. On 29 May 2020, *Siarhei Tsikhanouski* was detained in *Hrodna*. The brutality and brazenness of it all, the fact that it happened several months before the elections, and especially the scenario of a middle-aged prostitute being used as a full-fledged colleague of young policemen-simulators – all these factors had a "wow" effect.

During the signature collection, I saw long lines of people, comparable only with those I observed later when queuing to obtain an apostille to leave the country. These kilometre-long chains of people were brimming with sincere smiles as people recognised how many of their fellow Belarusians shared their experiences. It was then that the holiday began.

The next stage saw a complete purge of candidates: almost all of them were removed. The authorities mockingly threw a "bone" to the people by leaving *Siarhei Tsikhanouski*'s wife, Sviatlana, on the voting lists, intending to make a whipping doll of her. However, both the opposition and ordinary people saw in Sviatlana the only opportunity! Neither I nor any other Belarusian put down our phones so as not to miss the next piece of news.

Afterwards there was a series of rallies with their heroes and a trail of absurdity

And then the elections took place. Observers stood outside the polling stations, while inside, members of the election commissions, looking like shrunken lizards, began to falsify the first result certificates with trembling hands.

I visited my friends and brought them water; they were stationed at the "common sense defence" points on school grounds, or rather between the entrance to educational institutions and the beer stand frequented by regulars. I observed the "guardians of law and order" showing remarkable humaneness, I would even say some kind of special affection, towards the inebriated residents of our capital. In contrast, independent observers, people with higher education and binoculars in their hands, were surely of no relevance to our state.

9 August 2020 was the election day. I have never seen so many people dressed in white shirts with white bands on their wrists, and genuine smiles on their faces. It was as if the neighbours, after many years, had finally discovered that they could engage in conversations with other neighbours and enjoy each other's company, rather than just exchange brief nods when they met. It seemed that people all over the country got to know each other that day.

The procedure was marked by the police's brazen laughing in people's faces, which implied that nothing would go in the people's favour, as if they were worms and the authorities were kings. The election commission members maintained the same attitude on their faces, but the people remained optimistic and confident that in just a few hours they would throw off their shackles, knowing that it was impossible to deceive so many people. It was clear to everyone that Tsikhanoúskaja had won.

In the evening, I came to the polling station to see the preliminary election results. Several hundred neighbours also gathered there. At the school where my polling station was located, the windows were plastered with posters about brave pioneers. Then they started turning off the lights to obscure the view for us. The police arrived multiple times to disperse us from the windows. We sang and laughed at their cowardice, and then received the first SMS from our friends: "Riot police have arrived in neighbouring areas and are packing up people. Be cautious!" Indeed, as we sang near the secondary school where I used to study, the first arrests began, but they were carried out with minimal force. These people were fortunate; or rather, more fortunate than the other five thousand detainees that night.

Around nine in the evening, the polling station lights were completely turned off. The results were never posted. A woman police officer emerged and ordered everyone to disperse. People demanded to exercise their legal right to see the voting result certificate. The commission never came out to face the audience.

I left home, got ready, and made my way to the city centre. The night was meant to expose the blatant deception. As I walked, I saw groups of people – students, workers, doctors, architects, and bikers... We all converged by the *Stella monument*. Along the route, we were flanked by patrols of two or three policemen, who looked nervous as they faced the sheer number of people. Our excitement was electric, our eyes burning with anticipation. Belarus was finally coming to life!

Niamiha greeted us with a roaring sound. No one understood where it was coming from: a wild sound it was, as if hundreds of jackhammers were simultaneously breaking the asphalt. Paddy wagons drove across the bridge in large numbers. Less than three minutes had passed when the road to the Stella monument was blocked by several dozen identical black bodies with shields. If you've ever heard a hundred people banging hard rubber on metal, you'll never forget the sound. People started running away. Standing next to me was a man who shouted loudly: "We are not partridges. They won't treat us to sweets here. We either move forward or we will be killed." The crowd halted, turned around, and marched towards the riot police, their wrists bearing white ribbons. I'll admit upfront that this proved to be not the best weapon in the battle against evil. The girl in front of me was hit, and the force of the impact caused her hoodie fabric to roll up. The girl froze in shock and waited for the next blow to her small, fragile body. I pulled her out from the crowd and helped her sit on the curb. Of all my friends, only one stayed with me in the crowd; the others had fled. As I was pulling my friend away from the riot police, in those tense moments, we witnessed and heard the first detonations of the flash-bang grenades. I told others that we needed to run for cover, and none disagreed. We all knew that they would either put us in a vice, or we would have a few minutes to escape. We began to leave through the courtyards, using the bushes for cover, and we could hear the "valiant" representatives of the authorities hunting down people in the neighbouring nooks and crannies. We made our way to the avenue, where a friend was waiting for us in a car. The internet was down for three hours in the whole country, and I sent my first SMS in seven years. The avenue was alive with the honking: it was a long, continuous horn. Girls waved white-red-white flags from car windows. They celebrated without realising that a kilometre away, hunting and beating were taking place in the courtyards. The rest of the night, we were fixated on our phones, reading news on independent channels: someone was detained, someone was run over by a paddy wagon. They wrote about explosions, and that streets in *Pinsk* had run out of benches and riot police, and that a man had been shot.

    The morning brought a chilling silence. The only sound was the TV in the kitchen, broadcasting news of Lukashenka's victory. My friends and I had been sitting in a coffee shop since morning, and the city seemed to be going about its daily routine as if nothing had happened the night before. Then together with my friend we visited a hardware store, anticipating that the night would be the same as the previous one, if not worse. I wanted to be prepared with helmets at least, and it proved to be a good decision. We agreed that we would provide medical assistance to the victims and transport people to hospitals.

By evening, many drivers began attaching signs with red crosses to their cars, loading first aid kits, and driving into the city. Around nine in the evening, we started receiving messages that a civil war was almost breaking out at Puškinskaja. Uručča started to come out, and in Sierabranka, riot police were too afraid to approach the protesters. We were parked between the metro stations Piatroŭščyna and Malinaŭka, near the sculpture of a bison, in one of the large car parks. People started gathering near the park, initially numbering around 30. After about half an hour, the park and surrounding area were filled with people. The megaphone repeated chants without interruption, making it clear to everyone that no one had given up. Twenty minutes later, paddy wagons began to surround the park. About four hundred uniformed bodies, armed with clubs, mercilessly beat people, threw grenades, and shot rubber bullets. We stood across the road, unsure of what to do next. We began hanging first aid kits on poles. Later, we heard the sound of shooting behind us. A black jeep with shattered windows and a dented body pulled out. Four men stepped out from the jeep, their faces pale as death. They asked us to check for a safe exit route. One car went to scout the road, and we stayed in place, ready to jump into the car and rescue the remaining five if something happened. The men told us that they, like me and my friends, had been in their car with red crosses stuck to it when the first blows and questions from traffic police officers arrived: "You sons of a bitch, who are going to rescue?" By one o'clock in the morning, we went home. The next night and day, we stayed in.

Using a VPN, we finally gained access to the internet on the fourth day after the elections. The footage that followed made everyone shudder: hundreds of videos showed people screaming in agony outside police departments and *Akrescina*, photos revealed people bearing bruises and fractures. On the fourth night, a mix of emotions overwhelmed us: fear, pain, horror, and pride... Volunteer camp and solidarity... We discovered that our friends, former group mates, and work colleagues had endured torture. The next morning, I called a group mate, and we went to the emergency hospital, where we saw a friend of ours who was in a critical condition, with multiple fractures. No one could contain their tears or anger.

On Sunday, 16 August, the city centre was flooded with rivers of people waving white-red-white flags. It was the happiest day of 2020. Smiles, a lack of fear, and confidence in victory were evident on everyone's face. The beauty and pride I saw that day was something I had never seen before or since. As a pacifist, I never thought of myself as a patriot, but after the first news from *Akrescina*, I realised that in this case, a patriot and a pacifist are one and the same person.

What followed was an unforgettable month, with daily gatherings with neighbours, and weekly marches on Sundays. Ridiculous news spread, including reports about the former president running around with a machine gun, albeit without bullets, and even his own retinue laughed at him. Speeches on TV, where the former president publicly admitted that he gave orders to kill people... And constant lies, lies, lies...

People started organising themselves, creating independent trade unions, collecting money, and seeking ways to support one another. This was how we, as an entire nation, approached the beginning of the new academic year. On 1 September, students were not in their classrooms. Instead, they took to the streets, marching through the city and raising their voices.

On 4 September, riot police decided to make arrests at Minsk State Linguistic University. On 5 September, students marched through the streets with posters, proclaiming that they were not mere objects and would not be treated like slaves. I took a brief break from my French class, just for 15 minutes, to sing songs in the university courtyard. My teacher was really worried about me and didn't want me to leave, but I reassured him that everything would be okay, and I would definitely return to class. It wasn't until ten days later that we met again.

Every time I went out to protest, I longed for the violence to stop, so that people would be respected and no longer humiliated.

Later, my dean stated: "I will only be able to encourage students and teachers to go out when I can ensure their complete safety." On that day, part of the teaching staff joined the students in the street, with about 150 familiar faces from different faculties attempting to reach the avenue to join the general student march. However, five grey Sprinter minibuses prevented us from doing so.

With interlocked arms, with held back the initial attack. We even managed to have a few minutes of conversation with the police unit about the total injustice of what was happening. As our line began to break, I handed over my personal items to my teacher, asking her to give them to my parents if I were detained. The teacher and her son found refuge in a nearby café, not far from the Globus store. When they tried to strangle a junior student in front of me with a flag, my fear vanished for the first time and I came to understand that the bodies in masks were just ordinary people. I thought, I'm stronger than them! And I was able to save a friend from strangulation with one hand. They had been trying to break the line for about five minutes without success, and we managed to withstand. The minivans drove away, and some students returned to the university, while others continued towards the marching column. The minibuses returned a few minutes later. There were significantly fewer students than before. Those who remained stood along the restaurant wall, where we were pulled out of the line one by one. The girl nearby fainted, and at that moment, my fear vanished completely. I started shouting at *GUBOPiK* officers detaining us, demanding they call an ambulance. I recall the eyes looking at me from behind the mask. At that moment, the guy simply stood and shook in a daze. However, his pals began to wring my hands from behind. The last two phrases I managed to say when I was still free were: "No shit, guys, I'm not going anywhere with you... My mother will kill me at home." I asked an unfamiliar girl standing in front of me to give me a kiss, as I didn't know how long it would take before I might see the faces that were dear to me. The girl kissed me, and I smiled. From behind, several huge palms were forcefully pulling me away from the girl. Me and my companion in misfortune were detained by six seasoned muggers. We held each other's hands, feeling like sacks of potatoes – it's a national trait to compare ourselves with this particular root vegetable. They couldn't wring our arms, so they simply shoved us into the minibus and made us kneel. I tried to fake a heart attack so that they would call an ambulance and not take me to jail. The guy detained together with me began speaking in French, prompting me to cease my heart attack charade and play along: "This is an exchange student, he came right from France, and I am a translator." So we rode in the minivan for the next 40 minutes, whispering in French. When one of the policemen started to complain to someone on the phone that his work was very hard, one of the detainees loudly asked: "Shouldn't I feel sorry for you, son of a bitch?" This was the tensest moment of the arrest.

Following our detention, we were transported to the *Leninski* District Department of Internal Affairs, where we were processed – our photographs were taken and our belongings inventoried. I was summoned to the boss's office and informed that they would be charging me with organising mass protests. However, as later confirmed by a check of my phone and footage from the staff's cameras, I was merely an ordinary participant.

An hour later, a crowd of parents, classmates, and media representatives gathered outside the police department. The deans arrived and brought us refreshments, including juices, cookies, and crackers, which was a very ironic item to bring. They managed to secure the release of most of the students, but I was not among them. Instead, the police assured me that I would get to experience the full range of the penal system's delights.

Before we were taken away on a bus to one of the city's most unappealing destinations, we managed to shout out our gratitude to the relatives, thanking the dean for the food and support, and assuring them that everything would be okay with us. I decided to ask the major what he would do if the protest were successful. In response, he revealed that, in the event of a regime change, statements were already prepared and waiting in every policeman's home: "We'll simply tell them that we desperately wanted to leave, but were threatened with jail. I reckon they will believe us... And good luck to you, guys." They allowed us a few more smoke breaks before setting off. The scene was rather pathetic: a thin guy – the guard – in a balaclava, next to several big chubby students and a driver with disgusting music preferences and a vile sense of humour. We drove along to the song "Let's Get High" – I still have no desire to discover who its author is.

At *Akrescina*, we were placed in concrete "wells", with 2–3 people in each. Then, they took us out one by one, instructed us to undress, and asked us to confirm that our belongings matched the inventory protocols. They also inquired about any chronic diseases and returned us to the "wells". The process was relatively quick, taking about half an hour.

During that time, we managed to scribble yet another one of the hundreds of inscriptions on the walls of the "well", something like: "Students under *Article 23.34*, say hello to the next inmates"

– and the date. The entire "well" was covered in similar scratches. Then, they took me to a cell. We started making rosary beads from mouldy bread that was lying on the floor, asked for toilet paper and cigarettes, and managed to get another pen and a few pieces of paper. We also played a mafia game. We were fortunate: the young guard was eager to chat with us. He was totally green – I felt he was even younger than me.

Unfortunately, we didn't receive any food that day, and there was no way to light the cigarettes we had brought. We just talked a lot. The following evening, the same young guard came and brought his refreshments from home. He gave us a light every hour…

The interrogation was conducted by utterly despicable individuals. I don't know what they hoped to ascertain, given their restricted vocabulary, with predominant expressions starting with "fuck." After the interrogation, we were returned to our cell. When we asked the young guard what he was doing there, we heard: "If I weren't here, would it be easier for you?" The question was, of course, rhetorical. Almost at night, the first parcel arrived, containing a book that my mother had packed, with a message hidden between the lines on page 19: "There will be a lawyer."

The next day, the trial began. I was immaculately dressed in a shirt, vest, and trousers. What did you expect? The detainee was a personality. The trial took place via Skype: I was at *Akrescina* Street, while the court hearing itself – no one knows where. Behind me sat a district police officer who clearly understood the entire context. During the whole time spent in the room, he was never able to look me in the eyes. Everyone I had expected and not expected came to my trial: parents, best friends, group mates, and journalists. In total, about 50 people were present. The judge, judging by her face, did not seem to understand who was going to be on trial. The court hearing lasted for three hours. My parents and the guys from the university did everything in their power to ensure that I would be released on the same day. They brought three laptops to show the video recordings and secured a reference from the dean's office that would be the envy of any specialist. At that moment, it was crucial for me to see my parents: to make sure that everything was fine with them and that they were coping. We managed to exchange a few sentences, and I felt a sense of calm. Despite the three-hour court proceeding, the judge had the verdict written in advance – a 10-day arrest. I heard my mother ask, "For what?" My group mates started crying. I closed the laptop and went out into the corridor. Nobody stopped me. I just left, went to wash my face, and waited until they took me back to my cell. As soon as I sat down on a bench in the corridor, a man came in and asked from the doorway: "Well, did they give all the fascists several days of arrest?" Then, for the first time, my intelligence failed me: I asked who this son of a bitch was and where they taught him to talk like that. His speech was not even Trasianka (mixed speech of two languages), but some unknown language. It was immediately clear that he had studied extremely poorly at school and did not even know the basic rules of the Russian language, let alone the rules of etiquette. We started a skirmish, during which a few two-metre-tall detainees in the administrative case and even the investigators who were nearby at that moment took my side. They asked me not to touch the holy fool. The holy fool, with his tail and ears between his legs, quickly left. It turned out that he was an investigator, and I realised that our fate was being decided by complete rednecks. That night, we were transferred to the ICO (Isolation Centre for Offenders). We stood in the transportation "well" for several hours. I had stolen some cigarettes and matches from my personal belongings and we smoked all this time. The cramped space was filled with 13 strangers, including presenters from the Belarusian Television company, famous figures from the strikes, and unknown students. Only two of us were brought into the cell: me and the junior student with whom we were detained together. It was the coldest night of my life. A window that couldn't be closed, a mouse gnawing on the floor. Someone was being beaten in the corridor, groans echoing through the hall. And two students hugging each other for warmth, waiting for their turn to be beaten. Out of fear, we went to the toilet so often that in the end, all that came out of us was water.

In the morning, we were transferred to *Žodzina*. I managed to get to know my future cellmates while shouting from the police van. Upon arrival, we went through another procedure, which involved exposing the body and checking personal belongings and parcels. Then, we were grouped to be placed into cells and settled. The camp was not the one for children, but very, very adult. I was imprisoned together with two guys who had been detained with me. There were also several IT specialists, a marketing expert, some workers and one real prisoner who was clearly the "ears" of the administration. During those seven days, we managed to conduct several courses for general development, someone taught programming on paper, I taught English, and in the end it even came to a master class on pickup artistry. The rest of the time we read, learned prison jargon, and did crossword puzzles. They didn't take us to the shower. Throughout the whole time, we spent only 15 minutes walking outside, but thanks to the "skilly guys" (prisoners who served food), we could smoke relatively freely. The people serving the term with me were very nice, well-mannered, and educated, many of whom I later met in Warsaw. The days passed slowly, but I held on, especially thanks to my mother's notes in books; I recited them like a mantra, and every time I read them before going to bed, I grinned from ear to ear.

What stands out is that during this time, I came across many prison guards, but one in particular, Misha, left a lasting impression. He was the one who was constantly addressed by his superiors and colleagues with phrases like "Misha, fuck, damn you, come here". It seemed to me that Misha was the most well-known guard in *Žodzina*. In a word, he was the epitome of what you would imagine a schmuck to be like.

I was leaving the prison with a broad smile. Four cars were waiting for me: mum and dad, relatives and friends. I was greeted like a hero. My mum actually told me to eat a lemon, saying that people usually don't come out of prison with such a grin. The most memorable part was when my mother asked if I had smoked. To which she heard me answer in pure jargon: "When the skilly passed the matches to the hatch, we smoked, and then switched to butts". I got rid of slang quite quickly, but I would keep my hands behind my back for another six months.

Within ten days, my parents aged ten years

I was welcomed like a piece of good news in the yard of my house, being one of the first to serve my sentence. After me, nearly the entire yard followed suit. For so many years, I had been unaware of the wonderful people living nearby. Almost a hundred people gathered to welcome me, making it feel like a holiday. Our flag fluttered everywhere. At the university I was also hailed as a legendary figure from fairy tales, with everyone embracing me, including the dean and administration, not to mention the students.

Every time my mother allowed me to go into the city alone, she would become hysterical if I didn't answer the phone within two rings. She would clutch her heart and *Validol*. As a result, in January 2021, I decided to emigrate. Later, I returned to Belarus for a brief period, possibly on one of the last available flights, defended my diploma thesis, and then left again.

I learned the language, and worked on night shifts as a cleaner at a nightclub, although I was previously told that there were no janitors with a higher education. I got into trouble several times, including being pepper-sprayed, which only added to my already troubled face. Then I enrolled in four universities at once. I chose a speciality related to political science and left Warsaw.

Then the war started. Belarus became a direct participant on the aggressor's side. I did everything in my power to protect my reputation and my tribe. I travelled to the border, where I cooked meals, volunteered at train stations and hostels, and provided financial and moral support to anyone I could help. In fact, this is what I am still doing. I have seen so many devastated faces that through their prism, I have viewed life from start to finish. Many people in their entire lives would not be able to see as much grief and pain as these eyes have seen. Almost four years of continuous adventures and events, each of which is worthy of a separate book, were just a slight slap that Fate gave me compared to what these people experienced.

What's the end result? Am I happy with this life? Can I envision the future? Will I ever be able to return home?

In the end, I'm glad that my life has become truly unique, I'm glad that I see life as it is – multifaceted, beautiful and ugly at the same time.

I am a small but vital part of the world's history. I can only see a week ahead, but I am trying to make plans. Homesickness is deeply ingrained within me, and I think about it too often. Intellectually, I understand that I am not a representative of the first generation of Belarusian emigrants who hoped to return home soon, but were unable to. Despite this, I long to visit the graves of my relatives, as almost all of my living relatives also left their homeland. Therefore, I will continue to cherish the hope of returning.

I understand perfectly well that even after returning home, I will remain an emigrant

So far, I have not decided whether I have been given a golden ticket to a bright future or a lifelong curse of being away from home. I am unable to draw any conclusions yet, as my experience is still limited. I have met the leaders of the opposition, albeit briefly. I have immense respect for those who are working to make our future bright. By 2035, I will do my best to become a significant figure in my beautiful native country, and I will make every possible effort to return home.

How can I help myself and other Belarusians while in exile? I am pursuing my education and relying solely on my abilities. I am actively seeking a job in international organisations that have the opportunity to influence the situation in our country. I am currently serving as an assistant to a European Ambassador. Next, I will aim to secure a position within structures close to PACE and contribute to the betterment of my country. And I will work, work and work again. Develop my skills in all possible areas, so that when I return home, I can be useful.

What do I still desire? I long for pure love, happy parents, friends by my side, the opportunity to return home, I long for justice, and for the rednecks who abuse people to get what they deserve. I also yearn for a happy and prosperous life, and in the end, the longest and brightest obituary in the world.

I will burn and shine, I will burn and bring warmth.

Now I'm 23 years old. I am an emigrant, an MA student, a son, an assistant to a European ambassador, a bartender, a translator, a European, a Belarusian. I am both childish and responsible. People like me are often called the "lost ones," but it is through individuals like me that humanity will ultimately find its path.

Poland, June 2023
todarszpak@yahoo.com

WE DO NOT CHOOSE THE TIMES, WE LIVE IN THEM

Pan Robak

❝ We don't choose the times we live in, but we do choose the path we take." This is what *Viktar Babaryka*, the most popular presidential candidate in the Republic of Belarus, said in his video autobiography.

Like many Belarusians in 2020, I chose the route of confronting the regime's lawlessness, hypocrisy, and impudence. That year became a truly significant chapter in Belarus' modern history, as hundreds of thousands of concerned people united to challenge the dictatorship and began to fight for their rights. Millions of our fellow citizens followed the events with bated breath and offered each other support. We were confident of victory. This was the moment when Belarusian society demonstrated its maturity, readiness for change, and desire for a democratic state where the law is respected and the people's will is reckoned with. However, such a popular upsurge was not always present: even six months before the elections, few could have predicted the course of events.

I will attempt to reconstruct the timeline of the rapid evolution of Belarusian society and my own role as an integral part of this society, recalling the emotions that drove me, and examining the ideas and goals that fuelled the popular protest. I'll discuss the difficulties young Belarusians are currently facing, three years after the 2020 events, as they are forced to seek new homes in foreign lands. Let's try to imagine what other challenges we may have to face and what actions we must take.

The pandemic

The beginning of 2020 became a difficult trial for the whole world. Humanity was faced with a challenge for which it was completely unprepared: overcrowded hospitals, empty pharmacy shelves, cancelled flights, closed borders, hundreds of thousands of victims, as well as lockdowns. International organisations and governments around the world joined forces to combat the coronavirus pandemic.

Meanwhile, the authoritarian regime in Belarus appeared to be completely incompetent in the face of an unusual threat. This was precisely the turning point for Belarusian society. Officials and local leaders were largely ineffective: they were unable to make decisions, waiting for instructions from above. While Belarusians took individual measures to minimise the spread of the coronavirus infection, such as switching to remote learning and work, quarantining, and caring for their loved ones, the authorities not only ignored the problem, but made it worse through their actions. From television screens and newspapers, Belarusians were subjected to blatant lies and outright stupidity. While Lukashenka, to stroke his ego, did not notice viruses in the air and crowded the stadia with state employees, civil society united and took action. Volunteers and ordinary citizens collected funds and personal protective equipment. Commercial organisations purchased hundreds of thousands of respirators, medications, and other essential items for doctors and arranged for their delivery to hospitals. Meanwhile, the Ministry of Health either underestimated or failed to release data on the number of new cases of illness and death. As students fought for the right not to attend classes for safety reasons, the administrations of educational institutions struggled to find a compromise between criminal instructions from above and the reality of the situation. Through joint efforts, public initiatives and businesses were able to establish uninterrupted work in a matter of weeks, effectively replacing the state in this area. This was the moment when many people witnessed first-hand the unity, resilience, and perseverance of our society. Belarusians easily proved that they were capable of solving even the most complex problems without a "leader." Meanwhile, the authorities continued to make absurd statements that quickly spread among the population, further fuelling discontent and anger.

I clearly remember the palpable fatigue that gripped my friends, classmates, and acquaintances at that time. There was no strong fear, no doubt, no faith in a bright future, only fatigue. Although we were all aware that change was necessary, we lacked a clear understanding of how to make it happen. Many people no longer saw a future for themselves within the country and were planning to leave. At one point, I was also among them. I realised that if we failed to bring about change in 2020, I would have to leave to pursue my education and career in another country. It was while being forced abroad that many Belarusians felt what it was like to be deprived of their homeland.

Election campaign

May 2020 brought more than just the feeling of approaching summer. It was filled with a series of unexpected and exciting events. Initially, all attention was focused on Siarhei Tsikhanouski's statement of his intention to take part in the presidential elections. I must admit that I first learned about him after watching a video. A charismatic speaker, businessman, and blogger, *Siarhei Tsikhanouski* was undoubtedly popular with a part of the population, but this was not enough. At the same time, I hoped that other candidates would emerge who could gain the support of the majority of the population. The chances were slim, as everyone understood that the regime would stop at nothing to maintain power. However, such a candidate still came around.

Viktar Babaryka's decision to run in the presidential campaign changed everything. A successful banker, talented manager, intelligent and educated, he met all the criteria for a leader who could unite and lead the Belarusians. Respected among his friends and colleagues, *Babaryka* quickly assembled an effective team and got to work. Of course, some were sceptical about the sincerity of his intentions, viewing it as a cunning scheme of the regime or even the Kremlin. However, time has proven the absurdity of these statements. Regrettably, *Babaryka* paid a heavy price for this.

Events unfolded rapidly. Everyone understood that their contribution would be valuable. We spread information among family and friends, persuaded those who were unsure about the necessity for decisive action, joined initiative groups, collected signatures, and signed petitions. At that point, I no longer entertained any thoughts about relocating to another country. It became quite obvious that I was needed here, that I wanted to stay and contribute to changing Belarus for the better. Overnight, I saw the enormous potential of Belarusian society, how much we can achieve, and how I can be useful. The only things required were to defend our rights and freedom, and to build a system of state power that serves the people, rather than acting against them.

A period began that will leave a lasting impression in my memory. The spirit of freedom and hope was palpable in the air. People were joyful and brimming with confidence, making plans for the future. In our free time, we discussed the prospects for the development of Belarusian statehood, the merits and drawbacks of transitioning to a parliamentary or parliamentary-presidential republic, reforms in healthcare and education, and the necessity for the lustration of those in public office. Foreign policy was a topic of great interest to me. There was no doubt that in order to reduce Belarus' significant dependence on Russia, it was essential to focus on developing interactions with Western countries while maintaining relations with our main Eastern partners. Changes in legislation, the abolition of the death penalty, and the introduction of a system of checks and balances would enable us to lift existing sanctions quickly and increase trade volumes with developed countries. Democratic changes would enhance the stability of the system, which would, in turn, attract new investors. Talented young people would remain in Belarus, and experienced managers from the private sector could utilise their expertise and years of practice to benefit our country.

For all this to happen, it was essential to overcome the most daunting challenge — winning the elections. Few people had any idea how exactly to achieve this. Despite the impressive scale of social mobilisation, society still lacked the courage and determination needed to succeed. I remember how hard it was at first to convince my acquaintances to participate in public events officially approved and sanctioned by the authorities. People were threatened with dismissals and expulsions if they participated. There were reports of planned provocations and even terrorist attacks. These statements did not seem implausible to anyone. The regime was not shy about using its tools and methods of oppression. Over twenty-six years of authoritarian rule, people had developed a perception of the repressive machine's invincibility. I was convinced, nevertheless, that the apparatus of power had degraded over time, so I tried my best to motivate others to be more involved.

The summer and autumn of 2020 will be remembered as a time that will be documented in numerous books and film scripts. It was a moment of solidarity unparalleled in Belarus' history and marked by the rapid maturation of society. We saw a dramatic shift from sixty-thousand at sanctioned rallies to half a million concerned Belarusians on the streets of Minsk who put their freedom, health, and careers at risk to express their disagreement with the dictatorship.

The whole world witnessed first-hand the Belarusians' determination and, simultaneously, their peaceful approach, demonstrating that Belarus is distinct from the Lukashenka's regime. Meetings outside prisons with tears in the eyes of the detained loved ones, gifts for unknown individuals, solidarity chains and neighbourhood initiatives, vigils near polling stations, and truthful results from a few polling stations contributed to strengthening my affection for my country and fellow citizens.

Each time I attended a rally, I mentally prepared myself for the possibility of arrest, and my family had a plan in place in case I was detained. My friends and I developed communication strategies during the internet shutdowns, and we avoided bringing personal phones to protests to prevent them from being tracked. Upon reaching the protest sites, I often met protesters, we joked and sang songs, and public transport drivers refused to take money for travel. It was fascinating to see how many different people were united by a common problem. I recall a telephone conversation between a young man and his mother during his first rally. The son was surprised to tell his mother that everything was completely different from what was shown on TV: people were friendly, and they handed out water for free on the streets. Unfortunately, this rally, like many others, ended with stun grenades exploding at our feet and brutal arrests. I ended up spending the evening in an unfamiliar entrance hall to a block of flats, prudently left open by the residents, while police, whom Belarusians had nicknamed "cosmonauts" owing to their gear, were running around the building.

We designed posters for rallies and, when the rallies finished, we took care to clean up the area. We planned in advance our "retreat" routes in the event of police raids, which we had to use multiple times. We selflessly extended our help to strangers with the same enthusiasm as if they were our closest relatives. During neighbourhood events, where we brought tea and treats, people talked and recited poetry. I finally met the neighbours I had lived next to for many years. We went through a lot and learned a lot during that time.

Despite our efforts, we had not achieved significant progress. We were unable to win over representatives of law enforcement to our side. They were bound by complete permissiveness, constant psychological pressure, and the fear of losing their position, which led to the unwavering loyalty and unprecedented cruelty of the security forces. The years of negative selection had borne fruit: law enforcement representatives not only mindlessly executed all criminal orders, but also showed initiative in choosing violent methods. With a carte blanche to use violence, their lack of holidays and days off, constant training, and general fatigue were vented into their anger on the protesters.

We also failed to pool our available resources, reconcile differences among democratic leaders, and develop a clear plan of action. We were unable to secure timely external support, and it wasn't until a year later that the first effective sanctions against the regime were implemented. As a result, the voice of dissent in Belarus was completely silenced, and the protests were brutally crushed.

Unfortunately, there were also students who supported the government, although they were a minority. These individuals were primarily those who were unable to envision their future outside the system, as they were badly prepared and uncompetitive in a free market. To be part of the system provided a sense of belonging to something larger and more significant, giving their lives meaning. Additionally, some of them sought to capitalise on the lack of competition to accelerate their career advancement and personal enrichment.

Departure

I kept putting off my departure until the last minute and only recently left the country. I am still grappling with the fact that I won't be able to return for a very long time. Now, being safe abroad, I constantly reflect on the emotions and ideas that filled me at that moment and on things that could have been done differently. In the meantime, the Belarusian regime's repressive machinery is operating at full capacity. Over 1,500 political prisoners are being held captive. Prison inmates have to fight for their survival on a daily basis. Tens of thousands of Belarusians have endured arrests, fines, and days in custody. Unfortunately, there are increasing reports of prisoners' health rapidly deteriorating and of their deaths. *Viktar Babaryka* was hospitalised with signs of physical abuse. For almost three months, nothing was known with certainty about his condition. Eduard Babaryka was sentenced to eight years in prison just for supporting his father, and his trial lasted over three years.

However, a fragile hope still flickers in my heart. Despite the numerous challenges associated with emigration, including legal issues, finding housing and work, learning a new language, and continuing education, we must take action. It is necessary to seek out opportunities to support political prisoners and their families. It is important to highlight the Belarusian issue abroad through journalism and academic publications. We must continuously look for ways to weaken the regime and, of course, support Ukraine.

In the current situation, the independence and prospective future of our country are directly tied to the Ukrainian Armed Forces' achievements on the battlefield. It is evident that the Belarusian regime persists solely due to the economic and military backing of the Kremlin, which has recently made no secret of its intentions to incorporate our country into the Russian Federation.

Russia's defeat in this war will significantly alter the current situation and provide us with a new opportunity to implement democratic reforms in Belarus. This does not mean that someone else will do all the work for us. Even after Russia's complete defeat, the process will not be simple.

Those who remain in Belarus must preserve their ideals, values, and beliefs, and not lose hope. They should be prepared to take decisive action as soon as the right moment arises.

After a successful regime change in our country, Belarusians will have to tackle a multitude of complex problems. Critical economic issues and brain drain, a tarnished international image, and an unstable regional situation will necessitate determination, hard work, and willingness to make difficult decisions to overcome these and many other problems.

City N, 01.2024

(NON)CULTURAL ESSAY

Palina

My seventh grade: I faced a challenging period at this awkward age, full of emotional turmoil. I developed an interest in psychology, which helped me understand myself and my psyche better. I often took online psychological tests, including career guidance tests, which I found engaging.

"A person is a person" or "a person is an artistic image" — the tests revealed something of these kinds. I intuitively understood this perfectly myself, but it did not help me in planning the future. I couldn't draw or dance, or pursue music seriously, as I only played in an amateur orchestra without formal training and did not study at a music school. And what else? Nothing, just a lot of ideas in my head, a desire for creativity and love for people.

Travelling was another dream that I had. To be honest, I still have it! I yearn to travel around the world. I would often indulge in exploring themed communities in the *VK* social network, gazing at photos from different places of the planet, and imagining where I would go first.

My eighth grade: My mother was actively involved in helping me explore my future study options. The dilemma was whether I would leave school after the ninth grade or stay on to pursue university education directly after school.

One day, my mother stumbled upon an article about the Belarusian State University of Culture and Arts. "Oh, have a look!" she said without taking her eyes off the computer. "There is something called Management of International Cultural Relations."

It was exactly for me! It was a combination of art, culture, and even travel, which meant the exploration of different cultures. I yearned to enrol for this speciality. My opinion remained unchanged throughout all the following years.

Four happy years

I was admitted to university without any issues, except for the stress caused by the centralised testing process. However, I still left school after the ninth grade and enrolled in a secondary school in the heart of Minsk. My mother and I believed it would be a better fit for me, as the secondary school was located in the same building as the law college and positioned itself as a law school, offering an in-depth study of social subjects and history which I needed so much for the university admission.

I distinctly remember the elation I experienced that summer when I was informed of my admission. And not only that: additionally, I would be part of a much craved scholarship, being also among the top names on the admission lists.

The first year was quite calm. The first exam session was unsettling because it was something new for me, but everything was surprisingly simple and even enjoyable. From the very beginning of my studies, from the first lectures and seminars, I felt a sense of belonging. The words that best describe this experience are creativity, freedom, and inspiration — and I miss that feeling now.

Apart from my studies, I was engaged in different extracurricular activities. For example, I volunteered at various cultural events, contributing to their organisation. Back in my school years, I developed an interest in politics and sought to find my role within diverse political movements.

Of course, I had been familiar with the Belarusian state policies for a long time. It was clear, even with the naked eye, that "something was amiss", as they say, evidenced from such school practices, as extortions, the compulsion to subscribe to various red and green* newspapers, and information sessions for the whole class, where the greatness of a certain Christian saint was discussed.

In general, I was unsure of how to handle all of this, so during my school years and the beginning of my university studies, authoritarian politics simply existed for me in the periphery. I focused on studying more and earning money by writing all kinds of papers for my classmates, accumulating experience that would be essential for my future job — which, I must admit, I had only a hazy vision of. However, I clearly understood that it would involve what people refer to as working in one's "speciality."

My relatively apolitical nature didn't endure for long. The second semester of university started in 2017, the year when the decree "On Prevention of Social Dependence" took effect, mandating unemployed people to pay fees. The situation was a shock to me: I knew that in other countries, the government provided financial assistance to the unemployed, enabling them to make ends meet. Our system is the other way around: it seems to say, "Find your own way out". With my empathy and intelligence, I found it difficult to understand how the unemployed can survive when they are required to pay a fine with money they do not have.

Mass protests started in Belarus. I felt compelled to join in.

The initial demonstrations passed relatively peacefully for me. Yes, there were large crowds and paddy wagons nearby, but there were no arrests. I recall Mikalaj Statkievič delivering speeches, which were met with enthusiastic applause from the crowd. That's all.

Nevertheless, the atmosphere in the country, particularly among government representatives, was noticeably tense. A major protest was scheduled for 25 March, Freedom Day, and — what a coincidence! — we were given Saturday classes in a subject that was never part of the curriculum. I still remember how they made us stand in a line in physical training classes and informed us that protests were an evil thing and that participating in them would lead to expulsion.

It didn't stop me. I submitted an application to the dean requesting an exemption from classes as I was to attend my sister's wedding (which, in fact, was a fabrication, as there was no sister, let alone a wedding). I said I could not attend the newly created class, and asked for permission to be excused — "freedom for the parrots!" To my surprise, they either believed me or chose to pretend to, and granted me permission to be absent.

25 March 2017: I was eighteen years old when I saw for the first time how those who are supposed to protect us from violence use violence themselves. That day, I witnessed riot police beating an absolutely helpless elderly man who was lying on the ground. I

barely managed to escape myself. After everything I saw, I couldn't come to myself for a long time. I cried.

Then my life changed. I was still unsure of what I could do to end all this violence and coercion, but I started doing what was necessary. Politics somehow became part of everything. For example, at university, we had to write texts for different disciplines, and I always included political themes. Once, I had to write a speech about my hatred of tomatoes, and I wrote how I dislike tomatoes because of the evil Signor Tomato who made ludicrous laws. When my group mates and teacher heard this, they had a hearty laugh. Everyone understood who I was referring to.

In the second year, I continued to study, earn money, gain experience, and suffer under the dictatorial regime. It was a solace that the university had subjects like Belarusian literature. It was nice that some teachers spoke only Belarusian. I felt at home when I came to the university, when I was doing my homework, or participating in creative activities outside regular classes. It was then that I understood very well that there was an outside world — a violent world of dictatorship.

In the autumn of 2017, another issue was added to my activities — managing mental health. I had my first depressive-anxiety episode, which was influenced by the sudden death of a relative and complete lack of rest. I continued to study well, but I had to slow down. During this period, however, I was offered the opportunity to become a volunteer for the "Green Network", and I accepted. Then I realised that my political views were aligned with the greens.

Around the same time, I participated in my first Erasmus+ project. It turned out that the university was quite effective in supporting the participation of both male and female students in such activities, so I was excused from classes without any issues. Then I went on many more trips. It was likely during this period that the phase of my life I had dreamed of since childhood began — the phase of endless travels. It continues to this day.

The following years were not particularly notable. In 2019, I became an activist of the Young Belarusian Greens and further immersed myself in ecoactivism. My mental health was deteriorating. It would get particularly bad approximately every six months, during the spring and autumn seasons. Despite this, my studies remained unaffected, as I was aware of the need to be more mindful of my well-being.

During the Covid-19 pandemic, I completed my dissertation and received a degree with honours. Alongside this, I started taking my first antidepressants — and no, I was not feeling unwell due to my studies; rather, my studies brought me a sense of satisfaction. This was so positive that I decided to continue my education.

It was 2020.

Culture under violence

I decided that I wanted to teach: to teach at my university, because I had developed an incredible affection for it. It was my place of strength.

Belarusian culture was also my strength.

Gaining admission to the master's programme was slightly more challenging, as I had to pass an exam that was evaluated by a committee of three people. Studying during that period was not easy, as the antidepressants I was taking caused significant side effects, requiring me to rest frequently and avoid overexerting myself. Nevertheless, I somehow prepared for the exam and passed it with an 8 — a valuable lesson in learning to accept grades other than 9 and 10 and not to demand too much from myself.

Around the same time, protests were already taking place in Belarus due to the detention of *Siarhei Tsikhanouski* and *Viktar Babaryka*. It is amusing to recall how I learned about being accepted into the master's programme — during a peaceful demonstration in Braslaŭ, where I was taking a break at the time.

There was a palpable sense of hope in the air. People believed that, as soon as elections were held, that would be the end of Lukashenka's rule. It was obvious there were many of us. However, it seemed to me that not everyone understood that there would be violence, which I had witnessed first-hand in 2017.

I registered as an independent observer at the election precinct in my former school, the Minsk school where I spent nine years of my education, the same school where I first discovered my aspirations. It was in this school where I felt for the first time that something was wrong in the country, where they used extortion, the compulsion to subscribe to various "red and green" newspapers and information sessions for the whole class. I believed that the regime would ultimately come to an end for me just there, where I began to understand its existence. However, that did not happen.

I witnessed the falsifications, but I couldn't do anything about them. On the first day of the early elections, I counted twenty-eight people who came to vote, while the ballot results report stated ninety-seven. The next day, the commission at the polling station reported four-hundred people, which could not have happened. I asked why they were cheating people, but they didn't give me an answer.

On 8 August, the day before the main voting date, I narrowly avoided detention simply for being an observer. I managed to evade capture once again.

And then the violence erupted, which I had been prepared for. I was fully aware that this would occur, as I could not expect anything else from this state. It appeared that more people had started to join the peaceful protests not solely due to their opposition to the Lukashenka regime, but also because they were against the violence. People were shocked.

At the end of August, before the beginning of the academic year, "themed" protests started to take place. Entire universities began to participate in demonstrations, and there was a chain of solidarity near my own institution. It was impressive to see my teachers involved, and I even had a poster that read "Culture against violence".

However, not the entire "culture" shared this view. As the classes began, expulsions and dismissals took place. Our wonderful rector was fired, and the dean had to resign. They were replaced by someone from the Ministry of Culture or someone with an open pro-Lukashenka stance. Active students, including myself, started being invited to "conversations". Once, I even visited the Kastryčnicki district police department for a similar conversation.

A few months later, a terrible event occurred. They detained my close relative, and then in the police department, they raped him with a baton and beat him so badly that he had to spend two weeks in the intensive care unit. It was a shock and a great pain for me, and I could not accept the thing that had happened. Meanwhile, my friends were in prison.

Soon, my mental health began to deteriorate. Later, I discovered with certainty that I had developed PTSD, but my condition significantly impacted my studies. It was challenging for me to focus, I didn't want to leave the house, and I had a subconscious fear for my life. The realisation that I could no longer be myself at the university was that very "one step" from love to hatred — I felt that I no longer wanted to study there.

Despite everything, I persevered and managed to complete my master's degree. It was a surprise for me, as I had genuinely expected to be expelled at any moment, but it did not happen. Of course, the pressure on me continued, which may have been a deliberate tactic by the regime — to humiliate mentally vulnerable students to the point where they would no longer want to live.

They were informed about my health problems. I had to miss classes, and I presented certificates from a psychotherapist, but they were not accepted. For example, the university's new internal rules stipulated that the sick leave be documented within three days of resuming attendance. Unfortunately, I couldn't meet this requirement because the certificates from the psychotherapist were issued through the dispensary, which took at least five days. Due to this, I was once deprived of a stipend for a month, but it was more comical than frightening. Things were turning into a circus.

What happened afterwards?

Afterwards — obscurity. I still find it difficult to understand what happened and will happen to me, and I seem still to be recovering from my PTSD.

I no longer live in Belarus. I left for Latvia, and two months later, KGB officers came to my registered address in Minsk. I had managed to leave in time. Honestly, I don't know if I would be alive today if I had stayed in Belarus and ended up in prison. Mentally, I definitely couldn't have endured it.

I chose not to pursue a career according to the mandatory job assignment after university. Initially, I wanted to just ignore it, but after overt threats, I still had to pay my fees. I am very grateful that due to my involvement in ecoactivism and travel, I have many acquaintances in different countries who, within just four days, helped me collect the entire amount needed to pay for my education.

By the way, ecoactivism has become my job. What about culture? Culture, as it currently exists for me, is mainly linked to ecology and eco-art. I am eager to get back into this field, but I have not yet found something that works for me.

I truly long to return to Belarus, to go home. Even after all these events, I do not lose hope that it will happen. However, I no longer expect it to happen as quickly as I once did. But I do not give up, I continue to fight and inspire others to do the same — through ecoactivism, a little through culture, and a lot through my love for people and the place where I was born.

I miss you, Belarus.

City N, January 2024
polbrk99@gmail.com

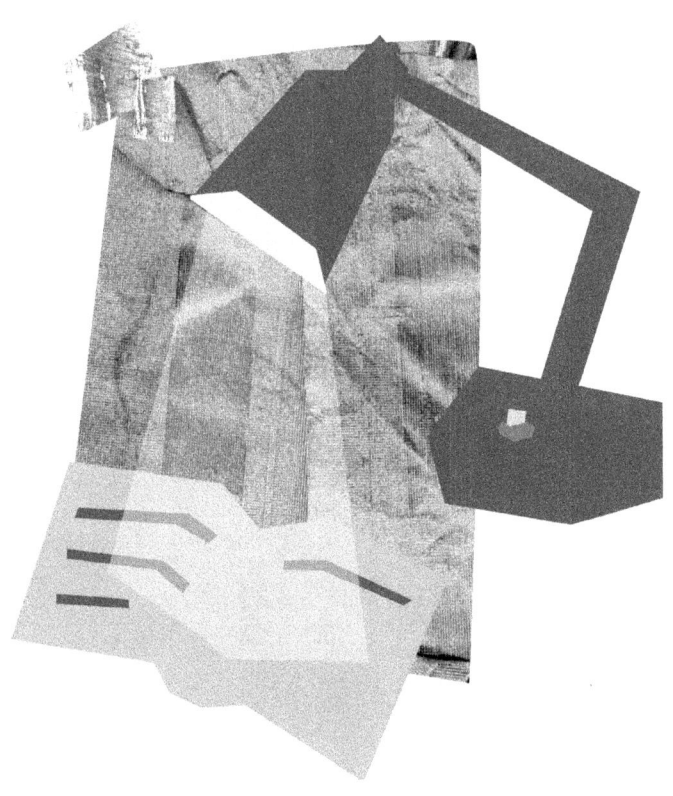

HISTORY IS FULL OF SURPRISES

Ne_avtor

A six for the "language"

I was born in the best of Belarusian cities (the name of which I cannot disclose for security reasons). I don't really like looking back on my childhood, but it was there that, through many events, I learned to manage stress, a skill that has helped me numerous times. I was fascinated by literature and devoured a huge number of books, which led me to consider a career in philology. However, I also liked history. My grandmother taught me about it in her own way, and therefore, as a child, I would often engage in debates with her about specific topics, such as, who was right in the Russian Civil War, was Tsar Nicholas II a criminal, and were the white generals heroes?

These topics, as you can see, are related to Russian history. As a child, I knew little about Belarusian history, partly because my family has Ukrainian and Russian heritage, which made it hard for me to immediately identify as Belarusian.

Despite this, when I was ten, I found it strange that everyone in Belarus spoke Russian. I mentioned this to my grandmother, saying that if we don't speak Belarusian at all, it will disappear. My grandmother, who was born in Russia and identifies as Russian, understands the Belarusian language. She agreed with the importance of the language and considered Belarusian beautiful.

I confess that I was embarrassed to speak Belarusian as a child, as it was associated with rural society. Now, when I start talking about the role of the native language, my mother reminds me of my high school grade of 6 in that subject.

Belarusian became one of the means of communication during my university days. Before that, I was a typical jabaćka, a Lukashenka supporter. In my final year at school, a teacher organised a debate on the Decree on the Prevention of Social Dependence. Based on what I had heard at home, I tried to convince the entire class that this law was the right one to have. I hope that time has erased this event from my classmates' memories.

Initially I didn't plan to connect my life with the History Faculty, but it once happened that a substitute teacher's captivating energy and reasoning during a history lesson amazed me. As with many life-altering decisions, I made the choice to enrol in the History Faculty in just five minutes, and I've never regretted it.

Awaken a Belarusian in yourself

The History Faculty was the place where I learned two things — how to think and how to drink. I arrived there as a modest jabaćka, but by the time of my expulsion, the administration seemed to view me as a real threat to Belarusian statehood. Perhaps if I had not been expelled, the regime might have fallen. But let's go through all of this chronologically.

At the History Faculty, I started my active student life. I became the group leader and an active participant in faculty events that weren't focused on the regime's propaganda. In my first year, I met many people who are commonly called "the civically-minded ones". My "red-green" picture of the world began to show "white" spots. By the end of my first year, I had come to understand that the elections were fraudulent, that Lukashenka was a dictator, and a mess was happening in the country. I was also deeply concerned about the topic of integration with Russia.

It is crucial to note that at the History Faculty, I interacted with very different people. Frequent discussions in the dormitory centred on the events unfolding in the country, and opinions varied significantly. At the same time I observed that, for example, a monarchist and a Stalinist did not attack each other with their fists. I was also surprised that someone in our time could hold such specific views, but the History Faculty teaches diversity.

Before the elections, I understood that the country's situation was not as it should be, but I believed that education and people with critical thinking could be the catalyst for change. After completing my bachelor's degree, I considered pursuing a master's and then a PhD. However, I wanted to try my hand at teaching, believing that young people in the education system could inspire a fresh outlook in children.

District Department of Internal Affairs, Akrescina, and the Dean's office

These and other plans went down the dumper in 2020.

The arrest of *Viktar Babaryka* was the turning point for me. Initially, I didn't plan to attend the rally on the day of his arrest, and decided just to walk by. Cars were honking and people were clapping tin responce.

At one point, I was walking past a bus stop. A man coming towards me said, "They're going to start grabbing us now."

I walked forward 15 metres and turned back to see a police minivan stop and security forces rush out and detain a man. Later, on the corner, when people started clapping again, I found the courage to join them. At that moment, I felt incredibly inspired.

I had signed up as an election observer. Of course, I was not permitted to serve in an official capacity. Instead, they designated me as being "on reserve". However, there were already many others in the "reserve" group ahead of me. As a result, on the first day of early voting, I and several other people stood outside the office and tallied the voter turnout. 34 people showed up at the polling station. By the end of the evening, the official ballot result report indicated 210 people. These intriguing mathematics impressed us, and our colleagues shared their comments with the press. The next day, a policeman "asked" us to leave the building.

From 9 to 11 August, I did not participate in the protests due to family obligations. What held me back was not wanting to upset my mother and grandmother; however, it was impossible for me to stay away. During those three days, several of my acquaintances were beaten: one of them was detained. Both I and those around me were shocked by the brutality. I attended the first Sunday march on 16 August with a sense of my own moral conviction.

Since it was a holiday period at the university, not everyone was in touch. It was hard to grasp the full scope of the situation. Some people participated in the protests while others opposed the violence and electoral fraud but were too afraid to join the demonstrations.

My first arrest happened a few months later. Several riot police vehicles arrived at the relatively sparsely attended march, and some not particularly friendly individuals jumped out. I was detained in a "polite" manner — they asked me if I would go with them voluntarily. When I tried to throw down the flag (the thought crossed my mind that it would cause more problems), the riot policeman "gently" tossed it back over my shoulders.

They put me in a small car, and another cop brought one more girl. We were ordered to sit down. There was only one vacant seat for two of us, and there was some kind of ammunition lying on the side, with a pistol sticking out of it. I automatically sat down on it. The policeman's reaction was swift:

"Are you crazy? Sit down on her!"

I ended up sitting on the lap of a girl I didn't know.

"Isn't it hard for you?" I asked, concerned.

"No, don't worry," she replied.

At some point, I accidentally glanced at the weapon lying next to me. Honestly, I still don't understand how one can leave ammunition so unattended while being involved in arrests.

The policeman noticed: "Are you going to shoot?"

I didn't know what to say, so I told the truth: "No, I can't."

The policeman lost interest in our conversation and turned away. Soon, his colleague got into the car. As I understood it, one of the protesters had tried to escape and accidentally hit him with his elbow, breaking the policeman's brow bone.

He was very angry: "Face down!"

We lowered our faces. From the context of the conversation, it was clear that he was removing his mask and his colleague was examining his face.

Later, we were transported in this car to a police van, which was already crowded with mostly young people. One of the riot police, who had guessed unmistakably that I was an interesting interlocutor, struck a conversation. It ended with me making a joke and everyone laughing except him.

I decided to save my comedic skills for the police department, so I fell silent. The guy sitting on the floor asked to loosen the zip tie binding his hands, but the request was ignored. One of the girls had something like a panic attack, and we started asking for water to be given to her. They offered water, but she refused it.

Soon we arrived at the police department, where there were many people. Some of them were marked with paint. It turned out that this was a message from the riot police to the police department, requesting special attention for these detainees.

We were kept in the district main police office for several hours. One of the policemen told me that *Nexta* was a fag, and that I joined the marches for *Nexta*. Involved in this fascinating dialogue, I tried to indicate that I had a positive attitude towards LGBTQ+ people, and I was protesting not for the sake of *Nexta*, but for justice. The conversation then shifted to a discussion about national symbols, during which I delivered a lecture to him about the white-red-white flag.

The following quote from one of the officers encapsulates our conversation: "No, he didn't score 80 percent. But he definitely scored 60!"

Later, one of the policemen took me to the toilet and said, "I could shock you and take you to a bad toilet, but I'll take you to a normal one."

One of the bosses allowed us to receive packages from our relatives and distributed food to us. Later, I discovered that one of the boys was taken away to be beaten. They let me call my mother and inform her of my detention. I wasn't scared, but I was worried about how my grandmother would handle it.

In the evening, we were taken to *Akrescina*. There, I quickly became friends with two girls. In the cell, we generally discussed political topics quite often and debated. Everyone endured imprisonment differently, so quarrels happened sometimes.

I was once taken for a talk with a security officer who – I later discovered – was from *GUBOPiK*. He was interested in the most active students at my university. I told him that because no one communicated with me at the university I couldn't provide any details. The officer responded by saying that I didn't understand the situation.

Sometimes I was overcome with wild anxiety about my grandmother. I was afraid very much that she would pass away. The girl I became friends with was extremely supportive, and we grew close — such conditions can foster strong bonds.

We were detained over the weekend, so the trial was not immediate. Before the court session, a policeman visited, who would later act as a witness against us. We gave him the numbers of our relatives so he could call them. I begged him to find out about my grandmother, but he never called my family. However, I have a vague memory that he did call one of my fellow inmates' relatives.

The trial was a circus. They read out my positive characterisation from the university (to give credit to the administration who signed the paper). I was very embarrassed to listen to all this, and I was also worried that I would miss lunch (the food was terrible there, but it was better than nothing).

Before me, everyone else had been sentenced to ten days, so I didn't think I would receive a different term. I was the only one with a lawyer (which was really unnecessary, but my family were worried), so the hearing dragged on. The trial was conducted via Skype, where I only heard the lawyer's voice and didn't see the judge.

As a result, I received a sentence of ten days and returned to my cell.

What did we want and why did we take to the streets? In the cell we were all students, and we actively discussed what was happening. Many came out to protest against violence. Those from opposition-minded families had more radical views. We often argued about the use of violence against security forces, and, at that time, almost everyone was in favour of peaceful protest.

We spent some time at *Akrescina*. On the day our packages were expected, we were woken up to learn that we were being transferred.

At first we didn't know our destination until one of the police officers casually dropped the word "*Baranavičy*". We thought he was joking, but it turned out that we were indeed being taken to *Baranavičy*. During our transportation in the "well", we sang "Play" until they knocked on our door.

A riot policeman talked to us through the keyhole for some time. It turned out that he came from the same place as one of the girls and, apparently, knew her; he was too surprised to hear her last name. He never told her his, though.

We spent five days in *Baranavičy* and were released. My mother met me and said that we definitely needed to go to the faculty, because they were waiting for me there. As a result, upset that there was no chance of a shower for me any time soon, another former prisoner-student and I set off towards Minsk.

During the journey, we were busy lacing up our shoes.

"The dean pleaded with you not to organise any actions."

"Mum, what actions? They even seised my phone," I responded.

"Well, it does not matter. They still asked you about it very strongly," she said.

Following a quick stop at a petrol station for a snack and a smoke, we went to collect our phones (they didn't return them, but we were told to come back later), and then made our way to the faculty.

I felt very awkward. After ten days of disconnection from the normal world I was tired, and all I could dream of was a room with the lights off where I could sleep. My classmates greeted me warmly. I knew that they were worried about me, because I had received a pack of fifteen letters in *Baranaviču*, including from my teachers. It later turned out that the letters were written by my entire course, but unfortunately, a portion of them never reached me.

Some guys met me in the corridor and we had a very warm conversation. I can't go into details, but many teachers showed amazing sensitivity. I couldn't talk much at that time, because people from the administration department were waiting. I didn't really want this conversation, because I was desperate for some sleep and a shower. I hadn't had a proper shower for ten days. To wash ourselves in the cell, we used a bottle to collect water from the tap and washed bent over the toilet.

The deputy dean also became interested in the issue of hygiene. She asked me, "How was the situation with your hygiene there?"

The dean gave a lengthy speech expressing his regret that his students were being used for someone's political purposes. I was not in the best condition, so I agreed to their request to write an explanation note for missing classes. They promised no expulsion and a reprimand instead. I must give them credit, I wasn't expelled during that period.

I would like to emphasise the solidarity among students. With some classes being online, my group mates accessed the learning platform using my account while I was in detention, making it seem like I was present in class. In fact, someone noted that I had signed up for one lecture five times.

Following my release from prison, *Kachanava* visited our university. I later learned that all the "protesters" had been invited to a meeting with her. It seemed that she believed her charisma could counteract the corrupting influence of the West, which she thought had affected us. However, it all ended quite comically. When students raised concerns about falsifications at their polling stations, she responded with a dismissive comment: "Well, there weren't any at mine."

In response to her phrase "Lukashenka is a great politician," I decided to ask why, with a great politician, people had such small pensions. In response to my question, *Kachanava* replied that her mother had to eat grass.

No report — no arrest

Nevertheless, the initial period after returning to university was difficult for me. My sleep was disturbed and my anxiety increased. It took me two months to "reel" from this state. I stopped attending protests due to concerns about my family, but then I joined an independent student union to continue defending my position.

As a consequence, we decided to organise a conference of independent student unions. On 5 March 2021, I and a number of other people gathered at the Imaguru business centre. I was asked to sit at the registration desk, to which I jokingly replied: "So, the riot police will tie me up first?" And so it happened. This joke became a sulf-fulfilling profecy.

When I was about to join the others upstairs, several cars pulled up to the building, and masked men got out and entered the room.

"Where are the trade unions?" they asked me, apparently mistaking me for an employee of the business centre. Deciding that this would delay them, I shrugged. After that they turned to the girl at the reception, and I ran upstairs. However, the security forces overtook me. In the end, it turned out that I ran into the hall right behind them. It was awkward: I had the feeling that I was at one with them.

"The police are working! Face the wall!"

As a result, I calmly walked around the security men and stood facing the wall along with the detainees. A little later, one of the security officials came up to me and asked:

"Were you the one who set us up?" Obviously, he meant that I "didn't know" where the trade unions were. I did not understand the prison jargon, so I was confused. As a result, he wrote down my last name from the badge.

Later we were taken to different police departments. There were interrogations. Most of the participants were released, but several people received administrative arrest.

Since there was no official detention report in my case, the lawyers advised me not to sign anything at the faculty: no report — no detention. This is what I conveyed to the administration when they asked me to provide an explanation. They told me that the document would definitely arrive, and it was better to write an explanatory note in advance. I said that when it came, then we would talk. I'm still waiting for this document.

Expulsion

This marked the beginning of the end for me at the faculty. In May, the deputy dean visited me at the dormitory and said that "from there" (she nodded upward) they had advised that it would be better for me to drop out voluntarily.

I refused and decided to sit the exams. The deputy dean assessed one of my exams, and despite my thorough preparation, he told me to retake it. Meanwhile, another student who could not even correctly name the dates of the Second World War managed to pass the exam.

For several months afterwards, I faced an epic struggle consisting of various manipulations, deceptions, and pressures. The administration used the phrase "we want to help you" to conceal their actions. Honestly, before they started 'helping', my life was fine. Eventually, I was expelled.

Around the same period, there was the so-called students' case involving my friend, who was arrested. Since only relatives were allowed to attend the court hearing, we (those who wanted to attend) came up with a life hack. We pretended to be siblings, explaining the difference in surnames by the fact that we had different fathers.

Following my expulsion, it became apparent that I would have to leave the country. And so it happened. A few months after Russia's full-scale invasion of Ukraine had begun, I left.

I have been in emigration for a year now. I long to return home, but I'm aware that we won't be able to go back to our homeland anytime soon. I continue to participate in Belarusian events and try to do everything I can to support those affected by the regime. While I feel that this is not enough, I do not lose hope. I know that history is full of surprises.

Poland, January 2024
snova_slovo@proton.me

OBSERVING ELECTIONS IN BELARUS IS DANGEROUS

Artsemi

I spent some time thinking about how to start. What can I tell people about myself? Finally, I decided to begin with my unusual name, Artsemi, which is not common in Belarus. I am from the small town of Viliejka, located in the Minsk region. While I lived and studied in this town, I often spent my free time in a nearby village, which is just a 15-minute drive away. Despite the short distance between Viliejka and the village, the atmosphere is remarkably diverse: the difference in people's perspectives is markedly tangible. As someone who values simplicity and sincerity, I found it refreshing to spend time in the village and engage with the locals. The forests and Viliejka Reservoir provide a wonderful setting for relaxation and solitude.

I attended secondary school no. 1 Logos. My desire to pursue a career in medicine prompted me to focus on biology and chemistry starting from the 8th grade. After the 9th grade exams, I had to choose a study area for the 10th and 11th grades. I opted for a physics and mathematics major. My decision surprised many, as everyone expected me to pursue medicine. However, I eventually realised that to be a doctor wasn't the right fit for me. This led me to explore new avenues. In the 10th grade, I studied technical drawing, which I enjoyed. Given my background in attending painting classes and a drawing studio since elementary school, I began to consider the option of enrolling in the Faculty of Architecture.

Lacking any family connections to this field, I sought information about exams and my future profession online. When I learned about the entrance exams required for a technical university, I recognised my knowledge gaps in this area. Therefore, from the third quarter of the 10th grade, I focused on intensive exam preparation. I regularly attended the studio, three days a week, to improve my drawing skills. In my free time, I focused on technical drawing and composition. I had a choice between Minsk and *Polack*, but I was more drawn to *Polack*, as I didn't have much confidence in my abilities. After passing my 11th grade exams in 2016, I decided to enrol at a university in Minsk. The admission process for the Faculty of Architecture involved three internal entrance exams (each with a maximum score of 100 points), plus the sum of my school certificate average and the results of centralised testing in the Russian or Belarusian language and mathematics.

For the first internal exam, I was tasked with drawing a plaster head. Unfortunately, I scored only 40 out of 100 points, which was a failure. Prior to this, I had consistently scored 70 to 80 points for this task in preparatory courses. Naturally, I was upset and started exploring alternative options. I considered the possibility of attending Belarusian State Pedagogical University if I didn't get into National Technical University (BNTU). I decided to take the next two exams. I scored 100 points in both technical drawing and composition. Despite the intense competition, with about five people vying for each place, I was accepted for the scholarship. My joy was overwhelming. Previously, I couldn't even imagine that I would be able to study in Minsk with budgetary support. It was as if a miracle had occurred.

In August 2016, I received a call from the dean's office informing me that I had been appointed leader of my group. I was thrilled to accept the role. Ours was a fantastic group. In my first semester, I made a concerted effort to excel academically. I actively participated in all conferences and various events organised by the *Belarusian Republican Youth Union* and the trade union committee of BNTU. Additionally, I served as the trade union chairperson in my first year at the Faculty of Architecture, and was later elected chairperson of the trade union bureau of the faculty at the beginning of my second year. Initially, I enjoyed social work, as we organised various events. The more I became involved in university life, the more I wanted to make a positive impact and create more comfortable conditions for students. However, I later realised that systemic changes are challenging to implement, as they often require significant time, financial resources, and a willingness to make changes. In my fourth year, I stepped down from the students' trade union committee of BNTU to focus more on myself. There were many issues that students were dissatisfied with, but we were ultimately unable to enact meaningful change due to the contradictions between the administration and the students. This became particularly evident after the 2020 elections, when the administration called in police to the university premises and reported on their own students.

My faculty was particularly "underprivileged". We didn't have our own building, as the Fifteenth Building had been closed for repairs for several years before I arrived. Instead, we studied in the Fifth Building. We were allocated an elongated, rectangular room, which was divided into five classrooms (students referred to them as "pens"). We didn't even have a toilet there — we had to use one in the main building. It was ironic that one of the most expensive faculties at BNTU, in terms of tuition fees, was forced to work in such unsuitable conditions. We were constantly fed promises that we would soon be moving to a renovated building and everything would be fine.

The pandemic

2020 was a year of surprises, starting with the Covid-19 pandemic. Students and teachers were anxiously waiting for the university's response to our safety concerns. We were waiting in vain. It was then that I realised the importance of students taking initiative and defending their rights independently.

The first Covid-19 infection in Belarus was recorded at BNTU. Initially, there was widespread panic due to the lack of understanding about the virus and how to handle it. I recall the sudden appearance of disinfectants at the university, which was a new sight. However, the supply of these items gradually stopped. After some time, statistics on infections started to circulate, showing that the actual numbers were several times underestimated. Covid-19 became a common occurrence. Despite this, students refused to tolerate the current situation. Our health was important to us. We began wearing masks and carrying our own disinfectants, as the university had already stopped providing them. At that point, I was still hoping that the university would take care of us and implement stricter safety measures if necessary. I thought the administration was gradually introducing these measures to avoid panic. However, it turned out that I was mistaken.

Protests

Before I discuss the protests in Belarus and the university, I would like to acknowledge that before 2020, I wasn't very much concerned with politics or related issues. I tried to focus on the positive aspects of everything. Even at the start of the election campaign, I didn't fully comprehend what it was about or how it worked. It was difficult for me to imagine a different government, so I was a standard observer in politics, staying on the side-lines and keeping silent. However, the 2020 presidential election was the first in which I could participate. This was something new for me.

Before the elections, I familiarised myself with the list of candidates. I knew one of them, but not the others. While living in a rented apartment on Niezaležnasci Avenue (just a three-minute walk from BNTU), I started noticing people waiting in lines to sign for presidential candidates. This was followed by the appearance of posters, police vans, and riot police. I started to explore the situation more thoroughly, trying to understand why people were taking to the streets and why the police were detaining them. Reading different news sources, I noticed significant discrepancies between the information provided by the current authorities and the opposition media. When I came across harsh propaganda, I realised that someone was lying. I continued to observe things from the side-lines until August, when I saw the mass detentions of familiar and unfamiliar people for their thoughts, words, and actions. Then I realised that a terrible injustice was happening. Although I was not well-versed in laws and human rights then, I understood that this was beyond the bounds of what was acceptable. I started thinking about how I could influence this situation. The only reasonable decision for me at that time was to register as an independent observer at the elections. I believed that I couldn't do anything else, but I was ready to see how the law was observed during the elections. I believed it was safe.

To become an independent observer, I needed to gather only ten signatures from citizens with voting rights at the polling station where I was applying. To stay informed, I started reading the news daily and monitoring the situation in the country. In my free time from work, I attended peaceful protests.

Having taken a day off from work and having obtained an observer certificate from the Belarusian Helsinki Committee, I travelled to Viliejka a week before the elections to register as an independent observer with the district election commission. This commission was responsible for collecting and tabulating voting results from the entire district, which were expected to be gathered there on 9 August after 9pm. That evening, I also registered as an observer at a polling station in a secondary school in the village of Rabuń. However, they did not immediately accept my application and the necessary signatures, as they were a little scared. They initially refused, arguing that they already had observers. After my request that they put the refusal in writing, they made a few calls to someone higher up. So I was finally registered as an observer. From Tuesday to Saturday, I was present at the polling station during early voting and counted the turnout of citizens. There were approximately 250 voters in this precinct. On average, about ten people voted each day. These were ordinary workers from collective farms and state enterprises who were forced to vote early. The turnout, which I counted, matched the figures in the ballot result reports, so I did not expect such serious violations from the commission that occurred in big cities.

One day, I did observe the commission's violation: a ballot paper was issued without an identification document. I promptly lodged a complaint to the chairman of the commission, noting all the "independent" observers and commission members were present but did not intervene. I also requested to attend the meeting on this case. Here is the spoiler: the meeting was held at 7am without my presence, with the excuse that they did not want to wake me up.

On election day, I was prohibited from being directly present at the polling station. Instead, I sat in the school hallway, counting the white signs (white bands made of various materials that were worn on the wrists of those who disagreed with the policies of the authoritarian regime). About an hour after the polling station opened, a police officer on duty at the school approached me, claiming that he had received a complaint that I was conducting surveys of citizens, which was illegal. The policeman asked me to leave the premises. In response, I inquired about the person who had made the complaint and suggested calling a different police officer to draw up a report for slander against me. After these words, the policeman left and never returned. Another policeman came to reinforce him. A deputy from the Viliejka district also appeared at the site and was present as an observer. Everything looked a little comical. By noon, the police approached me and kicked me out of the school building without explanation. I decided not to argue and left.

Around 3pm, I successfully registered as an independent observer at the secondary school no. 1 Logos in Viliejka. Yes, it was feasible! I collected signatures from voters within half an hour right in front of the school gates. The documents were accepted without issue at the polling station, but shortly after registration, I was asked to leave the building. Later, I was forcibly removed from the school premises, accompanied by several unpleasant talks with heated and threatening arguments. Without waiting for the end of the elections, I decided to head home, as I had a scheduled meeting at the district executive committee that evening in the capacity of a district independent observer.

I also served as the coordinator for observers in Viliejka district. It was a spontaneous development. In July 2020, I came across online information about the recruitment of independent observers. Later, I contacted the organisers, who invited me to become the district coordinator since Viliejka district was not yet represented in this capacity. I accepted the offer. There were over thirty polling stations in my district, but fewer than half of them had independent observers. We shared stories about the challenges we faced during registration, the threats we received from election commissions, and so on. On election day, many observers were detained, and it was unsettling to know that I could be taken away at any moment. I stayed in Viliejka for a couple of days after the election, participating in large-scale protests, unusual for our town. Seeing familiar faces and reconnecting with colleagues and friends was inspiring.

Then I left for Minsk. First, I became a member of *Viktar Babaryka*'s team, then took part in the revival of independent trade unions, and later — the BNTU strike committee. I wanted to seek justice and continue to make a difference. Initially, I was unsure where to begin, so I decided to find out what kind of support was needed for *Viktar Babaryka*'s team. Later on, I was given the opportunity to work on the revival of independent trade unions among students and teachers. Since the previous structures were outdated or ineffective, we had to start from scratch. This task was both challenging and engaging. Having experience in organisational work, I was able to adapt quickly to the new role.

Meetings with fellow students and friends at the university after the start of the academic year revealed that many of my acquaintances were dissatisfied with the election results and considered them false. As time passed, indignation grew among students across the university. A group was formed to coordinate the protests taking place at the university. Petitions, actions, and meetings became the daily activities of Belarusian students in September 2020. My involvement in this activism immediately drew attention from the university administration and law enforcement. As a result, on the night of 27-28 September, I urgently left for Ukraine. On 28 September, I became the first student expelled from BNTU and the first in Belarus to face such a consequence.

I had no plans, and my destination was nowhere, but I expected to return soon. Following my expulsion, a problem arose regarding my university documents. The administration refused to hand them over to either my authorised representatives or my lawyer. My school certificate, exam certificates, and a certificate of academic performance with grades for eight semesters were seized by law enforcement agencies as part of a criminal investigation. To this day, the whereabouts of my documents and personal data remain unknown, which hindered my ability to enrol at a foreign university.

During my time in Belarus, I chose to continue fighting for change while it was still possible and safe. It seemed that everything was moving towards the possibility of justice prevailing and power changing. And then, everything was expected to happen the way the free Belarusians, craving change, desired. The protests in Belarus were beautiful for their ideas, aesthetics, and thoughts. Following Sunday marches, I would return home with a surge of positive emotions, which lingered for a long time. I couldn't sleep as the thoughts were flooding my mind. I longed to share my thoughts, dreams, and impressions with loved ones. It was the only right choice for me at that time.

If we examine the reasons behind my actions, the main answer is that I realised I had been deceived. The truth was being hidden from me, and I faced the possibility of imprisonment for "revealing" it. I'm not talking about the entire nation, but rather my small town, where I encountered all this.

It was outrageously unfair! And the principle of justice is crucial to me. I was even more disappointed by the fact that my friends and teachers were at the heart of this deception. Those individuals who taught us in class that we should always tell the truth, be fair, and honest. Those, who corrected our mistakes with a red pen and gave us bad grades, were themselves committing a crime, while realising everything that was going on. The most important thing, however, is never to betray yourself and your students. Never to betray those who seek to bring about positive change, as they have more strength and ideas. I was unable to fathom how one could call the police on their own students. I couldn't wrap my head around it then, and I still can't now. I don't know if I'll ever be able to understand this. Certainly, there may be a hundred excuses given in response. But what these people did is detrimental not only for them, but for all of us.

It's difficult to challenge the system alone, but with many like-minded people, it became easy to make a positive impact. For the first time, I saw a huge number of Belarusians on the streets, united in their desire to change something, primarily in their lives. It was wonderful to communicate with teachers who had taught you at school or university, and honestly to discuss topics that interested both sides. It was wonderful to share your opinion and listen to theirs, grow as a person, and learn something new. For me, this moment held immense emotional and moral significance.

As I near graduation from a Polish technical university, I am looking for a job. I am focused on developing in the field of architecture and landscape design. I intend to continue participating in interesting social projects and improving people's lives. This will ultimately contribute to the growth of the New Belarus. I believe our country will eventually match the development levels of most European nations. We have a lot of areas for dynamic development, but the fact that many talented individuals have been forced to leave the country is a significant challenge for Belarus. However, I hope and look forward to the day when the world will not only admire the courage of the Belarusian people during the 2020 elections, but also their achievements in science, medicine, IT, and other fields. I wish for all of us to return home and enjoy life in our native country.

Warsaw, January 2024
artsemipopasporty@gmail.com

HOW I BECAME
A PROTEST COORDINATOR

Julija M.

"Do you think we have a chance?"
9 August 2020. Morning.
"Julija, let's go vote for *Tsikhanouskaya!*"
"Do you think we have a chance? Can anything change?"
"We ought to try. But what if?"
"Okay, let's go."

It's amusing, but that's exactly how my story began. I was studying at the Faculty of International Relations. Was I interested in politics? Of course, I was. In 2019, I even tried to engage in public life and make a change. A close friend once told me, "Julie, nothing will change in this country until thousands, hundreds of thousands of people take to the streets. And as long as people have something to drink and snack on, this won't happen." I took in these words. Who would imagine that they would be refuted.

To be honest, even on the morning of 9 August, I was sceptical. However, when we arrived at the polling station, I was astonished and inspired by what I saw. A massive line of people had formed at the precinct. Ninety percent of the crowd wore white bracelets on their arms. My hair was braided in a ponytail with a white elastic band. Without hesitation, I removed the elastic band and put it on my wrist.

We cast our ballots. The prospect that everything could change no longer seemed so illusory. Voting results from various polling stations started appearing online. There were many places where *Sviatlana Tsikhanouskaya* won by a significant margin. However, in the evening, the final results were announced — more than eighty percent had voted for Lukashenka. Everyone knew this was impossible.

Something terrible started to happen at night. My parents were away, and my sister and I were left alone in our flat in the Uručča district. The internet connection went down. The sounds of screams and explosions echoed outside our window throughout the night. Periodically, we saw large groups of uniformed security personnel rushing past our house.

The terror continued for three nights. On the next night, we saw security forces in the car park under our windows. They broke a car window, pulled a man out, and started beating him. My sister, our friends, and I watched this from our glazed and transparent balcony on the top floor. Over twenty security men crowded near our block of flats. One of them started shouting at us: "Bitches, whores, close the windows and get out of here, or we'll shoot!" We were frightened and turned off the light. Of course, we knew they wouldn't throw a stun grenade that high, so we continued to watch. Then, one of them ran to the minibus and returned with a grenade launcher. We all quickly lay down on the floor in shock. We remained in that position for over a minute until the security forces dispersed, then we returned to our room.

On the night of 11 August, motorcyclists were brutally beaten under our windows. We heard the sounds of riot police shouting and batons striking. We witnessed people lying motionless on the road, but they still continued to beat them. And we were unsure if all of them survived such atrocities.

Videos showed brutal beatings on the streets. Photos revealed the devastating consequences of torture at *Akrescina*. Victims and volunteers shared horrifying stories. There were missing friends and acquaintances. Several people were killed.

The events of August marked a point of no return. After witnessing and experiencing all that I did, it became simply impossible for me to remain uninvolved. I could no longer turn a blind eye to the situation in my home country or continue living as I had before. Attending university, doing homework, and writing my course paper felt meaningless.

Student protests

Our student protests began in August, and I was incredibly proud of my faculty, teachers, and fellow students for their active concern. Even then, we felt a unique new bond forming among us as we made our choice. This sense of unity was strong among all Belarusians, but within the student community it felt especially precious.

The first of September held much promise, and, it is worth highlighting, the students set a remarkably high standard. We showed the whole of Minsk the scale of our movement and what we were capable of achieving. Breaking through police cordons in the middle of the avenue? No problem.

But returning to university was a bit of a let-down. I walked into the German class with a red face, uneven breathing, and shifting eyes. The whole group stared at me in surprise. "Julija, why are you so late for class?"

"I was running away from the riot police," I replied. "Don't you know what's going on?"

Then I witnessed the other side of the coin. I found it absolutely impossible to comprehend how some could continue attending classes calmly, preparing for tests, and generally showing no interest in the ongoing events. A profound feeling of division had now been added to my sense of unity within the student community and the nation. There were students, who, apart from their personal concerns, were not interested in anything. They remained detached from the events and retreated into their own world. Unfortunately, there were also those who chose to inform on others. Things like this were truly creepy. Individuals were prepared to make a deal with their conscience and double-cross their fellow students, all in pursuit of a place in the ministry. I sincerely hope the informers did not imagine that their actions against those whom they had studied together with could culminate in prison sentences.

I now look at such matters with a greater sense of wisdom and calm. My experiences in recent years have better allowed me to understand people, learn to discern their true motivations, and come to the realisation that there are far fewer awful people than we commonly assume. Frequently, it is fear that drives people's actions, and they lack the strength to make the right choice.

University studies continued, but each week began with anticipation for Sunday. A black mask, sunglasses, a cap, and gloves. White paint; red paint. Don't forget to install another Telegram app on your phone. A toothbrush in your backpack, just in case. Dress more comfortably. "Mum, I'll be back soon. Don't worry, I run fast. But if I don't come back, here's a memo explaining what to do."

We sang songs, shouted chants, left drawings on the asphalt, ran from the police, and dodged shots. Then, the next day, it was back to our studies. But not everyone was able to return.

"Tell us the password, or we'll cut off your fingers"

Another Sunday in 2020. I chose not to join the march on that day, unlike some of my classmates. The city was unusually heavily militarised. This march was distinct from the previous ones. The dispersals and arrests started before people could even assemble. In the future, such tactics became a regular occurrence, but on that day, it was quite unexpected. The number of detainees reached one thousand people. I was extremely worried about my mates. At some point, one of them stopped responding.

I was overwhelmed with emotions that day. I felt a deep sense of injustice and anger. Although Vlad and I were not close friends, we shared a bond. In times of hardship, it's crucial to support one another.

Monday arrived, and as usual, we planned to attend a rally near Belarusian State University and then join the pensioners' march as a student column. However, that day was not quite ordinary. Vlad, our fellow student from the same course, had been detained the day before, and we had no information about his whereabouts, and no idea what was happening to him.

My emotions overwhelmed me, and I forgot to be cautious. During the march, I gave several interviews, came close to the minivans that accompanied us, and behaved, let's say, quite boldly.

The march passed calmly, and people began to disperse. We went through the subway, which could be considered the zeroing point, and, completely losing our vigilance, decided to grab a snack. Suddenly, I felt a hand on my shoulder. I jerked forward in surprise. With the words "Follow us, girl" they roughly grabbed me by the neck. I was still unable to see who was behind me and couldn't comprehend what was happening. Instinctively, I threw my phone onto the asphalt. My friend quickly tried to pick it up, but they pushed her away and took my phone. I tried to break free and realised that this was riot police. Several more police ran up, and the six of them carried me to the minibus. I was incredibly scared, I kicked, screamed, called for help, and I couldn't understand why no one was doing anything, why no one tried to help me.

They roughly pushed me into the minibus. A blow to my spine sent me flying to the back of the vehicle. A riot policeman approached me, threw me onto the seat, and then grabbed my neck, and forcing my head between my legs, he growled, "Face the floor, bitch." When he released me, I curled up, covering my head with my hands and begging him not to hit me.

"Please, guys, don't hit me, just don't hit me!" I cry out, completely unaware of what is going on and what awaits me.

"Last name, first name, patronymic and residential address?" asks a man in a balaclava, seated across from me, pointing the camera at my face.

"Please, let me catch my breath," I plead, "I can't speak at all, let me breathe, please".

The situation momentarily stabilised, giving me a brief moment to recover. There were six riot police officers in the minibus, also the driver and me. Two sat across from me, one beside me, while the others stood in a semicircle around us.

They started video recording my testimony. They asked my full name, address, and place of study, which was an ordinary procedure. They inquired if I had participated in the march. I replied affirmatively, explaining that I couldn't remain neutral because my friend had been arrested the previous day. They didn't comment on it in any way, they just listened to the information. I repeatedly requested to be released or allowed to contact my family, but was told that my family would be informed.

They demanded my phone password. The conversation took a very amusing turn. I began telling them that I was subscribed to all opposition sources, if that interested them. But they were not satisfied, demanding access to my correspondence and promising not to view my personal photos.

Our bickering went on for approximately five minutes. Until one of the individuals, who had remained silent throughout, spoke up:

"Bitch, tell us the password, or we'll cut off your fingers!"

"Why would you need my fingers? My Touch ID doesn't work anyway".

I have no idea how I managed to come up with such a brilliant joke in that stressful moment, but I consider it a masterpiece.

However, only one of the guys laughed. Probably because he was the only one who got it.

But in reality, I felt terrified. I had no idea where we were going and with whom. Now anything could happen to me, and then I wouldn't be able to prove it in any way, and I would be unlikely to find out who did it. I was aware that they wouldn't cut off my fingers, but breaking them or using violence of a different kind was quite in their style.

I was compelled to reveal my phone password. To be exact, I entered it myself to conceal the actual password from them. This action on my part could have had disastrous consequences, but, to my surprise, when they stumbled upon a photograph of me from the march, they cooled down. It seemed they just wanted to make sure they had caught the correct individual.

We drove to the police station, and I was handed over to other officers, along with my unlocked phone. They now had sufficient time to examine the mobile device, but even then, everything turned out fine. The police officer who communicated with me reviewed several phone conversations and then blocked my device. I breathed a sigh of relief as the panic faded away. But above all, I was deeply concerned about my family. The police still wouldn't allow me to contact them.

Fortunately, our conversation with the police department officer was quite positive. I explained to him the reasons why we attended the rallies: "We have the right to hold a different opinion and be against the current government, don't we?" "Yes, sure. But you can influence the situation through other means."

"How? The authorities do not issue permits for rallies, and opposition candidates are barred from elections. What options are there?"

"Well… You could propose amendments to the Constitution, for instance."

Our conversation was cut short by the major, who brought in a detained guy. The major was outraged by the fact that I was seated on a chair: "What kind of arrogant posture is this? Get up now and face the wall!" The guy I stood next to looked scared.

"Is everything fine?"

"No."

Later, when we were being transported to *Akrescina* in the same vehicle, the guy said that in the minibus, he had been beaten with a stun gun.

And prior to that, they took me to the police station for inspection. It was an assembly hall in which a young girl and I were left alone. We started talking. It emerged that she was also a third-year student at Belarusian State University, at the Faculty of Law. With sympathy in her voice, she asked how many of "our guys" were detained on that particular day. I don't believe she genuinely wanted to be there. At least I hope not. But the circumstances were very amusing. It reflects well the division in society that I have written about earlier.

Following that, I experienced an endless five hours in solitary confinement within the police department. There was only a concrete ledge in the wall, upon which I tried in vain to find a comfortable position and lie down. My mind was consumed with thoughts about my family and what was happening outside during that time. Additionally, I was also deeply worried about the possibility of being expelled from the university or failing to complete my course paper on time, should I be incarcerated for days. It would be a shame to drop out like this, after dedicating four years to studying.

We were transported to *Akrescina* in a patrol vehicle. I was travelling with the guy who had been struck with a stun gun, a police officer, and a traffic officer. The journey was rather positive, and the officers even offered their personal phones so we could call our loved ones.

"Mum, hello! Everything is alright, I'm almost at *Akrescina*!"

How absurd these words sounded. I was being transported to a location notorious for torturing people, yet we found solace in the situation. Well, at the very least, it provided some certainty. After such a journey in a minibus accompanied by individuals clad in black, things could have been worse.

Meanwhile, no one still knew where Vlad was.

Who will provide medical care and go out on calls — no one cares any more

Once at *Akrescina*, I was placed in a four-person cell, where four young women, all doctors by profession, were already present. The atmosphere was very amicable, and I introduced myself to them. They kindly gave me some bread and water. Unfortunately, those were the only provisions available. Shortly after, a lecturer from Belarusian State University was brought in to join our company.

On the subsequent day, we faced our trial. The proceedings took place at the temporary detention facility on *Akrescina* Street, where we were already being held. We were escorted into small office spaces, each with a staff member present to monitor us, and we sat before laptops to engage with the judge through Skype. Amazing! Yet, that was the Covid-19 situation.

What happened at the trial could be compared to a poorly rehearsed circus stunt. After all the formalities were completed, the judge invited a witness to testify. According to the stories shared by the other women, witnesses connected to the call online, whereas in my situation, the witness was already located within the temporary detention centre on Akrescina Street. He entered the office, and, adopting a commanding tone, directed me to stand facing the wall with my hands behind my back, and then seated himself in my place. They have intriguing arrangements there. No one even paid attention to the witness's actions towards me.

The man identified himself as an employee of the Ministry of Internal Affairs. His answers to the judge's questions were ambiguous, lacking in details. It was clear that he had never seen me before, just as I had never seen him. The judge asked him to describe me and the distinguishing features by which I was identified during my arrest. Instead of looking at me and describing what I was wearing (which was the only clothing I had at the time), he began detailing the items I supposedly possessed (bag, cap, protest insignia). I requested the judge to examine the inventory report of my belongings, which did not contain any information about these alleged items, but she apparently appeared uninterested. Perhaps it was due to such a stupid witness that her conscience prevented her from sentencing me to fifteen days. However, her conscience was sufficiently clear to impose a twelve-day sentence.

After the trial, I was even granted the chance to talk to my father. The verdict left me somewhat stunned, as, frankly speaking, I had been anticipating a fine. I also asked my dad to purchase a course paper for me.

A few hours later, I finally comprehended the reality of the situation and came to terms with it. On the whole, the circumstances did not seem all that dire. Spending twelve days in the company of fascinating and intelligent people could potentially be a great experience. The doctors and teachers provided us with lectures and shared unusual stories, while I came up with different games to amuse my fellow women. And we could talk about the current situation indefinitely. Everyone shared their arrest stories, each one unique in its own way. I remember the doctors recounting how they stood in the police department courtyard. There were approximately sixty people. A police officer asked if there were doctors among the detainees, to which he received a unanimous affirmative answer from everyone present.

"What, all are doctors here?"
"Yes."

Hope we win soon

Sometime later, it turned out that my close friend's grandmother was being held in the neighbouring cell. While she was imprisoned there, her husband died. She is a wonderful woman, and a professional in her area of expertise. She helped many during this time. I'm not sure that the doctors assigned to places like temporary detention centres or pre-trial detention facilities necessarily have at least some medical expertise nor that they arrive at work in a sober condition.

The day following the trial, our cell received about ten new occupants. The women looked very emaciated and exhausted. Prior to their arrival at the temporary detention centre, they had spent three days in *Žodzina*. During the initial two days there, they were given only bread; it was not until the third day's evening that they were served normal food.

We were among the fortunate ones to have guards who treated the detainees at the protests with kindness. It's possible that our pleasant and positive manners made it difficult for them to treat us differently. Back then, it was still possible to receive packages from relatives, and one of the guards brought me a bag from my parents. While we checked the parcel's contents against the list, we talked about unrelated topics and joked. Our conversation lasted for about fifteen minutes.

"You know, I really hope that we will win soon."
"Julija, I really hope so too."

This was the security officer's response. His tone was genuinely sincere and empathetic. Throughout my experience, he was not the only person within the system that I encountered who did not support the government but remained there to serve it. While I do not condemn them, I also do not support their actions. I understand why they made their choice and do not want to harbour resentment towards them. I sincerely hope that these people are working to undermine the system, do good, and help those they are forced to confront. I hope, when they have to make a choice again on day X, they will choose the right path.

Everything else can be resolved

I would like briefly to describe the remaining days. On the fourth day, before being transferred to the detention centre for offenders, new girls were brought in and told us about the death of Raman Bandarenka. This news shocked everyone; we were completely unable to understand how such a tragedy could happen during peaceful protests.

We only spent a few hours at the detention centre for offenders before being transferred to *Baranavičy*. During the journey, we even managed to reconnect with our relatives.

We only spent a few hours at the detention centre for offenders before being transferred to *Baranavičy*. During the journey, we even managed to reconnect with our relatives. We were met with shouts: "Hands behind your back! Keep your head straight, look down, don't turn your head! Run! Run faster, fuck you!" And we ran in sneakers without laces, with bags on our backs, to the prison guards' shouts. Then it seemed that it would be very scary here. And what cells awaited us! The atmosphere of a medieval castle dungeon reigned in *Baranavičy*. Political prisoners were kept in the old building. It seemed that, apart from the windows, nothing had been changed in these cells since the 1950s. The rough concrete floor, crumbling plaster on the walls, and iron beds. Mildew covered every surface, and everything appeared dirty, dilapidated, and rusted. There was also a severe lack of space. The cell designed for eight people contained four bunk beds, a table, benches, a toilet in the form of a hole in the floor, and a washbasin. The area of the cell was no larger than twenty square metres. The conditions were utterly inhumane.

Yet even in those conditions, we found ways to spend our time meaningfully. We shared our stories, composed and sang songs, crafted items from bread, read books, and solved crossword puzzles. We even received letters. God, how wonderful it was to receive letters! It was like a breath of fresh air — the news from freedom. When you are in prison and do not receive any information from the outside, you very quickly get the feeling that life is passing by somewhere without you, and everyone has forgotten about you. That's why receiving letters is incredibly important: it gives you strength. The guards didn't pay much attention to us; we could sleep during the day and go about our daily activities. The 8 days in *Baranaviču* passed quietly.

Although only twelve days had passed, readjusting to life outside was disorienting and difficult to comprehend. My family and friends met me, and during the journey home, we had a lot to discuss. On the way home, we called Vlad. At first, I was upset with him for not coming to meet me. However, it turned out that Vlad had endured more than I had: he suffered several injuries from rubber bullets, a concussion, and a closed head injury. During his imprisonment, he contracted Covid-19 and had a high fever. One day, his condition was so severe that he lost consciousness and hurt himself against the table in his cell.

This is how it was, my fourth year at university. I also fell ill with Covid-19 while in prison. And it was very difficult to return to my studies due to all the challenges. I needed time to recover, return to a normal routine, and overcome the lasting fear. It was difficult to concentrate on my studies when my thoughts were consumed by the awareness that every day ordinary people were suffering behind bars, their loved ones were suffering for their sake even more, and life had come to a standstill for them.

Though I was able to complete my studies, my life underwent significant changes after that experience. When you've been there [behind bars], you start to approach problems with a different perspective: being alive and free, with your loved ones also alive and free, is what truly matters, and everything else can be resolved. In fact, my life became somewhat happier until they came for me again on 19 February 2022.

Warsaw, July 2023
julija2001.mmm@gmail.com

I DO NOT CONSIDER THIS TIME WASTED

Maria

I am Maria, a former student of the Belarusian State Academy of Arts, where I studied in the Faculty of Design and Decorative and Applied Arts. At the Department of Industrial Design, my focus was on the design of industrial and household products. My field of study was Exhibition Design, which encompasses project conception and all stages of its development, such as choosing materials, designing, and determining colour and aesthetic solutions for small to medium-sized architectural forms. Exhibition design is not limited to exhibitions and museums; it encompasses a vast array of everyday objects that surround us, including bus stops, shops, shop windows, galleries, street lighting, and children's playgrounds. I thoroughly enjoyed my studies, the teachers, and the atmosphere at the faculty. We stayed in the classroom late into the evening; we ordered food delivery and prepared our projects for presentation. The teachers were understanding of our needs. Studying was challenging and time-consuming, as most of the programme was focused on developing a comprehensive project. The teachers encouraged creativity by not restricting our imagination, which resulted in interesting and bold solutions.

The Academy at the time of elections

The Academy I attended had a student body of just 1,400, whereas Belarusian National Technical University had 28,000 students. By

Belarusian standards, the Academy was a prestigious institution, where the high level of competition meant some applicants had to apply several times before being admitted. I was only successful on my second try. Upon completing my studies, I planned to further my career in product design and find employment in this field.

In 2020, I entered my fourth year and started combining my studies with activism. I must admit that I do not have a profound knowledge of the history of our Motherland. My family never had the habit of listening to TV opinions or getting news from state media only, so I also preferred to get information from different sources. The protest sentiment among the people began to emerge in May 2020, as the presidential election campaign began and the first arrests occurred. The evening of 9 August 2020 marked a pivotal turning point, with mass protests erupting as a response from citizens to the actions of security forces against those who disagreed with the falsification of election results. I believe many felt a sense of responsibility for the country's future, and the shared goal motivated people to protest repeatedly.

After the systematic mass detentions, the protest movement began to take on a more hybrid format. In addition to the large-scale Sunday marches, new forms of protest emerged, including women's marches, pensioners' marches, medical solidarity chains, neighbourhood actions, factory worker actions, and student protest initiatives. IT specialists were not silent either.

Prior to 2020, studies were quite engaging and did not have any "political tension," although some of the students' works contained implicit political messages. But with the start of the academic year and the first protests, the majority of students and teachers came together in solidarity to rally against the backdrop of the overall situation, attempting to support each other. Despite the hostility of some Academy employees towards the protesters, many students expressed their reflections through art and projects. The Academy's administration reacted aggressively, forcing them to remove these works from summer internship displays. Despite the displeasure shown by the rector's office, our students, along with representatives from other universities, stood in chains of solidarity every day, sang songs, and fought back with dignity in disputes with the regime supporters. The rector and vice-rector frequently summoned students for preventive conversations, which often included threats of expulsion and conscription into the army. In September 2020, the security forces' response to student marches was particularly brutal, with students increasingly being detained and added to lists of the arrested.

The student protest movement became more organised over time. After a month of regular mass detentions, student activists, of which I was a part, created university chats and Telegram channels where we could discuss the situation at our university and in the country more broadly. This helped establish ongoing communication. The coordination effort was successful, as the number of student arrests decreased. The chats discussed the format of legal actions, the general situation at the university, student detentions and expulsions, and the possibility of providing financial or legal assistance to the expelled students. I found this activity to be gratifying. Many students offered to help put up leaflets and stickers, and assisted in compiling lists of those who had been repressed. Protests and actions took place at other universities in Minsk and across the regions. However, when mass expulsions began, no one knew how to respond effectively. There were attempts to challenge the cases of expulsions, but they ultimately led nowhere. At the start of the academic year, universities introduced the position of vice-rector for security, which was filled by KGB officers. One of their responsibilities was to summon students for "preventive conversations." After issuing expulsion orders, they could then hand the student a summons to the army. New clauses and provisions were introduced in the regulatory documents governing mass events, including a ban on photo and video filming, which contravened fundamental rights and lacked legal justification. This period of three months saw regular student actions, expulsions, and threats.

Arrest

I was detained on 12 November 2020. As I was leaving my home to attend classes, several men approached me from behind. One of them presented his KGB officer ID and informed me that I was detained as a suspect, requiring me to return home so that they could carry out a search. After a lengthy and thorough search, the officers announced that I was under arrest. During the drive, we had a brief conversation about politics. They showed me the text of the Criminal Code, from which I understood that I was accused under Article 342, part 1: "Organisation of group actions that grossly violate public order and involve obvious disobedience to the legal demands of government officials or lead to disruption of the work of institutions." The KGB officer pointed his finger to the phrase "up to three years" prescribed in the text of this article. They asked me for my parents' phone numbers to notify them of my whereabouts. As it turned out afterwards, no one actually contacted my parents.

A few days later, while in the KGB pre-trial detention centre, I learned that there were twelve people involved in the so-called students' case. My cell held three female students who were part of this case. The conditions were deplorable — instead of a toilet, there was only a bucket in the cell that had to be emptied twice a day. The pre-trial detention centre officers peered through the peephole every couple of minutes, making it challenging to wash or use the toilet. Since our relatives were unaware of our location, for the first five days we had only the issued mug, soap, and half a roll of toilet paper. The staff did not respond to our question "What time is it?", so we had to rely on the bells of the nearby church, which rang three times a day. Apart from the sound of the bells, there was complete silence. The silence was so profound that it seemed like there were only three of us in the entire pre-trial detention centre. It was strictly forbidden to speak loudly; you had to say your last name very quietly. The only indication of other prisoners' presence was the garbage bags behind each cell door. Staying in the KGB pre-trial detention centre, we slept most of the time, and only woke up for breakfast, lunch, dinner, a walk, and investigative activities.

After eight days, we were transferred to Pre-trial Detention Centre no. 1, where we found many more political prisoners. Letters started arriving, and we had access to a TV. This made it easier mentally. The environment reminded me of a dormitory, but with a strict regime. We talked with the other students involved in the so-called students' case while reviewing the materials of our criminal case. When the trial began, we attended the hearings from morning until 6-8pm. We were thirsty and argued with the escort, as we were forbidden to bring water with us; they claimed there was tap water available in the toilet. After twenty-one court hearings that lasted for two months, the sentence was announced — 2 years and 6 months in prison. Before being taken back to the pre-trial detention centre, we all hugged and agreed to reunite in freedom. It was a very touching moment. Then I waited for the appeal in the *Homiel* pre-trial detention centre. The verdict was left unchanged.

The colony

It was not possible to communicate with everyone in the colony, as the prisoners worked in two shifts, with little overlap in schedules. Immediately after arriving at the colony, I was put on preventive registration, allegedly for a "tendency towards extremism and other destructive activities". This meant I had to wear a yellow tag. Throughout my entire term, I was transferred between six different detachments. According to the colony staff, this was done for "educational purposes". Special conditions with additional restrictions are created there for "extremists" in contrast to prisoners with ordinary criminal charges. Political prisoners are only allowed one day of extended visits, while other inmates receive two or three days.

For political prisoners, provocations are often staged with the help of other inmates to justify punishments like isolation in a punishment cell or deprivation of parcels and visits. Even minor infractions, like an undone button (violation of the uniform code), passing cigarettes, food, personal hygiene items, or any other item to fellow prisoners, can result in punishment. This behaviour is strictly prohibited in the colony — it is regarded as alienation or appropriation. Sometimes, they would plant needles and pills, sew them into clothes, or pour water into shoes. The colony administration deliberately creates a toxic environment, not only for political prisoners, but also for those who support them. The guards enjoy pitting the convicts against each other in order to make the conditions as uncomfortable as possible — the underlying belief being that "the prisoner must constantly suffer".

A lot of inmates in the colony have a strong dislike for "extremists". Despite the fact that many prisoners are themselves victims of the judicial system, regardless of the crime committed, they support the authoritarian regime. This is often the case even when the conviction was accompanied by violations of the Criminal Procedure Code. It seems to me that the judicial system embodies the core nature of the current regime in the country. Following the outbreak of the war, relations in the colony became highly tense, exacerbated by the inmates' exposure to state-controlled television. There are no alternative media channels available for viewing in the colony. The political prisoners would discuss the topic of the war quietly and only amongst themselves. We constantly talked about the news, the war, and the arrests, which led the staff to refer to us as a "group of interests". Political prisoners always maintained a distance from those convicted under conventional criminal charges. Regularly communicating with fellow political prisoners convicted for their civic position was a source of strength for me. Within our "yellow circle", there was always an atmosphere of sisterhood and mutual support.

Despite the fact that our expectations and hopes did not fully materialise, I believe it is impossible, in just three years, to dismantle a system that has been built over decades and has deeply entrenched roots. The repressive system has uprooted and exterminated any dissent. I believe that Belarusians should not think that everything was in vain, as this is precisely the mood that the illegitimate government of Belarus seeks to create. I genuinely hope that I will be able to return to Belarus soon without fear for my safety and without facing discrimination due to my criminal record. At present, there are nearly two thousand recognised political prisoners in Belarus, who, from day to day, lose their precious time, which could be spent with their family and friends. Now they live only on faith and hope that everything will come to an end soon, and they will be released. It was extremely difficult for me to bid farewell to my friend who had been by my side throughout the whole journey. She is the mother of two children, whose father is also imprisoned. My friend has always supported and protected me. Despite the significant age difference, our friendship remained strong. The repressive measures against political prisoners are becoming more severe, aimed at isolating them from the outside world. Since parting, I have received just a birthday card from my friend, and her children can only communicate with their mother ten minutes a month via a video call. The thought of my friends in the colony gives me the strength I need now, prevents me from forgetting the many wonderful people who are unjustly deprived of their freedom, and reminds me why I must continue to fight.

It appears to me that the primary reason for our detention was the suppression of student protests. I have a strong suspicion that mass student activism is now impossible in Belarus. The repression against students has numerous negative consequences. One of them is the significant decrease in university applicants after 2020, indicating students' reluctance to receive education in Belarus. The indictment against us stated that student protests led to a decline in the reputation of a number of Belarusian universities. However, the reality is that a university's reputation suffers due to the reluctance of the educational institution staff to address either student problems or socio-political issues.

Belarusians do not give up

During my time in the pre-trial detention centre and the colony, I found very close friends with whom I endured many hardships together. I believe that it is in difficult times that truly strong friendships can be born. Therefore, and for a number of other reasons, I do not consider this time wasted. Now, I have a strong desire to participate in Belarus' public life, to maintain communication with Belarusians inside and outside the country. To achieve this, we need to help ensure that Belarus remains a prominent issue on the agenda. It is important to continue promoting its culture and language. We must remind those in exile why they left, and not allow the democratic forces of Belarus to forget what they fought for.

I was released from prison 30 November 2022, after fully serving my sentence. Twenty days later, I left Belarus for Lithuania, where I have been living for the past six months. I am now preparing to study at the Vilnius Academy of Arts, as I want to obtain an education that I did not have the chance to complete in Belarus, because I was expelled on the day of my arrest. Being a student is an important milestone for me that can help guide the direction of my future life.

While living in Lithuania, I have managed to meet numerous Belarusians. Despite often hearing about a sense of fatigue resulting from the perceived lack of progress in the struggle, people persist in their efforts to confront the regime. The majority of them are employed in Belarusian media, NGOs, or are involved in volunteer work. They claim that this activity helps them not to lose sight of Belarus. I am heartened to see that despite the pervasive fatigue and burnout, people persist in their fight. I would very much like to continue my activist work to assist Belarusians who have suffered under the regime because of their views. I dream that our friends, someone's parents, children, brothers and sisters will be able to return home, and that all Belarusians forced to leave will have the opportunity to go back without fear of detention, and with the chance to experience freedom.

Vilnius, 01.2024
mashara259@gmail.com

THE WAY

Uladzimir D.

The protests that swept across Belarus in the aftermath of the August 2020 presidential election marked a defining stage in the country's history. As a person who experienced these protests directly, I can confidently state that they had a profound impact on my life. In this essay, I would like to share my personal story about the strong influence these events had on me.

The beginning of the story

It is crucial to comprehend the expectations of the Belarusian people when they went to the polls on 9 August 2020. For a long time everyone had known that there were no fair elections in Belarus, and the president could not be changed through a simple vote. All previous elections had ended in the same way. Did the Belarusians believe that the regime would change as a result of these elections? No one had prepared people for the protests and resistance to the law enforcement agencies, but each presidential candidate managed to "sell" the idea that significant changes would occur quickly. And some voters genuinely believed that they could influence the election outcome. I recall a fellow student who tried to persuade our group to participate in collecting signatures for candidates. I thought it was very naive, so I criticised the idea. What is the point? Why are we even discussing the elections? My answer was quite prosaic: the elections became an incentive for the regime to show its teeth. The regime had long operated without fear of punishment for its crimes, emboldened by the confidence in its own strength. The 2020 elections merely provided another opportunity for the regime to showcase its cynicism and cruelty.

The evening of election day was the most terrifying for Belarusian citizens, as they witnessed the true nature of the cynical authorities, which would not spare anyone. The main rule of the leader of any pack is that showing weakness is unacceptable, as it would invite a stronger leader to take over. On 9 August, a nationwide manhunt began. It was a people hunt! There were no longer any distinctions between "us" and "others"; it was now only "me and you", only "my strength" and "your vulnerability".

Beatings? Good!
Resuscitation ward? Even better!
Murder? No question!
Children, women, old people? What's the difference?

What could I feel witnessing all this? I watched and cried, just cried. There was no space for other emotions like anger or rage. There were only tears. These were human beings! I realised that all Belarusians were prisoners, with the only difference being the type of regime.

My path is not paved with sun and flowers

August. Protests occurred every day. At home, my mother worried and urged us to stay put. Must I do something? If I must, then what? Where could I find the answers to this? I had a huge number of questions overwhelming me, until I focused on the one that mattered most: how would I face my children in the future? In that moment, my doubts dissipated. I got dressed and went to join the rally in the city centre. There was no turning back. Once I embarked on this path, there would be no return. I recognised that anything could happen to me and my family. Fear was pervasive. Fortunately, I became afraid of the fear itself. This realisation was the only thing that truly helped me. One must be prepared for any potential consequences — arrest, interrogation, even death. Only then can you be certain that you are in control of the situation, rather than the situation controlling you. Prepare memos for relatives and colleagues with instructions for various occasions, so they can quickly orient themselves and avoid missteps. You must always remember your girlfriend — you cannot set her up. Maintain hope that your love will endure these tumultuous times.

Back in August 2020, it became evident that universities would become the battleground for future conflicts. It was obvious that it would not work without sacrifices. It was important not to show the white feather, it was important to save face, it was important to protect people. I had planned to become a scholar, but now I had to postpone those ambitions — such is the cost of the struggle. That is how your path shifts from scholarly pursuits to civic activism.

We are recording a video appeal to stop the violence in the country. Now, we are in the hands of the administration — both students and staff. On 26 October 2020, *Sviatlana Tsikhanouskaya* announces a national strike. Will it make sense? Shall I participate or not? The doubts swirl in my head. It remains only to support it, because this is a red line. If nothing works, the protest will come to an end.

Consequences

Every action has its consequences. There is a time to scatter stones and a time to collect stones. The red line has been crossed. Surprisingly, the administration is willing to start negotiations, but you cannot trust their words. The dean approaches me. I realise that a cross has been placed on my dream of becoming a Belarusian scholar. What, just expulsion? And that's all? A summons to the military enlistment office? They are prolonging conscription for our sake? Leave or stay? Is everyone leaving? Do I need to leave too? Is there any significance in this? What can I do there? Will I adequately assess the situation in the country when I am in Poland? Does this mean I have given up?

Information about blacklists has surfaced, and the authorities are not hiding it. Now, no one on this list can live peacefully in Belarus. One must forget about studies and work, as the only thing left is to wait for arrest. Doubts and more doubts. I must continue my studies, but I cannot cease fighting. I have to stay, for I am a fighter and have already taken this road. Arrests are starting to occur all around.

12 November 2020 marks "Black Thursday", when active students are arrested. I manage to avoid arrest, which I attribute to my caution. The arrests continue, and the exit is sometimes opened, and then closed. I believe they are trying to intimidate me. They are pressuring me to leave, but suddenly they impose a ban on leaving the country. Military conscription is extended again, and

everyone is taken into the army indiscriminately, without considering illnesses or contraindications. I must cling to any opportunity that arises. If I join the army, I do not know what will happen to me there. I might suddenly be sent to Piečy, where the reports of military personnel suicides are record breaking. It might happen that one's illnesses help you in life, which, however, the military enlistment office disregards. I undergo the medical examination twice, with the involvement of the State Security Committee. A genetic condition ultimately saves me from the army. To be able to battle the military enlistment office for six months is a true feat. Or is it a miracle?

The defeat of the protest is becoming more and more evident. And after defeat, there is always a chase. I must endure this moment. Perhaps I should go away for a while? I have been offered a one-year study programme in Germany — that suits me perfectly. Can I leave? Will they catch me at the border? I need to plan everything carefully. I am departing by a night bus to Ukraine. If I am arrested at the border, other people will know. On the same day, I am flying from Boryspil to Frankfurt. I have orchestrated my own escape. But have I truly escaped?

I believe in fairy tales, in happiness, and in miracles!

When you are safe, there is time for reflection. You start thinking about all the events, about friends, about people's actions. On the one hand, we have a picture where hundreds of thousands of Belarusians unite against the dictatorship and violence, but on the other hand, you understand that this is not enough. 500,000 out of 9 million? For the present moment, it is a substantial number, of course. But what next? The Soviet legacy has a profound influence on people, particularly that very indifference. Indifferent people are not our enemies, as they will not support the authorities, but they are not our friends either, as they will not help us. Could the protest have ended successfully with 500,000 protesters? It is impossible to predict with certainty, and fortune-telling is a futile endeavour. However, several objective factors suggest that a successful outcome was unlikely from the start.

Where were our political leaders? Viktar Babaryka was arrested; *Valery Tsepkalo* had left the country long before the elections; and *Sviatlana Tsikhanouskaya* was forced to leave Belarus under pressure after the elections. Who was there to negotiate with, to follow? How was the protest coordinated? The protest was chaotic, with no clear leadership. Gradually, the information space was captured by the *Nexta* Telegram channel, which does not represent an expert, political, or real mass community. During the entire first month of protests, when the regime was at its weakest, there were no clear political leaders, and a Telegram channel from Poland took their place. Was it possible to expect success in such a situation?

    The Coordination Council was formed. It meant to become a platform for dialogue. However, this occurred only a month after the protests, when the regime had already started the process of repression in society and in its own institutions. What was wrong with the show of force? Who would organise a show of force, and how would one resist an armed military force? It's no secret that Russian troops were stationed in Smolensk. Did we want to repeat the 2014 scenario of eastern Ukraine?

    Consequently, it turns out the 2020 protest was most likely doomed. One can assert with confidence that the probability of the regime's fall in 2020 was low. However, it is necessary to make the most of every opportunity, which the Belarusians did. Belarusisation after 2020 is simply astonishing: people are showing great interest in the rich heritage of Belarus — its history, culture, and language. This is a significant achievement, given that Belarusian is on the list of endangered languages. If Belarusians lack a linguistic identity, then why do we need Belarus at all? And what follows? From defeat to triumph? The high demand for Belarusian schools and clubs outside Belarus is a testament to the success of Belarusisation. Parents want to raise their children in a Belarusian environment. Even political actors in exile are starting to switch to the Belarusian language, which underscores their connection to the audience.

From defeat to triumph?..

"Our memory treads forest partisan paths, which could not overgrow in the people's fate" (Song lyric from the band Piesniary). What fate awaits us? What will happen to Belarus? Will it be independent? As sad as it is to acknowledge, the last century has shown us that Belarus has repeatedly failed in its quest for independence and neutrality. The West lacks the awareness of Belarus' significance. Belarus was left to be consumed by Russia a long, long time ago.

No matter how much the politicians talked about the support from Western countries, it was they who ultimately sold Ukraine to Russia by failing to block the "Nord Stream" and the Russian equivalent of SWIFT for financial transactions. This was a message to Putin that he could do whatever he wanted. As the war in Ukraine started, all the ambassadors fled and urged Volodymyr Zelenskyy to flee. In the early days, there was no international response. It wasn't until widespread protests across Europe that the policy shifted.

Europeans often fail to recognise the differences between Belarusians and Russians. We must rely on our own efforts, as even Ukrainians have a negative perception of Belarusians due to the country's role in the Russian invasion. Furthermore, some shelling of Ukrainian territory took place from Belarusian territory. Can we understand our southern neighbours? This is a challenging question. On the one hand, what can be the basis for dialogue when bombs are falling? However, there is another perspective, and it is encapsulated in one question: "What did you do to prevent this from happening?"

Who was the second main investor in the Belarusian economy after Russia in 2021?
— Ukraine!
Who, besides Russia, bought the *MAZ* buses?
— Ukraine!
Who played poker with Lukashenka?
— Ukraine!
Why was Lukashenka's support rating so high in Ukraine before the war? Why did Ukrainians call Lukashenka baćka (Daddy)?

It's always easier to identify the guilty parties. Why acknowledge mistakes? This is especially noteworthy against the background of the significant number of Belarusians fighting for Ukraine and numerous Belarusian organisations providing aid to Ukrainian refugees. Belarusians abroad are being viewed as accomplices of the aggressors, even those who were forced to flee their homeland. Meanwhile, those very countries that profess freedom, equality, and non-discrimination don't want to see them now.

The Belarusian people have withstood countless trials of the past centuries, which is why they will also endure now. We must stop relying on our powerful neighbours and instead become stronger ourselves, taking control of our own destiny. We are a resilient people who have always survived; this happened exclusively through our struggles. If we cease to fight, Belarus will cease to exist.

Me

Has my outlook on life changed after the protests? Have these events exerted a strong impact on my life? Regrettably, these occurrences have affected my outlook in such a way that it erodes my faith in people more with each passing day. One could attribute this to overly high expectations, but my expectations were not particularly lofty to begin with.

As for the impact on my life, it is only a speck compared to how the year 2020 affected Belarus. I can't go back home. Far from everyone in Germany welcomes me with open arms. I'm here on my own — without family, and without relatives. I don't have a defined legal status, and I haven't completed my university education. My career path as a scientist is now a distant memory. All these are drastic changes in my life. But, sorry, who said it would be easy? This was my choice, and I alone am accountable for it.

Conclusion

The year 2020 marked a pivotal turning point in the history of Belarus and in my own life. In many ways, the outcome was already evident within the first month of the protests. However, the unexpected cultural revolution demonstrated the Belarusian people's strong desire to transform their lives. Living under the harsh rule of a dictatorship, one is never truly free, as it is akin to existing in a prison. You can either fight for your home or seek a new one. This is the path to breaking free from the shackles that have held us captive for centuries. We must rely solely on our own strength if we wish to secure freedom for ourselves and our children. It is crucial to view things objectively and not make unrealistic plans. In this world, everything has a price, so you have to make a choice and sacrifice something. The struggle is meaningless if it does not carry any values.

Germany, June 2023
clever-20@mail.ru

AFTERWORD

The Future of an Independent, Democratic, and European Belarus Belongs to the Youth

Pavel Latushka

Deputy Head of the United Transitional Cabinet of Belarus, Head of the National Anti-Crisis Management, former Minister of Culture, Ambassador

I remember a story from the 2020 protests. Near one of the buildings of the Belarusian State University in Minsk, students took to the streets with white-red-white flags. Soon, security forces attacked the students. Trying to escape arrest, the young people ran away, but the security forces managed to catch a few of them. When a nearby professor saw this, he defended the students by stepping between them and the security forces, preventing the detention. The students managed to escape, but instead, the professor was detained. With his head held high, in a suit, unbroken. The professor who stood up for his students and their right to freedom of speech.

AFTERWORD

This story vividly illustrates the events of 2020 — events that were unique not only for our country but for all of Europe. All layers of Belarusian society, representatives of various professions and social groups united. Pensioners, workers, actors, and doctors marched with a shared sense of solidarity... They united to express their disagreement with violence, repression, and lawlessness — things that contradict a civilised society. People stood against lies, inhumanity, and crimes. Belarusian students were at the forefront of these events. During those fateful events, Belarusians were extremely proud of the Belarusian student community. We saw ambitious people who cared about the future of the country, the future of Belarus.

On the other hand, we also witnessed the atrocities committed by the regime against Belarusians. The machine of repression, which the regime unleashed in order to preserve its own power, touched the students as well. Young people — our young political prisoners — are still held in Belarusian prisons, imprisoned for their desire for a better future. Today, the youngest political prisoners are 18 years old... And they are in urgent need of support — we must remember them. Depriving the student community of freedom means depriving the country of its future. Repressing students means repressing those who will be responsible for the future of our country. Excluding young people from socio-political life today can lead to serious social consequences tomorrow. Dictatorial regimes fail to understand this, as they are primarily focused on preserving their own power — here and now. They do not realise the consequences their actions today may have in the future.

When the authorities violate the freedom of opinion of students, they commit a crime against the entire society. It is a crime against youth, against the future, and against the very idea of education. Education is not just a collection of knowledge; it is a key to self-realisation and to building a future life. The student community has a fundamental academic right to express its own views, including political ones. Limiting this right turns universities into places of ideological control rather than free spaces for the development of science, education, and research — places where there is no room for the free exchange of ideas. After all, it is freedom that acts as a catalyst for development.

Political prisoner students are the imprisoned future of the country because when the government detains students, it deprives itself of their new ideas, new talents, and new leaders. Students are the future scientists, engineers, and inventors. Persecuting them deprives the country of innovative development.

The socio-political events that began in 2020 are still ongoing. After the authorities' atrocities, we passed the point of no return. The thousands of political prisoners, the «student cases» and the shattered lives and futures — these will not remain without consequences. In time, these actions will be given the proper legal evaluation. We continue the struggle. We continue our work of documenting the regime's crimes. Accountability is inevitable.

And we remember and know: the future belongs to Belarusian youth. The future that will come in an independent, democratic, and European Belarus.

30 August 2024

GLOSSARY

80 percent
A meme referring to the 80% of votes awarded to Aleksander Lukashenka in every presidential election.

Akrescina
A large detention centre on Akrescina Lane in Minsk. It has become synonymous with the regime's cruelty towards political prisoners.

AMAP
A Belarusian abbreviation for riot police.

Amierykanka
A colloquialism for the KGB prison in Minsk. Literally means 'an American'.

Article 23.34
Article 23.34 of the Republic of Belarus Code of Administrative Infringements, titled "Infringement of the procedure for organising or holding mass events," has been used to prosecute thousands of protesters.

Azot
A large chemical plant in Hrodna.

Babaryka, Viktar
A political prisoner and former banker once known for significant investments in Belarusian arts. In 2020, he announced his intention to run in the presidential elections. The Election Commission rejected his application. He and his son, Eduard, were detained on 18 June 2020. Viktar Babaryka was sentenced to fourteen years of imprisonment.

Basic unit
A measure for state-regulated fines and other fees in Belarus. Its monetary value is regularly reviewed in line with inflation.

Belarusisation
A practice or policy aimed at reviving the Belarusian language and promoting Belarusian culture.

Baranavičy
A city in central Belarus, a large railway hub.

Belgazprombank
A Belarus-based bank controlled by Russian conglomerate Gazprom. Viktar Babaryka was Chair of its Management Board from 2000 to 2020.

Domino's
A fast food chain; protesters often hid from riot police in shops and restaurants.

Dormitory
Halls of residence for students. In Belarus, dormitories are routinely allocated as rewards for obedience and may also serve as venues for indoctrination.

BNTU
Belarusian National Technical University.

Braslaŭ
A town in northern Belarus.

Belarusian Republican Youth Union
A government-sponsored organisation for young people and students, a replacement for the USSR's Komsomol.

BSAA
Belarusian State Academy of Arts.

BSPU
Belarusian State Pedagogical University.

BSU
Belarusian State University.

BSUCA
Belarusian State University of Culture and Arts.

BSUIR
Belarusian State University of Informatics and Radioelectronics.

Dermatology and Venereology Unit
In Belarus, as in the Soviet era, skin infections and STIs are treated in the same departments. Modern and effective outpatient treatments for sexual health care are often unavailable, and patients requiring care are hospitalised for long periods. In Minsk, there is a large dermatology and venereology hospital for those requiring hospitalisation.

Fiaduta, Alaksandr
A thinker, scholar, and journalist. A political prisoner.

Frunzienski district
One of six districts of Minsk.

GUBOPiK
A Belarusian abbreviation for the Main Directorate for Combating Organised Crime and Corruption. Since 2020, it has been widely used for violent suppression of political dissent.

GLOSSARY

Hołas
A campaign for a smartphone-based alternative to Lukashenka's regime counting of votes in the 2020 elections.

Homieĺ
The second-largest city in Belarus.

Hrodna
A city in western Belarus.

Jabaćka
A dismissive colloquialism for Aleksander Lukashenka's followers. It comes from a Belarusian baćka, a Daddy.

Janka Kupała
One of the classics of Belarusian literature.

Kachanava, Natallia
Speaker of the Council of the Republic of Belarus since December 2019.

Kalinoŭski Programme
A Polish state aid programme for Belarusian youth who experienced persecutions established in March 2006.

Latushka, Pavel
A politician and diplomat, the Minister of Culture of the Republic of Belarus in 2009–2012. During the 2020 protests, he supported strikes by the theatre artists. On 19 August 2020, Latushka became a member of the praesidium of Sviatlana Tsikhanouskaya's Coordination Council.

Leninski district
One of six districts of Minsk.

Lukašuk, Žmicier
A radio journalist and founder of a Belarusian-language Euroradio station based in Poland. Under the Belarusian National Idea brand, he produced dozens of interviews with key thinkers, authors, and activists.

Liapis, Lyapis Trubetskoy
A Belarusian rock band.

Makei, Uladzimir
The Minister of Foreign Affairs of Belarus from 2012 until his death in 2022.

Malavanyč
A pseudonym of Alaksandr Zhdanovich, a popular children's TV presenter.

Matsiusheuski, Vasil
A banker, First Deputy Prime Minister of Belarus from 2014 to 2018.

MAZ
A manufacturer of large commercial vehicles based in Minsk.

Methodology Specialist (in Belarusian: метадыст)
In Belarusian educational institutions, a specialist in teaching a certain subject and a member of an academic department.

Mikhalok, Siarhei
A singer in the Lyapis Trubetskoy band.

Minsktrans
A state-owned enterprise for public transportation in Minsk.

Mukavozchik, Andrei
A newspaper columnist, one of the regime's most outspoken propagandists. He frequently called for violence against protesters. He is banned from travel to the European Union and a number of other countries.

Nexta
A YouTube and Telegram-based media, which acquired a huge influence during the 2020 protests. In 2021, the Belarusian authorities declared Nexta a terrorist organisation.

Niamiha
An area in central Minsk, one of the epicentres of protests in 2020.

NRM
A Belarusian rock band.

Pahonia
The first coat of arms of the independent Belarus. Its roots are in the coat of arms of the Grand Duchy of Lithuania.

Partyzanski district
One of six districts of Minsk.

Pieramožcaŭ Avenue
One of the epicentres of protests in central Minsk in 2020.

Podgaiskaya, Olga
A Belarusian composer. She currently lives in Poland.

Polack (pronounced: Polatsak)
A town in northern Belarus.

Postcrossing
A postcard exchange project.

Red Church (Belarusian: Čyrvony kaścioł)
A Roman Catholic church on the Niezaliežnasci Square in Minsk where many 2020 protests took place.

Red-green
A reference to the flag of the Republic of Belarus. A colloquialism for Lukashenka's regime and its followers.

Rumas, Siarhei
The Prime Minister of Belarus in 2018—2020.
SWIFT
A European network for international payments.
Stella monument
One of the epicentres of protests in central Minsk in 2020.
Šufladka
The Belarusian word for "desk drawer," also used by Russian-speaking Belarusians. It is often cited as a shibboleth representing Belarusian linguistic identity.
Tsepkalo, Valery
A politician and manager. In 2020, he announced his intention to run in the presidential elections. The Election Commission rejected his application. Shortly afterwards, he left Belarus due to safety concerns.
Tsikhanouskaya, Sviatlana
Following the Electoral Commission's refusal to register Siarhey Thikhanouski as a candidate in presidential elections and his eventual detention, his wife, Sviatlana Tsikhanouskaya, was selected as a unity candidate for Viktar Babaryka's, Valery Tsepkalo's, and Siarhei Thikhanouski's campaigns. Following the rigged elections, she was forced to leave Belarus. She lives in Vilnius, Lithuania, and is widely regarded as the 'leader of Democratic Belarus'.
Tsikhanouski, Siarhei
An entrepreneur and blogger. In 2020, he announced his intention to run in the presidential elections. The Election Commission rejected his application. He was detained and sentenced to eighteen years of imprisonment. A political prisoner.
Vaładarka
A colloquialism for a centre for temporary detention located in Piščałaŭski Castle in Minsk. The only prison in Europe where capital punishment is executed.
Validol
A widely used over-the-counter medication for heart-related conditions.
Veterans' House
An state-run institution in central Minsk providing cultural and social events for war veterans.
Viasna
The largest human rights organisation in Belarus. In 2023, the Belarusian authorities proscribed Viasna as an "extremist formation".
VK
A Russian social network, short for VKontakte.

Voblasć
An administrative unit of a similar scale to a province. There are six voblasćs in Belarus.

White-red-white
A reference to the first flag of the independent Republic of Belarus. A colloquialism for Lukashenka's opponents.

Zmahary
A dismissive colloquialism for Aleksander Lukashenka's opponents. Literally means "fighters".

Žodzina
A town in Minsk voblasć and a colloquialism for the prison there.

Note on transliteration

The traditional Belarusian Latin alphabet — łacinka — is best suited for Belarusian geographical names and anthroponyms. It was suppressed by Russian authorities in the nineteenth century. Since then, alternative transliteration (romanisation) systems have been adopted, with or without input from Belarusians. Among them, the most commonly used is the BGN/PCGN romanisation system, developed by Americans and British.

In independent Belarus, an attempt was made to develop a transliteration system for geographical names based on łacinka (e.g., *Homieĺ* instead of the Russian *Gomel*; *Hrodna* instead of the Polish *Grodno*). This system is known as the *Instruction on Transliteration of Belarusian Geographical Names with Letters of Latin Script*. It was adopted by the Belarusian State Committee on Land Resources, Geodetics, and Cartography and recommended for use by the Working Group on Romanization Systems of the United Nations Group of Experts on Geographical Names (UNGEGN).

After 2020, Belarusian authorities largely abandoned its use. Instead, Russian-style romanisation systems are now commonly applied, including for personal names. Additionally, some Belarusians use Russian-language versions of their names for Latin-script transliterations (e.g., *Olga* instead of *Volha*).

Despite the publisher's efforts to maintain consistency, a plurality of transliterations from Cyrillic alphabets could not be avoided in this publication.

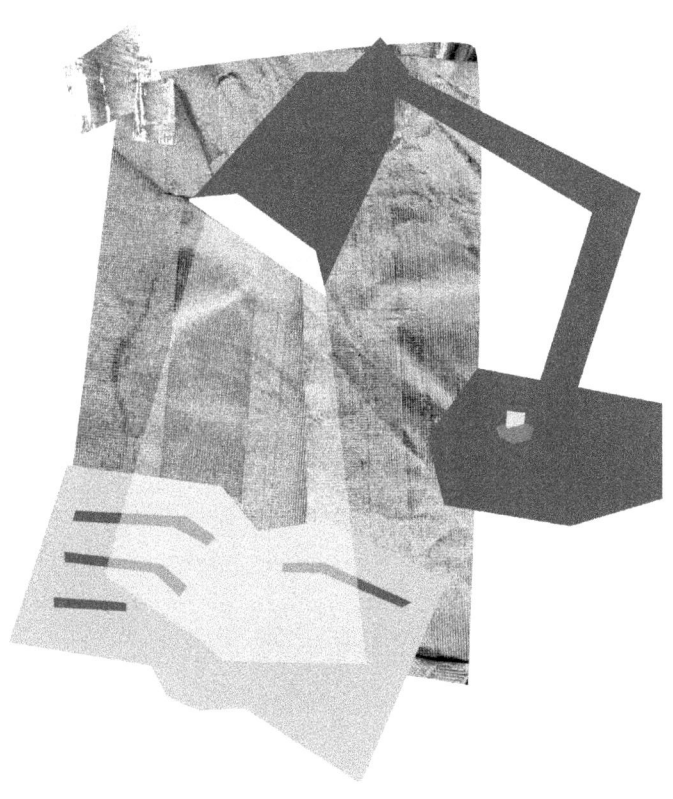

www.ingramcontent.com/pod-product-compliance
Lightning Source LLC
Chambersburg PA
CBHW070759040426
42333CB00060B/969